Catalyzing Reader-Response to the Oral Gospel

A Rhetorical Analysis of the Convincing and Convicting Devices in the Markan Text

Mwaniki Karura

MONOGRAPHS

© 2020 Mwaniki Karura

Published 2020 by Langham Monographs
An imprint of Langham Publishing

www.langhampublishing.org

Langham Publishing and its imprints are a ministry of Langham Partnership

Langham Partnership
PO Box 296, Carlisle, Cumbria, CA3 9WZ, UK
www.langham.org

ISBNs:
978-1-83973-007-8 Print
978-1-83973-008-5 ePub
978-1-83973-009-2 Mobi
978-1-83973-010-8 PDF

Mwaniki Karura has asserted his right under the Copyright, Designs and Patents Act, 1988 to be identified as the Author of this work.

All rights reserved. No part of this publication may be reproduced, stored in a retrieval system or transmitted, in any form or by any means, electronic, mechanical, photocopying, recording or otherwise, without the prior written permission of the publisher or the Copyright Licensing Agency.

Requests to reuse content from Langham Publishing are processed through PLSclear. Please visit www.plsclear.com to complete your request.

Scripture quotations, unless otherwise stated, are taken from the New King James Version (NKJV). Copyright © 1982 by Thomas Nelson, Inc. Used by permission. All rights reserved.

Scripture quotations marked (ESV) are from The Holy Bible, English Standard Version® (ESV®), copyright © 2001 by Crossway, a publishing ministry of Good News Publishers. Used by permission. All rights reserved.

Scripture quotations marked (NIV) are taken from the Holy Bible, New International Version®, NIV®. Copyright © 1973, 1978, 1984, 2011 by Biblica, Inc.™ Used by permission of Zondervan.

Scripture quotations marked (NASB) are taken from the New American Standard Bible®, Copyright © 1960, 1962, 1963, 1968, 1971, 1972, 1973, 1975, 1977, 1995 by The Lockman Foundation. Used by permission.

Greek Scripture quotations marked (NA28) are taken from Novum Testamentum Graece, 28th revised edition, Edited by Barbara Aland and others, © 2012 Deutsche Bibelgesellschaft, Stuttgart.

British Library Cataloguing-in-Publication Data
A catalogue record for this book is available from the British Library

ISBN: 978-1-83973-007-8

Cover & Book Design: projectluz.com

Langham Partnership actively supports theological dialogue and an author's right to publish but does not necessarily endorse the views and opinions set forth here or in works referenced within this publication, nor can we guarantee technical and grammatical correctness. Langham Partnership does not accept any responsibility or liability to persons or property as a consequence of the reading, use or interpretation of its published content.

To my wife,
Nyambura,
who has been a great source
of joy and encouragement.

To my children,
Ireri, Mũnyĩrĩ, Mũchiri and Mũriũki,
for their unfailing support and love.

Finally, to my parents,
Mr. Alexander I. Karura and Mrs. Stella Wacuka,
through their storytelling, I came to appreciate the faith and
behavior-changing power in telling and retelling stories.

Contents

Acknowledgements xi
Abstract xiii
Abbreviations xv
Chapter 1 1
Introduction
   1.1 Background 1
   1.2 Problem Statement 2
   1.3 Thesis of the Study 4
   1.4 Why Undertake the Study? 5
      1.4.1 Contribution of the Research to Markan Studies 6
   1.5 Hypothesis 6
   1.6 Outline of the Study 10
   1.7 Limitations of the Study 13
   1.8 Delimitations 13
   1.9 Methodology 14
      1.9.1 Necessity of a Text: Foundation of Rhetoric 19
      1.9.2 Hebrew Rhetoric in Genesis 26
      1.9.3 Comparison of Genesis and the Markan Text 30
      1.9.4 Hebrew Rhetoric in the New Testament 30
      1.9.5 Rhetorical Criticism 32
      1.9.6 Rhetoric and Rhetorical Situation 36
      1.9.7 Rhetoric and Meaning 38
      1.9.8 Use of Rhetorical Criticism in the Markan Study 39
   1.10 Summary 41

Chapter 2 43
"Gospelness" of the Markan Text
   2.1 Introduction 43
   2.2 The Salvific Episode and the Salvific Gospel 43
   2.3 Changes in the Referent of the Term Εὐαγγέλιον 44
      2.3.1 Etymology of the Word "Εὐαγγέλιον" 48
      2.3.2 Referents of the Word "Gospel" in Jesus's Time 51
      2.3.3 From "Gospel of God" to the "Gospel of Jesus Christ" 54
      2.3.4 Gospel during the Apostolic Period 57
   2.4 Effect of the Destruction of Jerusalem on the Term "Gospel" 66

2.5 Gospel in the Time of the Church Fathers 69
   2.5.1 Gospel in the Time of Clement of Rome 70
   2.5.2 Gospel in the Time of Papias Bishop of Hierapolis............71
   2.5.3 Marcion's Understanding of Gospel 72
   2.5.4 Gospel in the Time of Justin Martyr 73
   2.5.5 Gospel in the Times of Tertullian 74
2.6 Term "Gospel" in Mark's Text 75
   2.6.1 Reference of the Term "Gospel" in Mark 1:1 77
2.7 Content of the Oral Gospel 85
   2.7.1 Pointers to the Oral Gospel in the Markan Text................87
2.8 Summary: "Gospelness" of the Markan Text 89

Chapter 3 95
Contextual, Structural, and Form Analysis

3.1 Introduction 95
3.2 Socio-Religious Context of the Markan Text............................96
   3.2.1 The Christ Event as a Setting and Context of the
      Markan Stories..99
3.3 Structure of the Markan Text 100
   3.3.1 Outline of the Markan Text 102
3.4 Contextual Structure of the Markan Text...............................108
   3.4.1 Observations from the Contextual Strata of the
      Markan Text 110
3.5 Jesus's Retold Parables as Portraits of the Text's Occasion 111
   3.5.1 The Parable of the Sower as a Portrait of the Markan
      Audience..114
3.6 Purpose of the Markan Text 120
3.7 Literary Genre of the Markan Text...124
3.8 Summary 134

Chapter 4 135
Matrix of Interlocutors in the Markan Text

4.1 Introduction 135
4.2 Subject of Discussion in the Markan Text 136
4.3 Interlocutors within the Matrix of the Markan Discourse 140
   4.3.1 The Markan Text 140
   4.3.2 The Audience 148
   4.3.3 The Oral Gospel 149
4.4 Interlocutor Relationships in the Markan Discourse 152
   4.4.1 Dialogue between the Audience and the Oral Gospel 152
   4.4.2 Dialogue between the Markan Text and the Audience......153

4.4.3 Relationship between Rhetorical Situation of the
       Audience of Jesus and the Rhetorical Situation of the
       Audience of Mark 155
    4.4.4 Relationship between the Markan Text and the
       Oral Gospel 157
    4.4.5 Dialogue between the Markan Text, Audience, and
       Oral Gospel 158
  4.5 Summary 159

Chapter 5 161
Markan Old Testament Quotations as a Rhetorical Device
  5.1 Introduction 161
  5.2 Recent Trends in the Study of Old Testament Quotations in
     the Markan Text 162
    5.2.1 Review of R. E. Watts 163
    5.2.2 Review of Thomas R. Hatina 164
  5.3 Ideological and Religious Point of View 165
  5.4 Analysis of Old Testament Quotations in Mark 1:2–3 167
    5.4.1 Exegetical Analysis of Mark 1:1–3 168
    5.4.2 Rhetorical Reading of Mark 1:1-3 183
  5.5 Analysis of Old Testament Quotation in Mark 4:12 187
    5.5.1 Observations from Source Documents 188
    5.5.2 Comparative Outlines of Isaiah 1:1–6:10 and
       Mark 1:1–4:12 189
    5.5.3 Exegetical Analysis of Isaiah 6:9–10 194
    5.5.4 Exegetical Analysis of Mark 4:12 199
    5.5.5 Comparative Analysis of Isaiah 6:9–10 and Mark 4:12 201
  5.6 Summary 203

Chapter 6 205
Markan Miracle Stories as a Rhetorical Device
  6.1 Introduction 205
  6.2 Definition of a Miracle 206
  6.3 Miracles in the Old Testament 207
  6.4 Miracles Stories in the New Testament 209
  6.5 Extra-Biblical Miracle Stories 209
  6.6 Miracles as a Function of the Eschatological Kingdom 210
  6.7 Miracle Stories in the Markan Text 211
    6.7.1 Current Trends in Research on Markan Miracle Stories ... 211
    6.7.2 Mark's Commentaries in the Narration of Miracle
       Stories 214

    6.7.3 Genre of Miracle Stories 218
    6.7.4 Rhetorical Structuring of the Miracle Stories 219
    6.7.5 Function of Miracle Stories in the Markan Text 226
6.8 Summary 231

Chapter 7 233
Markan Passion Narratives as a Rhetorical Device

7.1 Introduction 233
7.2 Form of the Passion Story 234
7.3 Passion Was God Willed 235
    7.3.1 Passion Was Anticipated in Scripture 235
    7.3.2 Jesus's Predictions of the Passion 236
7.4 Passion in the Parable of the Tenants...237
7.5 Passion Was Sacrificial, Propitiatory, and Vicarious 238
    7.5.1 Interpreting the Passion in Light of Scripture....................238
    7.5.2 Passion Foreboded in the Lord's Supper Narratives. 239
7.6 Rhetorical Function of the Passion Narratives in
    Identifying Jesus...241
    7.6.1 Disclosure of the Person of Jesus in the Trial Narrative.....241
    7.6.2 Disclosure of the Person of Jesus in the Crucifixion
        Narrative 241
7.7 Rhetorical Function of the Narrative about Jesus's Prayers in
    Gethsemane 243
7.8 Rhetorical Function of the Narrative about Jesus's Arrest 244
7.9 Rhetorical Function of the Narrative about Jesus's Trial.............245
    7.9.1 Jesus's Trial before the Sanhedrin.......................................245
    7.9.2 Jesus's Trial before Pilate..246
7.10 Summary 247

Chapter 8 249
Conclusion

8.1 Introduction 249
8.2 Excursus 249
    8.2.1 Importance of the Longer Ending (Mark 16:14–20)........250
8.3 Summary 253

Glossary 257

Bibliography...261

Acknowledgements

I would like to acknowledge the gift of my family who have been a fountain of love, strength and comfort. Likewise, I extend my sincere gratitude to Gospel Outreach – Thika, for their financial support, time, and prayer over the years.

The faculty of Biblical Studies Department of Africa International University deserves mention, especially my lead supervisor, Professor Samuel M. Ngewa and the second reader Dr. Nathan N. Joshua for their guidance and encouragement. Special thanks too to Professor Peter Nyende, for his valuable challenge in my choice of topic during the seminar on Hebrews Exegesis. Thanks are also due to Dr. John F. Evans for introducing me to philosophical hermeneutics and biblical criticism without which I would have been incapacitated in handling the topic of this work. Dr. Joshua L. Harper also deserves mention for introducing me to Septuagint studies and Greek readings on the church fathers. My outstanding Greek lecturer Dr. Stephanie Black also deserves thanks. Thanks also to Professor Mark Shaw and Professor James Nkansah Ombrempong for their contributions in expanding my historical and theological horizons. Lastly but certainly not the least, I appreciate my internal examiner Professor Mumo P. Kisau and external examiner Professor Elizabeth W. Mburu for their input in enriching this little contribution to biblical studies.

To God be the glory.

Abstract

This study argues that the Markan text is a paraenesis[1] whose primary purpose was to catalyze reader-response to an oral gospel that was outside and independent of the text using Old Testament quotations, miracle stories, and the passion narrative as rhetorical devices. In 2006, Holly Heston identified a research gap in the study of the relationship between the written and oral forms. She identified "the reciprocal impact oral and written forms may have on one another and the implication of this for the development of biblical traditions, as an area that has not been researched and that should not be overlooked."[2] Notwithstanding her observations, there has not been any research on this important area in the Markan study. None of the research done this far, has analyzed the parable of the sower (4:1–12) from the point of view that it was retold to mirror the rhetorical situation of Mark's audience. The study has been conceptualized based on the supposition that Mark retold the parable of the sower and the parable of the wicked tenants (12:1–12) as portraits to mirror his audience's rhetorical situation and its exigence of obduracy and lukewarm response towards the oral gospel. A further supposition is that Mark's aim was to arouse abhorrence for his audience's obduracy and lukewarm response to the oral gospel. Paradoxically, he also aimed at arousing aspiration in his audience for optimal responsiveness in faith and obedience

---

1. This study defines paraenesis as a textual or oral work that is composed to exhort the audience to either believe its claims and act on its demands or believe the claims and act on the demands of a moral, social, or religious aspect that is outside and independent of the paraenetical composition. A paraenesis can first be categorized as a genre in as far as it is a literary type that is adopted to exhort. Second, it can also be categorized as a social function in as far as it functions to urge the readers to effect a moral or social change. Finally, third, it can also be viewed as a rhetorical device in as far as it is aimed at eliminating an exigence in an identified rhetorical situation. Grant R. Osborne identifies paraenesis as a genre (see Osborne, *Hermeneutic Spiral*, 183).

2. Heston, "Implications of Orality," 4.

to the demands of the gospel. However, from as early as the second century CE, when the Markan text was labelled "the Gospel according to Mark," it has been understood to be the written version of the oral gospel that was being proclaimed in Mark's milieu. This axiomatic stance has become a subjective presupposition that limits and bridles the questions that can be asked during the hermeneutical process. This presupposition has the potential to unduly skew the interpretive process. After delineating the labyrinth of the interlocutors that directly and indirectly interact within the matrix of the Markan discourse and, in particular, after analyzing the interaction between the text, audience, and oral gospel, it becomes clear that the rhetorical devices of Old Testament quotations, miracle stories, and the passion narrative were employed to catalyze audience response to the oral gospel.

Abbreviations

ESV	English Standard Version
HTS	*HTS Theological Studies*
KJV	King James Version
LXX	The Septuagint
MT	Massoretic Text
NA28	*Nestle-Aland: Novum Testamentum Graece*
NAC	The NIV Application Commentary
NETS	New English Translation of the Septuagint
NIBC	New International Biblical Commentary
NIB	The New Interpreter's Bible
NIBCNT	The New International Biblical Commentary on the New Testament
NICNT	The New International Commentary on the New Testament
NIGTC	The New International Greek Testament Commentary
NKJV	New King James Version
NTS	New Testament Studies
SacP	*Sacra Pagina*
SBL	Society of Biblical Literature
SPCK	Society for Promoting Christian Knowledge
RBL	Review Bible Literature
TCGNT	A Textual Commentary on the Greek New Testament
TNTC	Tyndale New Testament Commentaries
UBS	United Bible Societies

CHAPTER 1

Introduction

1.1 Background

The literary genre, "gospelness," and purpose of the Markan text have been disputed topics in Markan studies since antiquity.[1] In an excerpt quoted by Eusebius Papias, Bishop of Hierapolis (circa 110 CE), notes,

> Mark, having become Peter's interpreter, wrote down accurately everything he remembered, though not in order, of the things either said or done by Christ. For he neither heard the Lord nor followed him, but afterward, as I said, followed Peter, who adapted his teachings as needed but had no intention of giving an ordered account of the Lord's sayings. Consequently, Mark did nothing wrong in writing down some things as he remembered them, for he made it his one concern not to omit anything that he heard or to make any false statement in them.[2]

Papias's note, and especially his stress on Mark's relationship with Peter, suggests that he was writing a polemical treatise in support of the Markan text whose anecdotes, he notes, are not in order. This quote also suggests that, during Papias's time, there were concerns regarding both the reliability and chronological order (τάξις) of the episodes narrated in the text. He mitigates

---

1. Commonly suggested genres include, Greco-Roman biography, historiography and *sui generis*. This study has identified the genre of the Markan text as a paraenesis. See chapter 3, section 3.7, "Literary Genre of the Markan Text."
2. Eusebius, *Ecclesiastical History*, 113.

the text's seeming disorder by attributing it to the apostle Peter who, he says, had narrated the episodes not according to order ("οὐ μέντοι τάξει")[3] but according to need ("πρός τάς χρείας").[4] This need-based purpose of the Markan text is an area that needs to be researched in an effort to reconcile the different views on the genre, "gospelness," and purpose of the text.

Current research which includes analysis of the text's purpose, genre, and disputed endings has raised more questions than answers.[5] Indeed, research on the Markan text has not yet come to a consensus on some important hermeneutical questions that have been raised.[6] As such, most of the answers to these questions are tentatively held. They await further research so that the text can speak convincingly and order the lives of its readers.

1.2 Problem Statement

The second-century designation of the texts which narrate the life and times of Jesus as the gospel by Marcion[7] and the later identification of Matthew, Mark, Luke, and John, as the bona fide Gospels by "(*Irenaeus, AH 3.1.1*),"[8] a position that has since been held as axiomatic, arguably presents a subjective presupposition to interpretation of these texts. It unduly limits and bridles the questions that can be asked during textual interpretation. Pre-understanding predetermines both the mode and outcome of textual analysis. It is necessary to free studies of the Markan text from the subjectivity consequent of this pre-understanding. Hermeneutists should allow pre-understanding to be

---

3. Eusebius, 113, also quoted in Holmes, *Apostolic Fathers*, 738.

4. Holmes, *Apostolic Fathers*, 738.

5. The preface in Robert W. Herron, Jr.'s *Mark's Account of Peter's Denial of Jesus*, states, "It is not simply the quality of the secondary literature which makes an entrance into the Markan studies difficult. The task is aggravated by the absence of any consensus. Reading through the major literature confirms that specialists on Mark do not agree, and every year the number of contributors increases . . . The student of Mark, confronted with conflicting conclusions, will ultimately be driven back to a fresh consideration of the text of the gospel itself and to the discussion it has elicited over the centuries." (Herron, *Mark's Account of Peter's Denial of Jesus*, ix).

6. For example, research has so far not established a consensus on the text's purpose. Robert Gundry in *Mark: A Commentary on His Apology for the Cross* (p.1022), has suggested an apology of the cross. A political purpose has also been suggested. Many other reasons have been proffered. This work argues that the stories in the Markan text are narrated to catalyze audience response towards the oral and ritual gospel that was outside and independent of the text.

7. Koester, "From Kerygma-Gospel," 376.

8. Norris, "Apostolic and Sub-Apostolic Writings," 16.

reshaped by texts. Anthony Thiselton asserts, "The goal of biblical hermeneutics is to bring about an active and meaningful engagement between the interpreter and the text in such a way that the interpreter's own horizon is reshaped and enlarged."[9]

According to William W. Klein, Craig L. Blomberg, and Robert L. Hubbard, "Preunderstanding[10] may distort the reader's perception of reality and function like an unconscious prejudice adversely affecting the interpreter's ability to perceive accurately. It certainly determines how the reader will understand the task of reading the Bible."[11] Similarly, J. Scott Duvall and J. Daniel Hays argue that pre-understanding is "a major influence that can skew our interpretive process and lead us away from the real meaning in the text."[12] Moreover, introducing presuppositions[13] that are strange to the author's context distorts understanding of a text. This is highlighted by Peter Cotterell and Max Turner who note, "the significance an utterance has for any hearer depends not only on the sense of what is spoken, and on the shared presupposition pool, but also on the presupposition held by the hearer that he does not share with the speaker."[14] Effectively, an interpreter's presupposition that is outside of the shared presupposition pool becomes a blind and bridle to the interpretative process.

Current trends on Markan research are, in a fundamental way, limited and bridled by the pre-understanding that the Markan text is a "gospel." This has the following implications:

1. The text is a priori construed as the content of the gospel referenced in Mark 1:1. As such, proclamation of the gospel is understood as performing the text in either reading the text to a listening audience or in enacting its episodes.
2. The text is seen to be speaking to the reader in a linear communication.

---

9. Thiselton, *Two Horizons*, xix.

10. This book uses the terms pre-understanding and presupposition interchangeably

11. Klein, Blomberg, and Hubbard, *Introduction to Biblical Interpretation*, 157.

12. Duvall and Hays, *Grasping God's Word*, 89.

13. Due to the long period that the Markan text has been labeled "the Gospel according to Mark," this understanding has almost become a fixed presupposition.

14. Cotterell and Turner, *Linguistics and Biblical Interpretation*, 94.

3. The Old Testament quotations, miracle stories, and the passion narratives are identified as a repository of the life and times of Jesus Christ.

On the other hand, the implications of the supposition that the gospel referenced in Mark 1:1 is outside and independent of the Markan text are these:

1. The text is seen as a rhetorical communication aimed at catalyzing reader-response to the oral gospel[15] that was outside and independent of the text.[16]
2. The supposition illuminates the presence of four important interlocutors within the matrix of the participants in the Markan discourse: the text, the audience,[17] the mimetic world of the text, and the oral gospel.
3. The Old Testament quotations, miracle stories, and the passion narratives are identified as rhetorical devices that were employed to catalyze reader-response[18] to the oral gospel.

1.3 Thesis of the Study

Generally, this study offers an analysis of the Markan text that is freed from the limitation and bridle that is occasioned by the pre-understanding that the Markan text is the gospel that is referenced in Mark 1:1. Particularly, it argues that the Markan text is a paraenesis whose purpose was to catalyze its reader's response to an oral gospel that was outside and independent of the text using Old Testament quotations, miracle stories, parables, and the passion story as rhetorical devices.

---

15. According to Acts 1:8, the oral gospel was a pneumatically enabled witness. It is contrasted with the Markan text which has been identified as a narrative on selected episodes in the life and work of Jesus Christ.

16. Independence is construed to be in existence not in relationship.

17. The readers of the Markan text were simultaneously hearing the oral gospel. As such, the term reader-response and audience response will be used interchangeably.

18. Reader-response in this sense is the Markan reader's response to the oral gospel. It is distinguished from the modern hermeneutical philosophies and methods that are labelled reader-response criticism.

1.4 Why Undertake the Study?

Since the development of rhetoric as a systematized handbook discipline and with its recent development into a tool for biblical interpretation (by recent rhetoricians such as James Muilenburg, George Kennedy, Wilhelm Wuellner,[19] and others), rhetoric has been largely seen as an exclusively Greco-Roman literary embellishment. As such, New Testament scholarship has not made sufficient inroads in employing insights from Hebrew rhetoric in the study of the Markan text. No wonder Kota Yamada has downplayed the existence of any rhetorical order in the Markan text. He observes that "Mark's gospel is a series of notes without rhetorical order and embellishments."[20]

Second, there has been a gap in research on the effect of the Markan text on its reader's response to the oral gospel. This gap has been occasioned by the supposition, which is held as axiomatic, that the Markan text is actually the gospel that is referenced in Mark 1:1. This results in limiting instead of enlarging the scope of the Markan research. Similarly, no research on the Markan text has, to date, analyzed the controversy stories (particularly the parable of the sower) from the supposition that retelling them was indeed a Markan invention to mirror his audience's rhetorical situation and that this portrait was a distinct interlocutor within the matrix of the Markan textual discourse.

The difficulty in establishing the nexus between the oral *kerygma* and the written text has been highlighted by I. Howard Marshall when he says, in exasperation, "It is, however, notoriously difficult to proceed further than this and to find actual examples of the connection between the kerygma and the gospel tradition."[21] Commenting on the same issue, Heston identifies "the reciprocal impact oral and written forms may have on one another and the implication of this for the development of biblical traditions,"[22] as an area that has not been researched and that should not be overlooked. This gap in research, and specifically in the Markan text, is a call and motivation to undertake research in this fundamental area of biblical studies.

---

19. In his presidential address delivered at the annual meeting of the Society of Biblical Literature on 18 December 1968, James Muilenburg called upon scholars to embrace rhetorical criticism. Since then, George Kennedy and Wilhelm Wuellner and a host of other scholars have written extensively on the subject.

20. Yamada, "Preface to the Lukan Writings," 168.

21. Marshall, *Luke*, 49.

22. Heston, "Implications of Orality," 4.

1.4.1 Contribution of the Research to Markan Studies

This work contributes and integrates insights from Hebrew rhetoric to illumine use of rhetorical devices in the Markan text. It also shows that rhetoric is not a preserve of the Greco-Roman world but a universal language embellishment. Moreover, a rhetorical investigation of the Markan text that employs rhetorical precedents from the Old Testament is more rewarding because Mark narrated episodes that had their setting within the Hebrew religious and cultural context. Furthermore, the Hebrew use of storytelling in Genesis is comparable to the storytelling in the synoptic texts.[23]

Other major contributions of this study to scholarship are a fresh identification of a contextual structuring of the Markan text, identification of the interlocutors that participate within the matrix of the Markan discourse,[24] and a relook at the function of Old Testament quotations, miracle stories, Jesus's controversy with Jewish religious leaders, retold parables, and the passion stories. It has also contributed in (1) identifying the profile of the Markan audience and their religious context; (2) a new exegetical analysis of Mark 1:1–3 and Mark 4:12; (3) a suggested fresh designation of the book of Mark; and (4), in line with the thesis statement, a new perspective of the nature and function of the Markan text.

1.5 Hypothesis

The existence of an oral gospel prior to the written "gospel texts" has been noted by a host of scholars. Robert Gundry notes,

> τοῦ εὐαγγελίου carries the connotation of good news as preached, not just good news as such, much less good news as written in a book . . . The non-bookish meaning of εὐαγγέλιον elsewhere in Mark and the NT further rules out a bookish connotation here (again cf. Hos. 1:2 LXX, where "[the] beginning of [the] word of [the] Lord to Hosea" consists in an oral word spoken long

---

23. This position is argued in section 1.9.5, "Rhetorical Criticism."

24. The Markan discourse is understood to be a matrix of direct and indirect interlocutor relationships between a complex of interlocutors that are formed and addressed by the text. These include: the mirror image of Mark's audience's rhetorical situation as explicated in the parable of the sower, the mimetic world of the text, the audience, the oral gospel that was outside and independent of the text, and the Markan text.

before the written report of it). The later bookish meaning (first in Marcion – see Helmut Koester in *NTS* 35 [1989] 361–81) will grow out of an association of the oral proclamation with the books where the proclamation was recorded.[25]

Thus, Gundry suggests that before the texts were written, τὸ εὐαγγέλιον referenced an oral gospel. However, he holds the view that the written texts are a transcription of the oral gospel. This study's point of departure is the supposition that the gospel referenced in Mark 1:1 was an oral and ritual gospel that was outside and independent of the text and that it was circulating concurrently with the text.[26]

Gundry asks, "Does τοῦ εὐαγγελίου mean 'the good news' as such, as preached, or written up in Mark's gospel?"[27] This work answers Gundry's question arguing that τοῦ εὐαγγελίου references "the good news as preached." As such, the Markan audience were simultaneously dialoguing with the text and the oral gospel. This supposition is programmatic for reading and interpreting the Markan text in that it suggests and directs the questions that an interpreter can ask during the interpretation process. It also has the potential to redirect the present trends of the Markan research and to redefine the editorial title of the Markan text.

The introductory phrase, Ἀρχὴ τοῦ εὐαγγελίου Ἰησοῦ Χριστοῦ [υἱοῦ θεοῦ],[28] and the parable of the sower in Mark 4:1–12 are programmatic to the study of the entire Markan text. Whereas, by use of the noun Ἀρχὴ, Mark 1:1 introduces the subject of the text as the base on which the gospel about Jesus was premised, arguably the parable of the sower (4:1–12) was retold to paint a portrait of the rhetorical situation[29] of Jesus's audience and its exigence of obduracy and lukewarm response towards the word of God. It is also arguable that Mark employed this portrait to mirror his primary audience's rhetorical situation.

---

25. Gundry, *Mark*, 33.

26. It will be argued in 2.3.4, under the section "Gospel in performance of ordinances" that the oral gospel encapsulated the ritual gospel in the celebration of the Lord's Supper.

27. Gundry, *Mark*, 29.

28. Unless otherwise stated, Greek quotations are from NA28 and in English from the NKJV.

29. According to Lloyd F. Bitzer, the rhetorical situation is understood to be the occasion that prompts the production of a rhetorical communication (see Bitzer, "Rhetorical Situation," 5).

This method of painting a mirror image of the audience's rhetorical situation, which portrays both the exigence and the expected norm, is rhetorically rewarding in that it evokes both a dislike for the audience's exigence and at the same time an aspiration for the desired norm. In other words, the emotional energy generated by the audience's view of their obduracy provokes them to respond positively towards the oral gospel. Mark Wegener has aptly captured the evocative power of the Markan text and notes that "the evocative power of Mark's gospel resides in the force of the metaphorical and symbolic world it creates."[30]

In her introduction to Chaim Perelman's book, *The Realm of Rhetoric*, Carroll Arnold notes, "arguments are always *addressed to audiences* (possibly to the arguer's self) for the purpose of inducing or increasing those audiences' adherence to the theses presented."[31] The purpose of the Markan text was to increase Mark's audience's adherence to the oral gospel. James Hansen supports these sentiments in his postulation that, "that is precisely what Mark's narrative strategy attempts to do; make resistance to the 'gospel of Jesus Christ' difficult if not impossible."[32] Mark was also fortifying the oral gospel by showing that it was approved by God through the numerous miraculous signs that were performed by Jesus, and that it was the same gospel that Jesus had inaugurated (1:14–15) and commissioned the disciples to preach to the whole world (16:14–18).

The issue of authenticity is a question of reconciling values and opinions. Notably, the question before Mark is whether the oral gospel conformed to shared religious values and opinions. In this regard, Arnold asks, "By what process do we reason about values?"[33] Mark shows that the oral gospel was premised on fulfilled prophecies and promises that were part of his audience's "generally accepted opinions."[34] Perelman and Olbrechts-Tyteca refer to this kind of argument as "argument from authority."[35] The authority being

---

30. Wegener, *Cruciformed*, 5.
31. Arnold, "Introduction," x.
32. Hanson, *Endangered Promises*, 107.
33. Arnold, "Introduction," vii. Carroll argues that the question of values is inevitable because one cannot arrive at clear conclusions at how justice or any other value is distinguished from its opposite without considering how cases are made for or against that value.
34. Arnold, "Introduction," viii.
35. Perelman and Olbrechts-Tyteca, *New Rhetoric*, 305.

invoked in the Markan text is the voice of the Old Testament and the exalted persona of Jesus whose profile and ethos are highly pronounced by stories of his miraculous and grace deeds. This perspective informs Mark's choice of genre, structure, rhetorical devices of Old Testament Scripture citations, and the narrated anecdotes.

The rhetorical devices embedded in the text are aimed at catalyzing reader-response to the oral gospel. The obtaining scenario is similar to what John R. Searle has described as the relationship between rules of etiquette and inter-personal relationships in his observation that "many rules of etiquette regulate inter-personal relationships which exist independently of the rules."[36] Audience response towards the oral gospel[37] is catalyzed by the audience's observation and reflection on their undesirable rhetorical situation that is portrayed through retelling the parable of the sower (4:1–9) and the parable of the wicked tenants (12:1–12).

The literary method of narrating episodes from the audience's immediate and ancient history, to catalyze audience response to an interlocutor that is outside and independent of the text, is not original to Mark. The author of the book of Genesis narrated the episodes from his community's immediate and ancient history to the Exodus pilgrims, to catalyze a reflection on their obduracy, which is normally referred to as being stiff necked, to the covenantal stipulations. Particularly, the purpose of the episodic narratives in the Genesis text was to urge the Israelites to keep their newly established covenant, which they had already breached in making and worshipping the golden calf (Exod 32:1–6).[38] This supposition agrees with the assertion by Gordon Fees and Douglas Stuart that, "Narratives are stories – purposeful stories retelling the historical events of the past that are intended to give meaning and direction for a given people in the present."[39]

Narrating stories from Israel's pre-history, especially on the consequences of their forbearers' responses to the respective covenants that they had entered

---

36. Searle, *Speech Acts*, 33.

37. Henceforth, the term oral gospel will be used to stand for both the gospel that was orally and festally proclaimed through celebration of the ordinance of the Lord's Supper.

38. This notion is premised on the view that Genesis was written by Moses during the wilderness wanderings to urge adherence to the covenant stipulations. However, in case a different position is taken as source critics have suggested, then the audience changes but the argument is sustained albeit in a changed context.

39. Fee and Stuart, *How to Read the Bible*, 90.

with God, acted as echoes that mirrored the exigencies in the rhetorical situation of Moses's audience. According to Lloyd F. Bitzer, "some rhetorical situations persist over time and have resulted in a body of truly rhetorical literature."[40] As such, the Genesis stories acted as mimetic portraits of the reward of obedience and the wages of disobedience in which Moses's audience could mirror their own response to their newly established covenant and consequently abhor and turn away from their extant disobedience. The affective value of these echoes and portraits was in their efficacy to catalyze audience adherence to the stipulations of the covenant.

A study of the obedience and disobedience cycles in the wilderness wanderings, the book of Judges, historical books from 1 Samuel to 2 Chronicles, the Prophets, and the reformation cycles in church history shows that the rhetorical situations that are defined by a people's response to the word of God are a cyclical phenomenon. As such, a rhetorical communication that is aimed at eliminating an exigence in one epoch can be applied directly to future epochs. In line with Mark's literary and social background, he formulated a text that conformed with his Hebraic scriptural heritage. As such, the Markan text is Scripture per excellence. It addresses its primary audience albeit with an eye on the future generation of believers in similar rhetorical situations. In such circumstances, future readers of the text can apply the text as a mimetic exemplifier[41] and as a direct rhetorical communication that is aimed at eliminating the exigence in their specific and sometimes similar rhetorical situation.

1.6 Outline of the Study

Chapter 1 establishes the background and identifies the problem statement, the thesis of the study and the main hypothesis. Further, it presents an eclectic hermeneutical method comprising of rhetorical criticism as the major and most value laden hermeneutical method for interpreting a text with rhetorical features such as are in the Markan text. Complimentarily, speech act theory, discourse analysis and historical grammatical criticism have also

---

40. Bitzer, "Rhetorical Situation," 13.

41. Application of the text as a mimetic exemplifier is discussed in chapter 4, the section "Application of the Markan text to the secondary audience."

been incorporated to deal with specific topics. Specifically, the text has been identified as having been written in conformity with Hebrew rhetorical convention as opposed to Greco-Roman rhetoric.

Chapter 2 has investigated the "gospelness" of the Markan text. Primarily the study has used the diachronic approach. However, a synchronic approach has also been used. Particularly, the diachronic approach has been employed to examine the transmission history of the term "εὐαγγέλιον." According to Gerd Theissen, diachronic approach analyzes "texts as the product of developments in the process of tradition."[42] Particularly, this study illuminates the changes of the referent of the word εὐαγγέλιον from Jesus's milieu to the patristic milieu. The aim is to ascertain the most probable referent of the word εὐαγγέλιον in Mark 1:1 and to ward off any possibility of anachronistic reading of later-day referents of the term εὐαγγέλιον into Mark's milieu. Grant R. Osborne advises, "We must interpret a theological term not on the basis of what it came to mean later but rather on the basis of what it meant in the past."[43]

Chapter 3 surveys the context in which the Markan text was written. Of particular note is the consideration that the Christ event was an important context in which the Markan stories are set. The overarching religious worldview in which the text was written is that the prophetically anticipated καιρὸς (time) when the kingdom of God would be ushered into the world had already been fulfilled (1:15). As such, the Christ event was understood as a fulfilment of God's promises in Scripture which had become the eschatological hope of Israel. Consequently, stories on episodes within the Christ event are endowed with rhetorical value to authenticate and enhance the belief value of the oral gospel which is premised on the salvific episodes within the Christ event.

Chapter 4 discusses the nature and function of the interlocutors in the matrix of the discourse that is mediated by the Markan text. This discussion is the bedrock on which the work rests. It defines the Markan text and disentangles the labyrinth of the interlocutors therein. It also identifies stories of Jesus's controversy with the Jewish religious leaders and the retold parables as important rhetorical devices in the Markan discourse. The crux of this study is in identifying the interlocutors that dialogue within the matrix of

---

42. Theissen, *Miracle Stories*, 17.
43. Osborne, *Hermeneutical Spiral*, 90.

the discourse. It goes further to identify the nature and function of the interlocutor relationships in the discourse. The aim is to establish the connection between the text's rhetorical devices and reader-response to the oral gospel.

Chapter 5 argues out the supposition that the Old Testament citations in Mark 1:2–3 were used to show that Jesus was indeed the Christ. They are rhetorical devices that Mark used to convince his audience that the oral gospel was founded on the community's inherited faith and as such, it was worthy to be believed. Second, the analysis shows that the parable of the sower was a portrait of the rhetorical situation of Jesus's audience that Mark retold to mirror the rhetorical situation of his own audience and its exigence of obduracy and lukewarm response towards the oral gospel. Third, it unearths the underlying thought, ideology, and theology that influenced and directed the author in writing the text. In effect, it narrows the interpretative range to the most probable meaning and purpose of the stories, themes, and motifs that emerge in the text.

Chapter 6 argues the supposition that miracle stories are rhetorical devices which Mark used to convince his audience that the oral gospel was approved by God through performance of miracles that he, as the only source of numinous power, did through Jesus. It also argues that clustering the miracle anecdotes in one section of the text was deliberate and was aimed at intensifying the awe in the person of Jesus in order to evoke faith in the oral gospel that was premised on his work on the cross. It further argues that just as parallelism works to emphasize the issue under discussion, so also does clustering similar episodes in one section of the text. Overall, it is proposes that miracle stories are rhetorical devices that were used to awe the audience to the point of asking "what manner of man is this?" (4:41 KJV). This rhetorical question, in an indirect but powerful way, calls upon the audience to recognize both Jesus's divinity and divine commission. Consequently, this recognition evokes faith and an aspiration to respond towards the oral gospel.

Chapter 7 analyzes the passion narrative to show that the story and the subsequent resurrection were narrated for the purpose of connecting Jesus Christ and his death to the Old Testament promises. It also shows that Mark connected the passion story to Jesus's interpretation of his death by foreboding it in the inaugural words of the Lord's Supper. In effect, this connection was effective in changing the audience's view of Jesus's death from a mere human death to a sacrificial, propitiatory, and vicarious death. As such, the passion story functioned as a rhetorical device to convince the readers that the gospel was functionally salvific.

Finally, an apt conclusion has been appended to wrap up the entire work and to show that indeed the Markan text is a paraenesis and that it was meant to catalyze reader-response to the oral gospel that he and his contemporaries, who may have included the apostle Peter, were proclaiming.

1.7 Limitations of the Study

The work has deliberately avoided labelling the Markan text "a gospel" because of the hermeneutical presupposition consequent of such labelling. Other scholars have also noted the existence of an oral gospel before, during and after the writing of the New Testament texts and that it existed and functioned parallel to the written texts.[44] Though its ontology has been acknowledged, its relationship with the written text and the audience has not been adequately studied. As such, this study is not a novelty but builds upon what other scholars have affirmed.

Finally, the conflation of Mark the book, Mark the author, and Mark as the gospel can cause confusion. As such, the study has limited the use of Mark and its respective pronouns to Mark the author while the book has been designated the Markan text. This delineation brings more clarity in describing the different aspects of the text.

1.8 Delimitations

Whereas the Markan text contains more quotations and allusions of the Old Testament, this study has limited itself to explicit Old Testament quotations in Mark 1:2–3 and 4:12, which have a bearing in lighting up the thesis. Similarly, it has limited its discussion on miracle stories in the first half of the book, that is, up to Mark 8:26. It is expected that an analysis of this section will give a complete view of the nature and function of Old Testament quotations, miracle stories, and Jesus's controversies with the Jewish leaders. The passion narrative, which is in the second half of the text, has been analyzed to show

---

44. The concurrent existence of the written and oral gospel has been noted by Graham N. Stanton in, *Jesus and Gospel*, 58.

that it has been employed as a rhetorical device to catalyze reader-response to the oral gospel that was majorly premised on an interpretation of the passion episode. As such, the study has captured an overall view of the entire text.

1.9 Methodology

This section fronts and discusses rhetorical criticism as the major method of choice in explicating the Markan text. It has however been complimented with insights from other criticism methods especially speech act theory in chapter 6, discourse analysis in chapter 4 and historical grammatical criticism in chapter 5. In particular, the section has surveyed the nature and use of rhetoric and rhetorical criticism in explicating literary works. This method is not an innovation of this researcher but a biblical criticism method that has since been developed and adopted in biblical studies.

The aim of biblical texts is not just to inform, it is also to convince, convict and transform the readers. Thus, Scripture's aim is both informative and transformative. Scripture interpretation is often biased towards analyzing the informative aspect of communication. In other words, it answers the question; what are the referents of the syntagmatic and paradigmatic relations that constitute the text? Grant R. Osborne posits that "The former is linear and defines a word's relationship with the other terms that surround it in the speech act . . . A paradigmatic relation is vertical or associative, noting other terms that could replace it, such as words that are synonymous."[45] However, language is not just descriptive of the world in which it functions; it is also a medium of expressing and sharing the inner longings, attitudes, pains, and joys that are part of being human.

Language is therefore a medium of describing and communicating both the cognitive and affective aspects of the world and the inner human motions. Thus, it is both ideological and pathological. Socially and religiously, language also describes and communicates the desirable and undesirable states of affairs and urges abhorrence of the undesirable and aspiration to achieve the desirable. Perelman has described this state of affairs in his supposition that, "When we are dealing with theses presented in an argumentative discourse, these theses aim at times at bringing about a purely intellectual result – a

---

45. Osborne, *Hermeneutical Spiral*, 96.

disposition to admit their truth – and at other times at provoking an immediate or eventual action."[46] These provocative effects of speech are referred to by Kevin Vanhoozer as the "ulterior effects"[47] of speech, and are grounded in the purview of the speech's illocutionary acts.

The current hermeneutical trends in biblical research have not adequately explored these ulterior effects of speech. Such an understanding would benefit readers by illuminating the informative and transformative aspects of biblical communication. It is often thought that exploring questions that probe the effect of the text upon the readers may be overly subjective. This assumption overlooks the fact that much as texts are informative they are also transformative. As such, hermeneutics whose horizons encompass investigating both the cognitive and affective effects of textual transmission and reception would be more effectual in analyzing the nature and impact of the dialogue between the interlocutors within the matrix of a textual discourse. Its advantage is that it focuses on both aspects of communication – transmission and pragmatics.

Cognizant of the need to inform and transform their audiences, authors embed into texts both convincing and convicting enablers. These enablers include rhetorical devices that enable new understanding to take place, new worldviews to be created, new statuses to be conferred, and new destinies to be pursued. In evaluating narrative texts whose focus is to inform and transform its primary and secondary audience, it is necessary to analyze the effect of the text on the parties involved in the textual dialogue. The aim is to identify the author's intended reader's response towards the text or aspects outside the text. This enables the interpreter to locate not only what the text is saying but also what it means and what it is meant to accomplish. As such, hermeneutics should move the textual analysis beyond analyzing the locution to analyzing the effect of the text on the audience, that is, its rhetorical efficacy which is at times in the purview of the embedded illocutionary and perlocutionary acts.

David Rhoads, Johanna Dewey and Donald Michie have defined rhetoric as "the way in which an author writes so as to create certain effects on readers."[48] Dewey notes, "The rhetorical critic is asking the literary question

---

46. Perelman, *Realm of Rhetoric*, 13.
47. Vanhoozer, *First Theology*, 187.
48. Rhoads, Dewey, and Michie, *Mark as Story*, 137.

of how the rhetorical feature of the present text – structure, pattern, rhythm – affect the reader's response to an understanding of the text."[49] As such, rhetorical criticism can ably control and limit extraneous interpretations. It does not rely on conjecture since it analyzes both the *logia* and *pathos* which are aspects of the communicative process in which rhetoric and speech acts cohere and participate.

Bitzer posits, "Discourse is rhetorical insofar as it functions (or seeks to function) as a fitting response to a situation which needs and invites it."[50] This study suggests that the Markan discourse was a reaction to Mark's audience's obduracy and lukewarm response towards a contemporaneous oral gospel that was outside and independent of the Markan text. As such, in line with Bitzer's postulation, the Markan text is a rhetorical communication. Therefore, it invites rhetorical criticism into its analysis. This hermeneutical method will be used to analyze the function of the Old Testament quotations, miracle stories, and passion narratives which are presumed to be rhetorical devices in the text.

The advantage of using rhetorical criticism is twofold. First, it preserves the narrative as the primary context in which the Markan anecdotal narratives are expressed. Second, rhetorical criticism discusses aspects of the text that cut across the major communication domains of the author, the text and the reader. Madeleine Boucher supports the choice of rhetorical criticism in probing the relationship between the Markan text and the oral gospel saying, "Rhetoric is heterotelic: existing for the sake of something else; having an extraneous end or purpose."[51] Since the hypothesis that is fronted is that the rhetorical devices in the Markan text are aimed at evoking audience response to an aspect outside and independent of the text, then rhetorical criticism is best placed in explicating the Markan text.

Again, Boucher says, "Rhetorical speech has as its purpose to convince, to persuade, to move to decision or action. To persuade the hearer to execute a moral decision or action is one of the many possible goals of rhetorical speech."[52] However, some scholars have argued against use of rhetorical

---

49. Dewey, *Markan Public Debate*, 65.
50. Bitzer, "Rhetorical Situation," 6.
51. Boucher, *Mysterious Parable*, 16.
52. Boucher, 16.

criticism in biblical interpretation because of the possibility of rhetoric engendering a psychological purpose.[53] This study concurs that rhetoric does indeed engender psychological purposes. The affective realm, in which evocation occurs, is a realm of psychology. However, in addition to evoking free choices, the word of God is also meant to influence human behavior and desire, which are aspects of psychology. Elisabeth Schussler Fiorenza agrees with this proposition in her assertion that, "Rhetoric seeks to instigate a change of attitudes and motivations; it strives to persuade, to teach and to engage the hearer/reader by eliciting reactions, emotions, convictions, and identifications."[54]

Use of rhetorical criticism does not in any way circumvent historical and grammatical analyses of texts, it is a complementary method that goes further into investigating the text's convincing and convicting efficacy. Whereas this view does not invalidate the theological view that the nexus between hearing and the affective aspect of Scripture is abridged by the illumination of the Holy Spirit, it suggests that the Spirit is also responsible for embedding Scripture with apt rhetorical devices that are efficacious enough to convince, convict and transform the reader.

The importance of rhetorical criticism as an analytical tool is aptly captured by Benjamin Fiore in his statement that,

> Rhetorical (or pragmatic) criticism considers a work of art chiefly as a means to an end, as a vehicle of communication and interaction between the author and the audience, and investigates the use of traditional devices to produce an effect in an audience. It is an internal criticism that focuses on the rhetoric of the text itself, but also works outward to considerations of author, audience, and their interrelationships. The critics can detect some idea of the author, real and implied, from the text's rhetorical strategies. The critics can also derive information about the real and implied reader from the dispositions and desired effects of the work by the reader (implied reader) and from those elements

---

53. Thiselton puts a distinction between "'*illocutionary*' speech acts, which depend for their effectiveness *on a combination of situation and recognition*, and '*perlocutionary*' speech acts, which depend for their effectiveness on *sheer causal (psychological or rhetorical) persuasive power*." Thiselton, *First Epistle to the Corinthians*, 51.

54. Fiorenza, "Rhetorical Situation and Historical Reconstruction," 387.

of the work which are capable of producing an effect on certain kinds of audiences.⁵⁵

The choice of rhetorical criticism in explicating the Markan text is premised on the need to investigate the text's cognitive and affective impact on the audience and the need to identify and probe the relationship between the text and other interlocutors that are outside and independent of the text. John Verbin avers,

> Social-rhetorical approaches ask what the genre of the text and method of its organization imply about its intended audience; how the author diagnoses the situation addressed; and how arguments are constructed so as to be persuasive. It is not only the explicit arguments that are important, but the way they are constructed – their selection of metaphors, their choice of evidence, and the conduct of their arguments.⁵⁶

As such, rhetorical criticism can facilitate understanding of how authors diagnose and address exigencies presented by their audience's rhetorical situation and how they plan to persuade them to act in order to eliminate these exigencies.

By definition, rhetoric refers to "the art or science of literary composition, particularly in prose, including figures of speech."⁵⁷ However, this definition is narrow in the sense that it assumes that texts are set only within a systematized handbook literary convention. It does not account for scenarios where the text is produced within rudimentary rhetorical conventions. A fuller definition should capture these rudimentary aspects of rhetoric. Peter Phillips notes, "Rhetoric as a strategic communication attempts to mould another person's view of the world in which he or she lives; it invites its audience to reconsider their existing worldview in the light of the worldview promoted through strategic communication of one kind or another."⁵⁸ Phillips has stretched the definition to include reader responses resultant of textual imperatives and evocation. These imperatives and evocations may be viewed

---

55. Fiore, "NT Rhetoric and Rhetorical Criticism," 716.
56. Verbin, *Excavating Q*, 196.
57. Guralnik, *Webster's New Wolrd Dictionary*, 1220.
58. Phillips "Rhetoric," 241.

as the speech acts embedded in the text. As such, a working definition of rhetoric can thus be restated as "the art of literary or speech composition that is aimed at convincing and convicting the audience by means of the speech acts that are deliberately embedded in the particular text or speech."[59]

Arguably, in any intentioned communication, the text is given force of comprehension and eventual appropriation by the rhetorical devices that are embedded in the text's form and structure. Another special aspect of rhetorical analysis has been captured by Patrick Dale and Allen Scult as they note,

> Rhetorical analysis can and should be both an explanation of how a text might have persuaded audiences of its truth and a means by which interpreters can experience that truth for themselves. Indeed, this latter goal becomes an essential tool in the realization of the former. Additionally, this affirmative version of rhetorical approach can serve to integrate the interpreter into the mainstream of the text's readership.[60]

Whereas biblical rhetoric is "the art of persuading individuals and communities to accept the Bible's worldview,"[61] rhetorical criticism "is the analysis of the strategies of persuasion within a text . . . It is the study of how the Bible seeks to offer the reader a new way of seeing the world, of establishing a new community, a new way of being human."[62] Thus, rhetorical criticism is an apt hermeneutical method of investigating the persuasive power of the Markan text and thus a useful tool for identifying the text's nature and purpose. This is aptly captured in George Kennedy's definition of rhetoric as, "that quality in discourse by which a speaker or writer seeks to accomplish his purpose."[63]

1.9.1 Necessity of a Text: Foundation of Rhetoric

The aim of authors of biblical texts is to impact its readers. Nicholas Wolterstorff has captured this aspect in saying, "by uttering and inscribing

---

59. This definition captures both the literary and speech aspects of communication. It also takes care of the rudimentary language conventions whereby rhetoric is not developed as a formal discipline.
60. Dale and Scult, "Rhetoric and Ideology," 66.
61. Phillips, "Rhetoric," 260.
62. Phillips, 260.
63. Kennedy, *New Testament Interpretation*, 3.

words, we do, typically, influence others, in fact and by intent."[64] Clarence Walhout refers to aims of biblical texts as "teleology of texts."[65] This description suggests that texts are not written for their own sake but to impact the audience. As such, though texts are cognitively read, they are also aimed at impacting the reader affectively. Consequently, the hermeneutic horizon should be enlarged to include the analysis of the evocative power of texts on the reader. Jerry Camery-Hoggart has aptly captured this need in saying, "literary scholars have understood 'meaning' more broadly to include the range of reactions evoked within the reader."[66] Thus, texts urge audiences into particular actions. They also create faith through their convincing and convicting rhetorical power. Fiorenza agrees with this proposition in her assertion that, "rhetoric seeks to instigate a change of attitudes and motivations; it strives to persuade, to teach and to engage the hearer/reader by eliciting reactions, emotions, convictions, and identifications. Furthermore, the evaluative criterion for rhetoric is not aesthetics, but praxis."[67] This is affirmed by Frances Young in his postulation that,

> Texts were meant to "mirror" life and to be a "possession forever" able to teach by exemplar. But attention to rhetoric may take us even further. In seeking to instill the techniques of persuasion, teachers both analyzed texts and offered theories. Things can be said in a variety of different ways; the subject matter was clothed in diction, and the choice of style, of vocabulary, of figures of speech, had to be appropriate to what was said if it was to carry conviction . . . But *pistis* (belief, conviction) depended also on the *ethos* (character and lifestyle) of the speaker, as well as the audience's *pathos,* its response, its being moved by the speaker and the message to the point of acceptance.[68]

Generally, biblical texts are born out of a need to immortalize historical phenomena and to revivify their intended effect on readers. They are also

---

64. Wolterstorff, *Divine Discourse,* 75.
65. Walhout, "Narrative Hermeneutics," 90.
66. Camery-Hoggart, *Irony in Mark's Gospel,* x.
67. Fiorenza, "Rhetorical Situation and Historical Reconstruction," 387.
68. Young, "Towards a Hermeneutic," 107.

written "to make ideas known to absent persons."[69] As the time and geographical distance from the time and place of the historical phenomenon increases, historicity gives way to a mythological perception of the phenomenon. Its finer details become hazy and the perception of its significance wanes. Therefore, biblical texts are useful in revivifying the impact of the salvific episode and transmitting it to communities in diverse geographical areas and to successive generations of readers. The need for an authentic and reliable record, with the aim of affirming the believer, correcting and affirming the faith, or stirring the religious practice of the successive believers becomes inevitable. As such, though, to a large extent biblical texts are occasioned by a need to eliminate an exigence in their time, they are also directed to secondary audiences. As Bitzer avers, "some rhetorical situations persist overtime and have resulted in a body of truly rhetorical literature . . . these are rhetorical responses for us because they speak to situations which persist and which are in some measure universal."[70]

The form and content of a text are, therefore, determined by the author's perception of the exigency presented by the audience's rhetorical situation. Bitzer notes, "It is situation that calls discourse into existence."[71] However, Richard Bauckham argues against attaching any need in the audience that may have occasioned the writing of the gospels. He says that "the most essential and, at the same time, the simplest way in which the early Christian movement strove to transmit Bible texts was for their own sake and in their own right, not as part of something else."[72] However, Bauckham has not accounted for the obvious difference in the choice of episodes and styles adopted by the different evangelists or even the explicit identification of the paraenetic purposes by some of the New Testament writers as in John 20:31.

In his reference to the writings of the apostolic fathers and his note of their conspicuous lack of quotations from the texts labelled "the gospels," Bauckham has not explored the possibility that they may not have been privy to these books, or if they were, then they had not yet ascribed scriptural value to them. His supposition is that the contents of the gospels were so

---

69. Smith, "Limited Inc/arnation," 117.
70. Bitzer, "Rhetorical Situation," 13.
71. Bitzer, 2.
72. Bauckham, *Jesus and the Eyewitnesses*, 278.

prevalent that it would have been superfluous to cite them explicitly. On this point, Bauckham has followed a preferred point of view without adducing adequate supporting evidence. In view of the strong textual evidence adduced by the form critics, it is safe to support the position that the texts by the four evangelists and particularly the Markan text are purposeful treatises which addressed particular rhetorical situations. The "view that missionary preaching was the primary *Sitz im Leben*"[73] cannot be easily ignored in any hermeneutical enterprise.

In Jesus's earthly mission, he directed and cleansed his disciples by his word (John 15:3). However, after his death, resurrection and ascension, the reminiscences of his life, word and work were passed on as oral tradition by eyewitnesses. As time passed and the distance from the geographical location of the salvific episode increased, by reason of the expanded geographical reach of the missionary work, the memory of the salvific episode was bound to wane. The attendant risk of not having a living record of the reminiscences of the salvific episode was that, it would, with time, recede into a myth. Though scholars have expressed frustration in defining myth, this study will take myth to be the antithesis of historical. Consequently, the salvific message, which was and is orally transmitted, would also, with time, be viewed as mere folklore.

As such, in addition to its paraenetic purpose of catalyzing reader-response to the oral gospel by enhancing its belief value, the Markan text was also aimed at immortalizing the salvific episode. For that reason, it was incumbent upon the synoptic writers to record genuine accounts within the Christ event in an understandable, convincing, convicting, and transformative form. During the lifetime of the eyewitnesses of the salvific episode, they transmitted the oral tradition about the life and times of Jesus (Luke 1:1–2). However, after their demise, believers interacted with the salvific episode through exegesis of the written records. The text became the only medium of ascertaining the salvific episode. Aware of the faith affirming and ascertaining value of biblical records, their writers were obliged to embellish them with apt rhetorical devices to enable the primary and secondary readers to not only comprehend their meaning but to also achieve the performative purpose of engendering faith in the salvific message.

---

73. Bauckham, 275.

Greco-roman rhetoric in the Markan text

Rhetoric as a way of persuading people concerning the truth of certain propositions is an old art. Extant records of court and political speeches in the Greco-Roman world show that it was used in arguing out court cases,[74] in political speeches,[75] and even in social spheres like in delivering funeral speeches.[76] Rhetoric as a discipline in speech communication was developed in Greco-Roman antiquity by philosophers like Aristotle, Cicero and Quintilian.[77] Rhetoric that focuses on literary production in its three main genres, judicial, deliberative and epideictic is what is commonly known as classical Greco-Roman rhetoric. Kennedy refers to this type of rhetoric as secondary rhetoric. According to Phillips, "it is handbook rhetoric – the conscious development of primary (oral) rhetoric into a practical (textual) skill, fully conceptualized, with developed theoretical framework, education system and supportive literature."[78] Primary rhetoric, however, is the "the art of persuasion per se, usually experienced largely within a largely oral culture: the practice of rhetoric within a society whether conceptualized or not."[79] Classical rhetoric has been adopted into the interpretation of biblical texts and is currently advanced by scholars such as George Kennedy, Wilhelm Wuellner and James Muilenburg.[80]

According to D. F. Watson, Kennedy proposed this five-step methodology to "determine the rhetorical unit; define the rhetorical situation; determine the rhetorical problem or stasis and the species of the rhetoric; analyze invention, arrangement and style; and evaluate the rhetorical effectiveness."[81] In his analysis of Greco-Roman rhetoric, Watson seems to support the notion that biblical interpretation would associate more with epideictic rhetoric which "praises and blames, and concerns itself with what is honourable or the

---

74. Demosthenes, "Prosecution," 57–139; Aeschines, "Defence," 143–188.
75. Demosthenes, "For Megapolis," 169–249, see also other speeches in the same volume.
76. Thucydides, "Pericles' Funeral Speech," 33–38.
77. Phillips, "Rhetoric," 233–234.
78. Phillips, 235.
79. Phillips, 235.
80. See Kennedy, *New Testament Interpretation*; Wuellner, "Arrangement," 51–87; Muilenburg, "Form Criticism and Beyond," 1–18.
81. Watson, "Rhetoric, Rhetorical Criticism," 1041.

dishonourable with a view to increasing or decreasing assent to values."[82] His method can be useful in analyzing the synoptic writings since they concern themselves with the person of Jesus, his mighty works, teachings and their impact on their audiences.

However, it should be noted that though the New Testament texts were authored within the Greco-Roman milieu, it cannot be conclusively stated that all New Testament writers were well versed with Greco-Roman rhetoric. Furthermore, rhetoric is not exclusively a Greco-Roman literary convention. Every spoken language has its unique kind of rhetoric. As has been affirmed by Richard Burridge, "the general awareness of rhetoric and of literary training permeated much winder society than just the formal training. Furthermore, much of rhetoric was a formalization of natural patterns of argument, which can be found in most human societies."[83]

He further avers,

> Due to the position of most Christians in the social strata, which probably was in the middle of the social classes, a general awareness of Hellenistic culture and education can be assumed, if not higher rhetorical training. This means that it is not unreasonable to study the gospels carefully for forms of rhetoric in all senses of the word, but we must be cautious about reading off a direct connection between their narrative biographical texts and the formal oratory of the law court or assembly.[84]

As such, rhetorical criticism of the New Testament must, of necessity, consider probing New Testament rhetoric as part of Hebrew and Aramaic rhetoric which was part of the language conventions of the writers and characters in the New Testament texts.

A study of the structure of the Markan text shows that to some extent, Mark may have employed Greco-Roman rhetorical conventions. It shows aspects of a well-thought-out and well-structured text with an apt *exordium* (1:1–15) and *inventio*. According to Burridge the invention stage of compilation "involves thinking through the subject matter, clarifying what is the

---

82. Watson, 1041.
83. Burridge, "Gospel and Acts," 510.
84. Burridge, 510.

key issue, στασις or *status*, and discovering the best way of persuading the audience: the practice of rhetoric within a society, whether conceptualized or not."[85] The evident *exordium* and *inventio* in the Markan text suggests that serious thought and planning and style discrimination were meticulously done prior to writing the text. This observation goes against Papias's observation that "Mark, having become Peter's interpreter, wrote down accurately everything he remembered, though not in order, of the things either said or done by Christ."[86] Like many scholars after him, he was wrestling with the unusual structure of the Markan text.

This study argues that the Markan text enhances believability of a contemporaneous oral gospel by showing that it is anchored on the community's faith matrix as recorded in the Old Testament Scripture. The body of the text (*argumentation* or *confirmation*)[87] is also noticeable in the way Mark persuades his audience to accept his proposition that the Jesus of the gospel message was indeed the Christ of the Old Testament Scripture and that the gospel message was approved by God through the miracles that Jesus performed which included resurrecting Jesus from the dead.

In summary, consciously or unconsciously, Mark seems to have employed some aspects of Greco-Roman rhetoric. However, introducing a text and arguing out its major proposition was also an aspect of Hebrew rhetoric. It is therefore plausible to argue that rhetorical conventions among different peoples in the world followed the similar patterns although they may not have been studied, conceptualized, defined, and systematized like in the Greco-Roman literary world. J. David Hester says,

> It was through its (*rhetoric*) institutionalization in the education system (*paideia*) as one of the three liberal arts, reinforced through centuries of perceptive instruction, that rhetoric was perceived as a closed system of rules for composition . . . It has only been recently that the work of historians of rhetoric has helped us to appreciate the diversity of rhetoric (as theory and practice) reflecting the variety of values and systems of the

---

85. Burridge, "Gospel and Acts," 382.
86. Eusebius, *Ecclesiastical History*, 113.
87. Watson, "Rhetoric, Rhetorical Criticism," 1042.

complex cultures that comprised not just classical antiquity, but each culture's historical development.[88]

Hester's contribution challenges rhetoricians to expand their horizons beyond the usual Greco-Roman rhetoric in identifying the particular rhetorical convention used by biblical writers.

1.9.2 Hebrew Rhetoric in Genesis

Hebrew rhetoric is in the purview of "primary rhetoric."[89] This is rhetoric that is common to all language conventions but that is not developed into text book rhetoric. Phillips contends, "We shall not expect to find pure, theoretical rhetoric in these texts (*New Testament*), but rather living, vernacular fusion of primary rhetoric drawn from both Greek and Hebrew rhetorical traditions."[90] As such, a rhetorical study of the Markan text should explore further than the Greco-Roman rhetoric per se to investigating Mark's use of primary rhetorical conventions that include Hebrew rhetoric.

Genesis as a rhetorical treatise

J. H. Walton says, "The overall purpose of the book of Genesis is to chronicle the history of the development of the covenant."[91] Arguably, Walton has premised his supposition on the doctrine of progressive revelation.[92] This work proposes and argues that the Genesis episodes are narrated for their rhetorical efficacy in urging the Exodus community and their progeny to adhere to the Sinaitic covenant. In analyzing the function of Genesis, and in particular the Adamic, Noahic, and Abrahamic covenant narratives among Moses's audience, this study supposes that the book of Genesis was authored by Moses.[93] Adducing the reasons for or against this supposition is outside the scope of this work. Certainly, Genesis contains aspects of Hebrew rhetoric. It can

---

88. Hester "Wuellnerian Sublime," 7.
89. Phillips, "Rhetoric," 235.
90. Phillips, 251, italics added.
91. Walton, "Flood," 323.
92. Progressive revelation suggests that throughout the Bible, revelation develops with time and as such interpretation of later revelations can be illuminated by interpretation of earlier revelations. Osborne, *Hermeneutical Spiral*, 361, says that this can lead "one to read later texts into earlier ones as when one sees the Old testament as a Christological case book."
93. Harrison, *Introduction to the Old Testament*, 551, intimates that "it seems legitimate to suppose that the redactional activity was by and large the work of Moses."

provide a comparative treatise that aptly mirrors the Markan text's rhetorical choices, purpose and genre.

Arguably, the dating of Genesis was during the wilderness wanderings. Specifically, it can be located after the community had entered into a covenant with God at Sinai. As such, it is also arguable that the rhetorical situation that may have called for the rhetorical communication such as the narration of the Genesis account was the community's constant breach of the covenant through unbelief and idolatry (Exod 32:1–6).

The creation story as a rhetorical device

The creation narrative shows that the gift of Eden with the accompanying promises of provision, God's presence, and progeny upon obedience not to eat the forbidden fruit is very similar to God's promise of land, provision, God's presence, and progeny in the Mosaic covenant. M. D. Gow suggests, "the frequent use of the compound name Yahweh Elohim emphasizes that God is not only the creator but also the covenant God who enters into relationship with his creatures."[94] Thus, this conditional promise to Adam constituted a covenant. Whenever the story about Adam's breach of the covenant (the fall) and the resultant penalties was narrated, it acted as a profound warning to the Israelites who had likewise shown signs of obduracy in breaching their newly established covenant.

As such, the creation narrative, and in particular the narrative about Adam and Eve's breach of God's command, was directed to the Israelites during the wilderness wanderings. Arguably, Moses narrated his community's history and especially the consequences of their first parent's disobedience as echoes to awaken the community to their own disobedience and to spell out the consequences if they failed to repent and hearken to God's entreaty for rapprochement. Observably, the story of creation and subsequent stories are not mere historical treatises. They do not call for proof much as they are not provable. Their value is not in the authenticity or truth value of the episodes, but in the efficacy of the stories in urging adherence to the covenant that God had entered with Israel at Sinai. As such, proving whether the serpent actually spoke or whether creation took a literal six days, as a historical treatise would demand, is not an aspect of religious treatises. The gist of the text is in

---

94. Gow, "Fall," 286.

its efficacy to mimetically guide the audience and evoke obedience to their own covenant with God. In other words, the text is a rhetorical communication aimed at eliminating the exigence in the extant rhetorical situation of the audience.

A leading question at this juncture is, how do such stories impact the audience? Noticeably, the narrator sets a storyline and portrays a setting that is similar to the rhetorical situation of the audience. According to Bitzer, a rhetorical situation is "a natural context of persons, events, objects, relations, and an exigence which strongly invites utterance."[95] Similarly, the narrator narrates a story that presents a rhetorical situation and an exigence that mirrors the rhetorical situation of the audience and the exigence therein. The challenge of the narrator is to create a meaningful mimetic communiqué between the rhetorical situation of the narrative world and the audience. Such communiqué is similar to John Sailhamer's understanding of Moses's intention in writing the Genesis accounts. He posits, "Moses intended to draw a line connecting the God of the fathers and the God of the Sinai covenant with the God who created the world."[96] By identifying Israel's Yahweh who had sent him to deliver them and who had entered into a covenant with them as the God of creation, Moses achieved two purposes. First, it raised his ethos as a knowledgeable and trustworthy mediator of God's covenant. Second, it served as a rhetorical embellishment of his narrative with a rhetorical device that was apt in convincing and convicting his audience to reconsider their disobedience and adhere to the covenant.

The story of Noah as a rhetorical device

The story about Noah's salvation from the deluge is comparable to that of Israel's deliverance from Egypt. The punishment of Noah's generation for their sins and the redemption of Noah and his family are portrayed side by side to show the paradoxical and parallel existence of God's abhorrence of sin and the multitude of his mercies. Therefore, the narrative shows God's fidelity in keeping his covenant with those who, like Noah, are faithful. It also shows his righteousness in punishing the wayward sinner.

---

95. Bitzer, "Rhetorical Situation," 3.
96. Sailhamer, *Pentateuch as Narrative*, 81.

As such, the Noahic narrative functions as a rhetorical device that is aimed at portraying a vivid mimetic exemplifier to Moses's audience. It is used to challenge the audience to learn from their forefather's successes and failures. Particularly, the story portrays God as faithful in keeping his covenant and as such urges the Israelites to reciprocate and maintain fidelity to their obligations in the covenant. However, Walton has posited that the flood narrative "is intended to reveal the character of God."[97] Though this historical treatise no doubt teaches aspects of theology, its rhetorical situation suggests that the original purpose of narrating the story to the children of Israel was to urge faithfulness to the Sinaitic covenant.

The story of the patriarchs as a rhetorical device

Narrating Abraham's story was a masterpiece in use of rhetoric. Abraham is portrayed as a man who faithfully upheld his covenant with God thereby receiving the fruits of obedience. The story was, no doubt, meant to mimetically exemplify faithful adherence to God's covenant. It was used to urge the community to faithfully uphold their newly established covenant with Yahweh. The stories connected the God who had revealed himself as Yahweh to God the creator who was also the God of their progenitor – Abraham. As such, Moses used the stories of the patriarchs to urge the Israelites to adhere to the covenant stipulations.

Instead of analyzing the significance of the text to the reading community, the common trend in hermeneutics has been to reconstruct the world of the text. The exercise is driven by the desire to know God as he is revealed in his works throughout history. Unfortunately, this method overlooks the need to analyze the author's message to his primary audience. Such reading and interpretation, though driven by a genuine desire to know and understand God and his attributes, ends up alienating an important dialogue partner in the textual discourse matrix – the audience's rhetorical situation which happens to be the text's *Sitz im Leben*. Textual stories are told with the aim of eliminating exigences that authors identify in their audiences' rhetorical situations. The exigence that Moses was dealing with in the Genesis narratives was the possibility of Israel breaching God's covenant. He may also have

---

97. Walton, "Flood," 323.

been dealing with a worse situation of obduracy after they had broken the covenant stipulations by making the golden calf (Exod 32:1–8).

1.9.3 Comparison of Genesis and the Markan Text

Observably, the Genesis account and the Markan text are similar in their nature and function. In both instances, episodes in history are narrated as rhetorical communication to catalyze their audiences to respond favorably to covenants that were outside and independent of the texts. According to Bitzer, "rhetoric alters reality by bringing into existence a discourse of such a character that the audience, in thought and action, is so engaged that it becomes a mediator of change. In this case rhetoric is persuasive."[98] This work shows how the Markan text, as a rhetorical communication, impacts its audience's rhetorical situation. This is achieved by narrating episodes within the Christ event, which was the immediate history of Mark's audience, so as to (1) anchor the gospel of the new covenant on a historical phenomenon that was part of the inherited belief matrix of the Markan community and (2) provide a mimetic portrait through which Mark's audience are urged to abhor obduracy and aspire to obey the gospel message.

1.9.4 Hebrew Rhetoric in the New Testament

Phillips has postulated that

> rhetoric was an everyday aspect of the strategic communication in Israelite society, although it was not as developed as the secondary rhetoric in Greco-Roman literature. . . . This means that we do not have the specific categories to name the commonplaces, devices or tropes, or to analyze whether they conformed to any putative standards.[99]

Some scholars have argued that biblical rhetoric is special in that it does not conform to human standards in proving its truth claims. This position disregards the nature of incarnation whereby God did not only incarnate himself in human flesh (John 1:14), but also in human culture which includes language with its idioms, metaphors and rhetorical conventions. As such, both the Old

---

98. Bitzer, "Rhetorical Situation," 4.
99. Phillips, "Rhetoric," 235.

and New Testaments have employed Hebrew, Aramaic, and Greek language conventions in their various linguistic expressions.

The noticeable stating of facts in biblical phraseology without elaboration using enthymeme is not proof of uniqueness in biblical phraseology. It is, rather, dictated by the fact that these texts were mainly written to believing communities who had taken the communicated truths as normative. However, any introduction of new and unprecedented concepts is normally elaborated by use of enthymeme.[100] An example is the unprecedented virgin conception of Jesus. The angel explained to Mary how it would happen (Matt 1:18–25). Similarly, John explained the divinity and humanity of Jesus Christ (John 1:1–14).

Hebrew rhetoric appears to be an entrenched method of embellishing texts and endowing them with efficacy to convince and convict their audiences. From his writings, it is noticeable that Moses was concerned with the question of how his message would be believed. Embellishment of his message to both Pharaoh and the children of Israel with the saying "thus says the Lord," (Exod 9:1; 11:4; 32:27) that identified the speech as from God and as such carrying the authority of God himself, was to urge belief and enforce performance of its demands. Using this identification formula is an embellishment of the speech with efficacious rhetoric illocutionary acts not only to convince and convict the audience but also to confer new statuses and to enforce obedience to its demands.

The formulaic saying, "thus says the Lord," was later adopted by the prophets in their many oracles to either Israel or the nations. Their epoch can be classified as the era of God's oral and direct communication through his prophets. This direct communication was later put into script. Nevertheless, it still carried the same divine authority and the same cognitive and affective effect on the audience. After the writing of the prophetic oracles and recognition that the written texts had canonical value, references to the written oracles used the identification formula, "as it is written" as in Mark 1:2.

Other rhetorical embellishments that were common from the Mosaic period were narrating God's actions in history which included his miraculous and redemptive works and invoking God's covenants with Israel's forefathers to endow the speech with illocutionary and perlocutionary efficacy.

---

100. Enthymeme is used in this sense as the premise on which a proposition is based.

For example, "I am the God of your father, the God of Abraham, the God of Isaac, and the God of Jacob" (Exod 3:6) or "I am the Lord your God, who brought you out of Egypt, out of the house of slavery" (Exod 20:2) are rhetorical embellishments aimed at enforcing performance of covenant stipulations.

In circumstances where God introduces himself as the God of Abraham, Isaac and Jacob, he identifies himself with Israel's revered forefathers thereby enhancing faith in his word. Again, in the preamble of the covenant at Sinai, Yahweh's identification with the God who delivered them from Egypt is a rhetorical device that shows his rights over the Israelites. The statement's illocutionary act confers upon the Israelites a new relational status as God's people. As such rhetorical embellishments such as invoking the name of God and Israel's forefathers evoked obedience and fidelity to the covenant stipulations. This was enhanced by the fact that the word was being read within a faith community that had a common faith heritage and reverence for the God who is revealed in Scripture.

In summary, rhetoric is not exclusive to the Greco-Roman literary convention. It was and is a universal aspect of both oral and written discourse. As Whitney Shiner posits, "Rhetoric is a communal activity. The meaning of any oration is found only in that communal context as it is presented by the orator and as it is received by the audience."[101] However, in the Greco-Roman world, rhetoric was identified, formalized and institutionalized as an important aspect of the learning process. Nonetheless, rhetoric is encapsulated in the language conventions of communities that have not identified and formalized and incorporated it into their formal learning process.

Rhetoric transcends the form and structure of speech and texts and incorporates use of idioms, hyperbole and stories within the text that enhance the aesthetic and belief value of the text. Awareness of how authors employ rhetoric is important to interpretation of biblical texts. The hermeneutical method that investigates texts by examining their rhetorical embellishment is known as rhetorical criticism.

1.9.5 Rhetorical Criticism

Like many other criticism methods, rhetorical criticism has taken various forms. In his review of the current trends in rhetorical criticism, Gustavo

---

101. Shiner, "Applause and Applause Lines," 130.

Martin-Asensio has identified three strands. The first analyzes scripture following the "convention and rules of classical rhetorical texts."[102] The weakness of this method in studying biblical texts is its assumption that all Bible writers were conversant with elements of classical rhetoric. As such scriptural texts are not evaluated based on the individual writer's language convention but on a criterion that could have been foreign to them. Consequently, the interpretation process may yield a mismatched meaning.

The second trend is represented by what Martin-Asensio describes as one that "sees some value in studying the Greco-Roman manuals, while at the same time issuing words of caution in regard to a mechanical or slavish application of the classical rhetorical categories to the books of the New Testament."[103] Thus, it opposes a "straight jacket" application of the method to all texts but advocates discrimination based on the particularity of the literary composition. Martin-Asensio sees this group as less creative in developing new insights in rhetorical criticism.

The third trend is followed by scholars who support a method that incorporates both ancient and modern insights into human communication. These writers "argue that it cannot be demonstrated that the New Testament writers were familiar with and adopted, whether consciously or not, the complex structures taught in rhetorical manuals."[104] These scholars further argue that "the term 'rhetoric' encompasses much more than Aristotle, Quintilian or Seneca ever envisioned."[105] Martin-Asensio concludes by saying that "rhetorical analysis has succeeded in 'highlighting the importance of *function in context* in our study of New Testament documents.'"[106]

After analyzing the merits and demerits of the three trends, Martin-Asensio has suggested that, for rhetorical criticism "to be more fruitful, a more 'productive match' must be sought between the biblical texts and a critical method. . . . Such a method, in short, must be aimed at the study of language as a means, indeed the primary means of social interaction."[107] He then introduces "Michael Halliday's 'functional grammar' as an ideally

---

102. Martin-Asensio, "Hallidayan Functional Grammar," 86.
103. Martin-Asensio, 86.
104. Martin-Asensio, 89.
105. Martin-Asensio, 89.
106. Martin-Asensio, 92.
107. Martin-Asensio, 92.

suited method for achieving the aims of rhetorical criticism."[108] This study, while noting the contribution of the three trends and their use today, builds upon the foundation of the third trend which suggests that classical rhetoric is too limited to analyze the varied and sometimes very rudimental literary types contained in the New Testament. However, to meet Martin-Asensio's genuine concern of the need to incorporate into the rhetorical criticism a system that can connect biblical literature with real life; this study has proposed to complement rhetorical criticism with insights provided by Austin's speech act theory. This hybrid method is more fruitful in investigating both the cognitive and affective impact of the text on the audience. The whole purpose of an author's employment of rhetoric is to enable and enhance the communication process.

Literary criticism presumes that, consciously or unconsciously, the author structures a text in a way that would direct its understanding, interpretation and effectiveness in its evocations. In this connection, Vanhoozer avers, "using language to communicate is not an arbitrary happening . . . the 'design plan' of language is to enable communication and understanding."[109] It is with this teleological view of language use that Bernard Lategan says, "The term 'rhetorical' is synonymous to 'pragmatic intent.'"[110] In this premise, literary critics hypothesize that by analyzing the textual structure and form, it is possible to identify the literary and structural pragmatic markers that the author used in constructing the text. Identifying and analyzing these markers would in turn guide the interpreter into the purpose and meaning of the text. These literary and structural clues may be in the form and structure of the literary units, in the choice of the syntax, metaphors, idioms, parables, allegories, genre, and even in the artistic arrangement of the information which include parallelism and chiastic formations. As such, as Michael E. Vines says, "The literary work not only makes claims, evaluations, and judgments concerning previous utterances; it also makes assumptions, and anticipates and parries possible counter responses."[111]

---

108. Martin-Asensio, 92.
109. Vanhoozer, *First Theology*, 167.
110. Lategan, "Textual Space as Rhetorical Device," 397.
111. Vines, *Problem of Markan Genre*, 58.

Rhetoric in speech and literary structure can be used not only to convince but to convict. That is, rhetorical formations are aimed at both informing and forming. In other words, they affect both the cognitive and affective aspects of the audience. This position is supported by Vanhoozer's assertion that, "language is transformative as well as informative . . . Hence we are interested in the pragmatics as well as the semantics of language."[112] This view of rhetoric integrates semantics, which is the function of the author, and pragmatics, which is in the purview of the audience.

Aware that after leaving his or her ambit, the text is an independent agent, the author is obliged to embed it with every available literary device that would encapsulate and articulate the facts and meaning of the message to enable the reader understand it without recourse to the author. These enablers of comprehension and understanding are the rhetorical devices that are consciously embedded into the text. The responsibility of interpreters is to identify and analyze these cues in order to comprehend the text's message. Rhetoric is effectual in convincing and convicting the reader about the truth and belief value of the message in which it is embedded. Wilhelm Wuellner describes rhetoric "as power of the sublime"[113] to which he says "it brings to awareness and into focus how the spiritual is working in the physical."[114] Thus, the sublime nature of rhetoric enables the affective efficacy of speech or text to impact the audience.

The first task in rhetorical analysis is, therefore, to identify a text's rhetorical devices. These cues could be aspects of the text's structure, syntax, argumentation, anecdotes, and speech acts. The second task is to investigate and interpret how these rhetorical cues contribute to the textual function of convincing and convicting the reader, the former being cognitive and the latter affective, concerning aspects that could be within or outside the text. Third, a consideration of the rhetorical situation that prompted the writing of the text is analyzed to identify the purpose for which the text was written. These are the three major tasks in analyzing a rhetorical communication. The final task is to apply the message of the text depending on the interpretation that is directed and illuminated by the rhetorical analysis of the text.

---

112. Vanhoozer, *First Theology*, 164.
113. Wuellner, "Reconceiving a Rhetoric of Religion," 26.
114. Wuellner, 26.

Peter Nyende avers:

> The critical reading of a text rhetorically is in part carried out by determining its *effects* on its audience; in part, too, by examining the strategies (*invention*), such as discussing techniques, argument structure, use of evidence, treatment of subject, control of emotions etc., that a rhetor marshals to create those effects; and, not least of all, by considering the *exigences* that occasion a text's emergence in the first place. The amalgam of these three components of rhetoric, but especially, if not primarily, *exigences* is at times known as the "the rhetorical situation" of a text. It is this rhetorical situation that allows the rhetorical critic to make sense of a given text.[115]

As such, the aim of rhetorical criticism is interpretation of texts. It identifies the nature and function of the rhetorical devices that originally structured the text. Through rhetoric's evocative power, the reader is drawn not only to believe but also to practice that which the text urges. Since, ontologically, all Bible texts have embedded rhetorical devices, rhetorical criticism is an important and complementary method in biblical hermeneutics.

1.9.6 Rhetoric and Rhetorical Situation

Bitzer says, "Rhetorical discourse comes to existence as a response to a situation."[116] Since most biblical texts are occasioned communications, they are rhetorical discourses. They are birthed out of a desire to change the audience's perception and disposition to the author's perception and disposition. Authors use texts to inform their audiences and at times to urge them to act in certain ways that are either prescribed in the text or in an aspect that is outside of the text. The author is therefore obligated to embellish the text with rhetorical devices that prompt the audience to act to solve the exigence presented by their extant situation. Rhetoric, in this case, acts as the agent within the communication process that catalyzes the audience to comprehend, aspire, and strive towards acts that would solve such an exigence. Thus,

---

115. Nyende, "Hebrew Exegesis," PhD seminar, author's notes.
116. Bitzer, "Rhetorical Situation," 5.

rhetoric is a function of the author and is informed by the audiences' need as it is perceived by the author.

Bitzer describes the text's prompting occasion as a "rhetorical situation."[117] He defines rhetorical situation as "a complex of persons, events, objects, and relations presenting an actual or potential exigence which can be completely or partially removed if discourse, introduced in the situation, can so constrain human decision or action as to bring about the significant modification of the exigence."[118] A discourse that is geared at influencing the removal of the actual or potential exigence would of necessity demand deliberate and choice rhetorical devices that highlight and prompt action towards resolution of the exigence. Bitzer defines exigence as "an imperfection marked by urgency; it is a defect, an obstacle, something waiting to be done, a thing which is other than it should be."[119] As such, an exigence is an anomaly whose removal changes the rhetorical situation to a norm that is envisaged by the author.

Therefore, effective rhetorical constructions must, of necessity, use rhetorical conventions that are shared by both the author and the audience. If the author is bereft of sufficient rhetorical acumen to aptly embellish the text, the readers find it difficult to understand and work towards actualizing the desired norm. This means that if Mark's audience was rudimentary in terms of understanding Greco-Roman rhetoric, his use of this type of rhetoric would not have evoked the intended reactions due to barriers in rhetorical conventions. The audience's exposure to the writer's rhetorical conventions is a major determinant of the rhetorical devices that the writer adopts. As such it is also possible to reconstruct and identify the implied audience from the kind of rhetoric used by the author. Use of complex rhetoric suggests an audience that is exposed to complex rhetorical conventions but use of primary and rudimentary rhetorical cues suggests a simple, rudimentary, and at times a semi-illiterate audience in as far as handbook rhetoric is concerned.

Thiselton has identified an aspect of rhetoric in biblical texts that need to be interrogated. He posits, "I distinguish between illocutionary speech acts, which depend for their effectiveness on a combination of situation and recognition, and 'perlocutionary' speech acts, which depend for their effectiveness

---

117. Bitzer, 6.
118. Bitzer, 6.
119. Bitzer, 6.

on sheer causal (psychological or rhetorical) persuasive power."[120] Thiselton is in effect drawing a line between speech effects that are prompted by persuasion through the text and effects that are prompted affectively by the Holy Spirit. This view seems to have been influenced by his theological understanding of the doctrine of the Holy Spirit's illumination in understanding Scripture. While acknowledging the work of the Holy Spirit in illumination of Scripture, it is the position of this work that the doctrine of incarnation suggests that God uses human language in all its facets to express the gospel in a simple-to-understand form. As such, the Holy Spirit inspires writers to use apt rhetorical devices that are understandable to the readers.

1.9.7 Rhetoric and Meaning

Osborne notes that "an extensive debate rages today over both the possibility and the importance of a critical examination of Scripture (or any other text) in order to ascertain its original message."[121] However, it is incontrovertible that biblical texts are written with a pragmatic intent. Therefore, they are written in a form and structure that attract readership, enable effective transfer and understanding of the author's intention to the intended reader.[122] In situations where the author shares the same context with the primary reader, the author's intention is synonymous with the meaning of the text.

However, in a situation where secondary readers do not share the same presupposition pool with the author, the readers approach the text as eavesdroppers to the textual conversation between the author and the primary reader. In such situations, the intention of the author and the textual meaning may differ depending on the new context and presupposition pool of the secondary reader. Therefore, a probe and reconciliation of the contexts and presupposition pools of author and secondary reader is necessary in any hermeneutical enterprise.

As such, meaning can be defined as the intention of the author that is communicated to the reader through the medium of the text. Intention in this sense could be the author's aspiration to communicate a point of view, urge an action, or influence a change of character. Vanhoozer states, "one's

---

120. Thiselton, *First Epistle to the Corinthians*, 51.
121. Osborne, *Hermeneutic Spiral*, 465.
122. Osborne, 465.

intention refers to what one plans to do."[123] Thus intention consists of a desire to change the perception or state of the reader to agree with the writer's perception or desired state. The text is therefore a conveyor of intention and a catalyst of action.

According to Vanhoozer, "there is a determinate something 'in' the text – intended meaning – that remains fixed and unchanging throughout the history of its interpretation."[124] He further says, "meaning can refer to the doing (action) and to the deed done (act)."[125] Thus meaning happens upon hearing, seeing, or touching and being impacted by these acts after duly interpreting and understanding what has been sensed. In other words, meaning happens when the text evokes the intended effects or prompts the reader to act and react to change the extant perception or disposition towards the norm that is described and encouraged in the text. Meaning is neither inherent in the author, text nor reader, it is a function that can be aided or thwarted at either stage of the process depending on the effectiveness of the medium of communication. As such, the rhetorical embellishment of texts aids interpretation of the intention of the author.

1.9.8 Use of Rhetorical Criticism in the Markan Study

In the present study, rhetorical criticism has been used to assess the strategies that Mark used to order his text so as to effectively communicate his message and to eliminate his audience's rhetorical situation's exigence. It explores issues like structure and the literary conventions that Mark used in compiling the text. It also explores the textual embellishments which the author used to effectively meet his pragmatic concerns. Rhetorical devices and speech acts are part of these effectual textual embellishments. Dewey considers rhetorical formations in the Markan text as embellishments to create audience appeal, understanding and buy-in to the text and its teachings. She says that Mark's rhetorical embellishments are used to lead the audience into the story through statements that "set the stage for the episode to follow."[126] However, this study has identified rhetorical formations in the Markan text that draw

---

123. Vanhoozer, *Is There a Meaning in This Text?*, 75.
124. Vanhoozer, 259.
125. Vanhoozer, 226.
126. Dewey, *Markan Public Debate*, 68.

the audience to an appeal and buy-in to an oral gospel that was outside and independent of the text. As such, the audience was hearing two messages; first, the oral gospel that was outside and independent of the text and second, the paraenetic evocations that are prompted by the Markan text. Therefore, the text acts as a catalyst to audience response to the oral gospel.

Being a work of art, the textual structure, which entails the arrangement and interrelation of the parts, can serve as a rhetorical device since it contributes to motivating the reader and illuminating the textual context in which each thematic formation is set. Therefore, the text's artistry contributes to the effectiveness of articulation of its message and hence its rhetorical efficacy. Structuralism has however acquired a place of its own as a discipline in literary criticism. As such, it has been used sparingly in this study to explain Mark's reason for clustering miracle stories in one section[127] and in explaining the noticeable contextual stratification of the episodic themes in the text.[128]

Analysis of the syntax contributes the most to rhetorical analysis of texts. It presupposes that textual composition follows commonly used literary conventions. This is noticeable in works of well-trained rhetoricians and elitist writers like Luke, Paul, and in a more polished form, the author of Hebrews.[129] However, in pre-conceptualized writings like the Markan text, a view that is demonstrated by the pleonastic presentation of its content, whole forms[130] are better units of analyzing the rhetorical value than syntactic formations. This study, therefore, focus more on analyzing thematic forms in the Markan text. These forms will be limited to Old Testament quotations, Jesus's controversy stories, parables, the miracle stories, and the passion story. Stanley Porter and Dennis Stamps note, "one aspect of rhetorical criticism is that of assessing the nature and strategies of argumentation."[131] Though the Markan text does not

---

127. This issue is discussed in chapter 6, the section "Clustering the miracle stories as a rhetorical device."

128. This issue is discussed in chapter 3, section 3.5

129. Luke's Luke-Acts is an example of the work of a writer from the higher echelons of the literary community. His exordium, body and peroration show use of classical rhetoric. Similarly, Paul's Epistles follow the Greek introduction argumentation and conclusion method of literary outlay. Hebrew's use of *synkrisis* (Peter Nyende, NEGST, AIU, March 2015) also shows the work of an accomplished rhetor.

130. Forms in this case is defined aptly by the "form criticism" of the twentieth-century scholars like Dibelius in *From Tradition to Gospel*, 6.

131. Porter and Stamps, "Introduction," 18.

constitute argumentation, but rather an exhortation, a rhetorical analysis of the text is more helpful in identifying its purpose and meaning.

Rhetorical units have been identified at three levels. First, the structural construction of the text has been examined to identify the reason for Mark's structural biases (i.e. why he structured his message functionally and geographically). Second, the textual units have been investigated to identify the text's literary convention. In particular, the question of the text's "gospelness" has been analyzed in order to identify the referent of the term gospel in Mark 1:1 and to show that the textual label "the Gospel according to Mark" in the second century CE imposes a hermeneutical presupposition in the interpretive process of the text. A delineation of the interlocutors and their relationships has been analyzed to explain the flow of the Markan discourse. Third, the Old Testament quotations, miracle stories, and passion narratives have been investigated to identify their rhetorical nature and contribution in catalyzing audience response to the oral gospel that was outside and independent of the text.

1.10 Summary

When faced with a book such as the Markan text in which the text's occasion is not explicitly stated, much conjecture is relied on in trying to interpret the text. Rhetorical analysis "serves as a control to exegesis, limiting the possibilities of understanding, excluding some interpretations on the ground that they conflict with the rhetorical feature of the passage."[132] Rhetorical analysis shows that the Markan text had paraenetic value to the primary audience and also to the secondary readers including us. The study is useful in subjecting the Markan text to greater scrutiny thereby enlarging the scope of Markan research.

---

132. Dewey, *Markan Public Debate*, 6.

CHAPTER 2

"Gospelness" of the Markan Text

2.1 Introduction

This section analyzes the referent of the term εὐαγγέλιον (gospel) from Jesus's milieu to the patristic milieu. The analysis is aimed at clarifying whether the gospel referenced in Mark 1:1 and the content of the text were synonymous. In particular, this analysis will show that the referent of the term εὐαγγέλιον in Mark 1:1 is the oral gospel that existed outside and independent of the text. In addition, it also identifies the content of the oral gospel. The study has used both diachronic and synchronic approaches.

The "gospelness" of books which were designated "το εὐαργέλιον" in the second century is an issue that should attract interest in biblical scholarship. Claudio Moreschini and Enrico Norelli have posited that "the multiplicity of the gospels was to some extent a problem for the early Church."[1] The widely accepted ascription of "gospelness" to the contents of the four treatises by Matthew, Mark, Luke, and John and the apparent eclipsing of the one and only oral gospel that was circulating simultaneously with the written texts introduces a pre-understanding that impacts interpretation of these texts.

2.2 The Salvific Episode and the Salvific Gospel

A study of the relationship between the salvific episode, the Markan text, and the salvific gospel is crucial in identifying and understanding the referent of

---

1. Moreschini and Norelli, *Early Christian Greek*, 205.

the word εὐαγγέλιον in Mark 1:1. This work supposes that the salvific episode is the entirety of the Christ event which encapsulates the birth of Jesus, his teachings, his passion, resurrection, the outpouring of the Holy Spirit, the continuous work of the Holy Spirit in the church, and the awaited parousia. As such, the salvific episode constitutes already accomplished and yet to be accomplished episodes. It engenders human response by faith to its author and fulfiller – Jesus – and his vicarious death (blood) that was "poured out for many" (14:24 ESV). As such, the significance of the salvific episode to humanity's redemption demands that it be proclaimed to the heirs of salvation.

In New Testament parlance, proclamation of the certainty and significance of the salvific episode to God's redemptive agenda constitutes ευαγγελιζεσθαι while the content of the proclamation is το εὐαγγέλιον. In other words, the contents of το εὐαγγέλιον is the news concerning God's gracious fulfilment of the promise to usher into the world the salvific episode coupled with a call to a response in faith towards Jesus and his salvific work on the cross. In this understanding, the contents of a book that announces the fulfilment of the salvific episode, its salvific significance to humanity, and enjoins a faith response towards Jesus (Roman 10:10), can be regarded as "το εὐαγγέλιον."

In trying to establish the "gospelness" of the Markan text, it is necessary to ascertain whether its content can be considered as a proclamation of the fulfilment and salvific significance of the salvific episode coupled with a call to respond by faith in Jesus Christ and his salvific work on the cross. Another question that should concern the hermeneutist is, what is the relationship between the salvific episode and the salvific gospel? Whereas the salvific episode is a historical and propitiatory episode, the salvific gospel is a rhetorically efficacious proclamation that is used to draw the hearers into faith and trust in the salvific episode (Romans 10:17). In addition to its thesis, this study ascertains the significance of the Markan text and, specifically, the significance of its rhetorical devices in this salvific transaction.

2.3 Changes in the Referent of the Term Εὐαγγέλιον

Current usage of the word εὐαγγέλιον is a good example of the changes in the referent of a word and how such changes can affect biblical interpretation if their inherent impact is not accounted for in the hermeneutical process. The referent of the word "εὐαγγέλιον" has mutated over the years to stand for different referents in different eons. According to Helmut Koester, εὐαγγέλιον was, "originally a term for the early Christian proclamation."[2] Similarly, Graham Stanton says, "in the earliest post Easter decades, τὸ εὐαγγέλιον refers to oral proclamation of the significance of the death and resurrection of Jesus, not to a written account of the story of Jesus."[3] However, through the succeeding eons, this word's referent, as used in the Bible, mutated to refer to different things. Stanton further posits that "there is general agreement that by no later than the second half of the second century τὸ εὐαγγέλιον was used to refer to a 'gospel book.'"[4]

The question under focus is whether, consequent to the changes of the referent of the term εὐαγγέλιον, interpreters have been reading back its referent during the patristic milieu into its referent during the Markan milieu. As N. T. Wright has posited, "of course, a later writer recording an earlier division may well project backwards an anachronistic understanding of that division."[5] A changed reference to a word, in time, is likely to lead to an anachronistic reading of the same word in an earlier time and context. As such, as Roger Lundin has posited, "to understand the words in a text, we must have a related understanding of the human actions involved in the use of these words."[6] The secondary reader of a text needs to take into account the context that produced the word in order to align his or her understanding with the situation that occasioned its use. This study is useful in identifying the most probable referent of the word τὸ εὐαγγέλιον in Mark 1:1. It eliminates the possibility of imposing later-day referents to the Markan milieu when the word may have had a different referent.

C. C. Broyles notes,

> the reader of the gospels must be wary of reading a post-Easter definition into the evangelists' use of the term *gospel* . . . In the Synoptics it is found in the mouth of Jesus at the beginning of his ministry: "The time is fulfilled and the kingdom of God is at

---

2. Koester, "From the Kerygma-Gospel," 361.
3. Stanton, *Jesus and Gospel*, 52.
4. Stanton, 52.
5. Wright, *New Testament and the People of God*, 346.
6. Lundin, "Interpreting Orphans," 58.

hand; repent and believe the gospel" (Mk 1:14–15; cf. Mt 4:17; Lk 2:18, 43).[7]

As such, to Jesus, εὐαγγέλιον referenced the proclamation that the kingdom of God,[8] which had been anticipated in the Old Testament promises, had finally been inaugurated. As such, redemption through Jesus's work on the cross, which was part of the accruing benefits to those who would accept to be subjects of the kingdom, was available. Being the subject of Jesus's gospel, an interpretation of what entailed the kingdom was an important aspect of proclamation of the gospel. However, this understanding mutated as history progressed and by the "second half of the second century, το εὐαγγέλιον was used to refer to a 'book.'"[9] This change needs to be accounted for in textual interpretation otherwise the ensuing presupposition that the texts by the four evangelists are the gospels can limit and misdirect interpretation of these texts.

The transition from Jesus's proclamation to the apostolic proclamation witnessed an incorporation of the salvific significance of Jesus's passion and resurrection into what was, by then, Jesus's proclamation of the fulfilment of the time and the nearness of the kingdom of God (1:15). As such, during the time of the apostles, the referent of the term εὐαγγέλιον encompassed the interpretation and proclamation of the nature and salvific significance of the incarnation, death, and resurrection of Jesus Christ followed by a call to audience response in faith towards Jesus for the remission of sins and adoption into the church (Acts 2:22–40; 3:12–26; 27–53; 10:34–48). In the era of the apostolic fathers of the late first century and early second century, the term referenced the oral proclamation of the nature and significance of the Christ event and the consequent ethical demands as shown in the *Didache* titled "Διδαχὴ κυρίου διὰ τῶν δώδεκα ἀποστόλων τοῖς ἔθνεσιν (Didache 1:1),[10] that is, *The Teachings of the Lord to the Nations*[11] *by the Twelve Apostles*.[12]

---

7. Broyles, "Gospel (Good News)," 283.

8. The kingdom of God is taken to be the rule of God through Jesus Christ.

9. Stanton, *Jesus and Gospel*, 52.

10. Didache accessed via BibleWorks [c:\program files\x86)\bibleworks 9\init\bw900.swc].

11. The word ἔθνεσιν could as well be translated as nations or peoples. As such, though some have translated it as Gentiles, Didache was not specific to Gentiles but to all peoples including the Jewish Christians.

12. Homes, *Apostolic Fathers*, 345.

From the era of the church fathers, in the second-half of the second century, to the present, the term εὐαγγέλιον has been used in reference to the written "prose narratives of Jesus' life and ministry."[13] Within sections of biblical scholarship, gospel is also seen as an unprecedented literary genre (*sui generis*) that narrates the life and times of Jesus Christ. Currently, in its popular usage, the term gospel refers to any saying that is believed to convey a truth proposition. These changes need to be accounted for in the process of interpreting the Markan text.

Stanton avers, "Gospel may have been adapted from its usage in the plural in the imperial court or from its secular usage, in which it meant simply 'good news' without any religious connotations."[14] This position suggests that the gospel authors used the secular connotation to describe a like phenomenon in the religious circles. However, this book is of the view that, its use in New Testament circles was rather an adaptation from its usage by Jesus in his native Aramaic or Hebrew to describe the news that, at last, God had fulfilled the promise, that was anticipated in Scripture, of ushering into the world his kingdom and that Jesus was its embodiment, king, mediator and herald. In agreement with this proposition, William Horbury observes that,

> Aramaic, including Aramaic renderings of Hebrew Scripture, such as where it is used in the participle form in Isaiah 52:7 (εὐαγγελιζομένου ... εὐαγγελιζόμενος ἀγαθά) who brings good news, . . . who brings glad tidings of good things (NKJ), would have formed the immediate background of the Christian use of the Greek noun.[15]

The change of the referent of the term "εὐαγγέλιον" in the time of Jesus to the referent by the church fathers is problematic to hermeneutics. This problem is aptly captured by Harry Gamble in his assertion that,

> The emergence of written gospels in the second half of the first century posed two problems for the early Church. The first was owing to early Christian use of the term gospel, which from the

---

13. Hutardo, "Gospel (Genre)," 276.
14. Stanton, *Jesus and Gospel*, 35.
15. Horbury, "'Gospel' in Herodian Judaea," 13.

beginning had been used to designate the fundamental message of salvation, emphatically understood to be single and unified.[16]

As such, in interpreting New Testament texts, it is necessary to locate the primary referent and meaning of biblical terms within the social and religious context in which the books were written so as to avoid the pitfalls of anachronism. As Ludwig Wittgenstein has posited, "we gain an understanding of the meaning of a word, phrase, or text by examining its place in the surrounding context of human action."[17]

2.3.1 Etymology of the Word "Εὐαγγέλιον"

The etymology of words for the purpose of ascertaining their meaning has recently been criticized. James Barr states, "the main point is that the etymology of a word is not a statement about its meaning but about its history . . . It is quite wrong to suppose that the etymology of a word is necessarily a guide either to its 'proper' meaning in a later period."[18] While this study agrees with Barr's statement, it notes that etymology is useful in establishing the historical development of a word and in pinpointing its usage of a word at a given epoch. Awareness of the different referents of a word in different epochs is necessary in warding off anachronistic reading of their referents in one epoch into another. This study probes the historical development of the word εὐαγγέλιον and hence the use etymology.

The word εὐαγγέλιον was not original to Bible writers. It was first used in the LXX as a Greek equivalent of the Hebrew word בְּשׂרָה. According to O. A. Piper, "as many Hebrew verbs, it has an ambivalent meaning, designating the public announcement of something wrought by God – e.g., a defeat (1 Sam. 4:17) or a deliverance (Ps. 96:2) – that is of special importance to the group or collectivity which receives the news."[19] In its Greco-Roman political context, it was generally used as a referent to any good tidings. According to Verlyn Verbrugge, it was "chiefly a technical term for a message bringing joy . . . it is mainly in connection with oracles (i.e., the promise of some future event) and in the imperial cult the term *euangelion* acquires a religious

---

16. Gamble, "New Testament Canon," 276.
17. Wittgenstein, *Philosophical Investigations*, 11.
18. Barr, *Semantics of Biblical Language*, 109.
19. Piper, "Gospel," 443.

meaning."²⁰ In this latter referent, "news of a divine ruler's birth, coming of age, or enthronement as well as his speeches, and acts, are glad tidings that bring long-hoped-for fulfilment to the longings of the world for happiness and peace."²¹ Thus, the term's use in biblical circles predates the New Testament. In the Old Testament, it is used in the LXX in 2 Samuel 4:10.

Verbrugge also argues that,

> The verb *euangelizo* . . . comes to stand for the Hebrew *bissar*, to announce, tell, and publish (e.g., 1 Ki. 1:42; Jer. 20:15). This verb is used in Psalm 40:9; 68:11; 96:2; Isaiah 52:7, to herald Yahweh's universal victory over the world and his kingly rule . . . This 'gospel' is effective speech, a powerful saying, a word בְּשׂרָה that brings its own fulfilment. In the mouth of the messengers God himself speaks and his word is accomplished; he commands and it is done (cf. Ps. 33:6, 9).²²

Burridge says, "Within the Old Testament the verb εὐαγγελίζεσθαι has theological sense, e.g. Isa. 52:7; 61:1 (LXX)."²³ Therefore, the referent of the term εὐαγγέλιον and its cognate verbs as used in the New Testament should rather be understood from the Hebrew context and not the Greek context. After all, their Greek equivalents in the New Testament are translations of Jesus's use of the terms in either Hebrew or Aramaic into Greek by the writers of the New Testament.

As such, designation of the writings of the four evangelists, Matthew, Mark, Luke, and John as the gospels was a paradigm shift. The implication of the ensuing presupposition to interpretation needs to be taken into account in every instance of interpreting these texts. Carson, Moo and Morris have rightly said that,

> Nowhere in the New Testament is any of the four accounts of Jesus' ministry called a gospel (εὐαγγέλιον [*euangelion*]); . . . "Gospel" and the cognate verb "preach the gospel" (ευαγγελίζομαι [*euangelizomai*]) are used in the New Testament,

---

20. Verbrugge, *New International Dictionary of New Testament Theology*, 213.
21. Broyles, "Gospel (Good News)," 283.
22. Verbrugge, *New International Dictionary of New Testament Theology*, 213
23. Burridge, *What Are the Gospels?*, 187.

and especially frequently in Paul, to denote the message of God's saving act in his son (see, e.g., Mark 1:14–15; Rom. 1:16; 1Cor.15:1; Gal. 1:6–7).[24]

It is arguable that, some of the write-ups by the evangelists and even some of the writings by the apostles were initially understood as exhortations to their audiences to believe and appropriate an oral gospel that was outside and independent of the particular texts. This raises a fundamental question: What entailed the oral gospel? In his commentary on the ministry of the non-writing apostles, Eusebius argues, "using only the proof of the divine Spirit, who was working in them, and the miracle-working power of Christ that was being carried out through them, they were proclaiming the knowledge of the kingdom of heaven to all the inhabited world, caring little for attention to writing books."[25] This note shows that, to a large extent, proclamation of the gospel involved a Spirit inspired oral proclamation of the in-breaking of the kingdom of God and its significance to God's redemptive agenda.

Casurella notes, "An examination of the *euangel*-word group gives an idea of what Christians until about 150 AD understood by the term *gospel* . . . the words belonging to this group refer to grace of God in Christ rather than to a written gospel."[26] To enhance the belief value of this oral gospel, the Old Testament Scriptures were used to ground it on the promises and stipulations of the community's inherited faith. The stories of the holy life of Jesus, his deeds of love, passion, and resurrection were also recalled to validate the oral gospel message. It is also apparent that the teachings that were encapsulated in the two ordinances that Jesus inaugurated and commanded the church of all time to be performing and celebrating were complementary to the oral gospel (Mark 14:22–26; 16:16; Acts 2:42; 46; 1 Cor 11:23–26).

In summary, as used in the New Testament, the word εὐαγγέλιον should rather be seen as a translation of the Hebrew word בְּשׂרָה or its Aramaic equivalent. As such it should be seen to be a derivative of its cognate in Hebrew or Aramaic. It derives its meaning from the proclamation of the soteriological significance of the person and work of the Jewish Messiah, whom, variously, Jesus alluded to be (8:27–29; 14:61–62). Thus, the word

---

24. Carson, Moo, and Morris, *Introduction to the New Testament*, 46.
25. Eusebius, *Ecclesiastical History*, 3.24.1–5.
26. Casurella, "Gospel," 431.

"gospel" as used in Mark 1:1 refers to the message of joy about the dawning and soteriological significance of the kingdom of God and its king – Jesus. As such, gospel is more than an announcement of the coming of the Messiah; it includes an interpretation of what his incarnation, death and resurrection mean to humanity. This is evident in the message of the angels upon the birth of Jesus in Bethlehem; that "for unto you is born … a saviour, who is Christ the Lord" (Luke 2:9–14).

An announcement of the birth and deeds of Jesus without an interpretation of their significance to God's salvific agenda constitutes a mere story of a personality who appeared in history. The message acquires the privilege of the title το εὐαγγέλιον when it relates the soteriological significance of its subject. This is the criterion that ought to guide the determination whether the Markan text or any other writing merits the dignity of the label το εὐαγγέλιον.

To Mark, gospel is the good news about the nature and salvific significance of the kingdom that had been anticipated in Hebrew Scripture and that had been inaugurated in the coming of Jesus Christ (1:14–15). However, the question that confronts the interpreter is this: Is this gospel, to use the words of Gundry, "the good news as such, as preached, or as written up in Mark's gospel?"[27] Prophecy, precedents in Scripture, and later proclamations show that gospel announced the fulfilment of the time when the anticipated kingdom of God was to be inaugurated, the coming of Jesus Christ, and the significance of his death to humanity's salvation (Acts 2:14–40; 3:12–26; 10:36–43).

2.3.2 Referents of the Word "Gospel" in Jesus's Time

The first mention of the word gospel by Jesus Christ as recorded in the Markan text is Mark 1:15, "πεπλήρωται ὁ καιρὸς καὶ ἤγγικεν ἡ βασιλεία τοῦ θεοῦ· μετανοεῖτε καὶ πιστεύετε ἐν τῷ εὐαγγελίῳ" (NA 28). Mark refers to the gospel that Jesus proclaimed as "τὸ εὐαγγέλιον τοῦ θεοῦ" (1:14 NA 28). It is apparent that Jesus's concept of "gospel" was a proclamation about the fulfilment of the eschatological expectation that had been ushered in by his coming, and as such repentance and membership into the kingdom of God were consequently available. However, Mark distinguishes between the gospel about Jesus Christ (1:1) and the gospel of God that Jesus preached (1:14). During Jesus's lifetime, part of the Christ event – his death and resurrection

---

27. Gundry, *Mark*, 29.

(Isa 53:1–12), that became part of the contents of the gospel proclamation (1 Cor 15:1–3) after Easter, had not yet been fulfilled. Therefore, the gospel of Jesus Christ the Son of God (1:1) encapsulated the proclamation of the death, resurrection and the second coming of Jesus Christ.

Mark saw Jesus's proclamation of τὸ εὐαγγέλιον τοῦ θεοῦ as the precursor to the gospel that he and his contemporaries were proclaiming – τὸ εὐαγγέλιον τοῦ Ἰησοῦ Χριστοῦ [υἱοῦ θεοῦ]. The gospel proclamation during Jesus's time entailed urging his audience to repent and believe the good news of the fulfilment of the promises of God and the "nearness" of the kingdom of God. Nearness, in this case, should not be seen as an aspect of time or distance; it references ease of reach and availability to whosoever wills. This nuance is more in line with the declaration of the fulfilment of the time when the kingdom was to be ushered in the world. Use of the indicative perfect passive πεπλήρωται ὁ καιρὸς shows a complete action whose impact continues after the occurrence of the episode. Similarly, "ἤγγικεν" in "ἤγγικεν ἡ βασιλεία τοῦ θεοῦ," a perfect tense "indicates a past action with a continuing result . . . The emphasis is on present nearness rather than on future arrival . . . perhaps the appropriate question to ask about the kingdom in Mark 1:14 is not a question about the time of arrival, but about how one can respond to what is already near."[28]

Jesus was proclaiming a gospel about the fulfilment of a previously promised kingdom of God. Apparently, this time had been fulfilled in his coming and the benefits of forgiveness of sins could then be availed through faith in the gospel. As such, τὸ εὐαγγέλιον was first and foremost the news about an occurrence of an efficacious salvific episode, otherwise labelled the Christ event. However, its efficacy is inert until it is activated through faith in Jesus. As such, the occurrence of the salvific episode and its soteriological significance need to be communicated in a way that convinces and convicts the would-be beneficiaries concerning its salvific value.

The salvific episode was not a one-off event but a progression of events that will culminate at the parousia. The content of the gospel continued to be expanded as the anticipated aspects of the salvific episode continued to be fulfilled throughout the progressive realization of the kingdom of God. The vicarious death and the outpouring of the Holy Spirit on Pentecost were other

---

28. Dobson, *Learn New Testament Greek*, 330.

aspects of the benefits of the kingdom that were later-day manifestations and thus additions into the gospel proclamation (Acts 2:1–39). After Pentecost, the only episode forming part of gospel proclamation that was yet to be fulfilled is the anticipated second coming of Jesus Christ. Therefore, it is proclaimed as the eschatological hope of the church (Rev 22:12–14).

Preaching the gospel therefore entailed a proclamation that the kingdom of God was now at hand, that is, within reach and available, and that people should come forth and partake of its salvific benefits through repentance (1:15). It is apparent from the Old Testament Scriptures, which anticipated the eschatological kingdom, that miracles, controversy with religious leaders, passion, and resurrection would be episodes that would be witnessed in the time of the servant king (Isa 53:1–12). As such, Jesus performed miracles as a strategic act to prove that the Christ event, to which they were bearing witness, was indeed, the event that had been promised by God and that he was both the herald and conveyor of its benefits.

As the term εὐαγγέλιον was transmitted through the successive generations, its referent mutated into different things. This change is resultant partly from the progressive fulfilment, in time, of the eschatological promises within the Christ event. It was also due to the interpretation of what entails the gospel by the second-century church. During the earthly ministry of Jesus, God's fulfilment of the promise to usher in his kingdom was interpreted to be the gospel of God (1:14).

Response to the gospel in the time of Jesus

Response to the gospel message in the time of Jesus entailed repenting and believing the gospel message. The following questions call for answers that shed light on the understanding of the pre-resurrection response towards the gospel: what does repenting for "the kingdom of God is at hand" (1:14–15) entail? What obligations did the gospel impose on the believer that may constitute the praxis of the gospel?

The gospel message entailed a proclamation of the fulfilment of the time when God was to usher the kingdom of God into the world (1:15). As such, the audience were being called upon to believe the message, put their faith in its subject, Jesus, and repent of their sins. At the same time, the gospel message obligated the audience to praxis in line with the status conferred by believing the gospel. Praxis is summed up by Jesus's response when he was asked "which commandment is the most important of all?" (12:28 ESV). His answer was "'love the Lord your God with all your heart and with all your soul and with all your mind and with all your strength.' The second is this: 'Love your neighbor as yourself.' There is no commandment greater than these" (12:30–31 ESV).

A comparison of instances of teachings and sayings of Jesus in the Markan text and the other synoptic texts shows that Mark was not keen to record the teachings of Jesus on Christian praxis. The teachings on faith in Jesus and Christian practice must have been an integral part of the oral proclamation of the gospel. Mark's near silence on such an important aspect of gospel proclamation suggests that the audience were aware of the contents of the oral gospel. It also suggests that the Markan text was not written for catechetical purposes like Matthew's text, which is replete with explicit teachings by Jesus (Matt 5:1–7:29; 13:1–53; 24:1–25:46).

Awareness of the contents of the oral gospel by the audience of Mark suggests that the text was written to an audience that was hearing an already thriving oral gospel. As such, among his many concerns, Mark must have been concerned with his audience's response to the oral gospel. Therefore, the first line of investigation into the purpose of the Markan text should be its connectedness to the audience's response to the oral gospel that he and his contemporaries, who may have included the apostle Peter, were preaching. Actually, the structure, form, and nuancing of the Markan miracle stories and the paraenetic entreaty in the parable of the sower (4:1–12) show that his intention was to draw his audience to respond to the gospel. The above argument suggests that the Markan text is better comprehended with some awareness that its primary audience was simultaneously hearing the text and an ongoing oral gospel that was outside and independent of the text.

2.3.3 From "Gospel of God" to the "Gospel of Jesus Christ"

It is evident that from the time of Jesus to the time of the patristic fathers, the referent of the term gospel changed significantly.[29] Jesus proclaimed "the gospel of God." This gospel message simply announced that the scripturally

---

29. Koester, "From the Kerygma-Gospel," 361. He posits that "Εὐαγγέλιον, originally a term for the early Christian proclamation became the designation of a certain type of literature."

anticipated eschatological kingdom of God had been fulfilled and as such, forgiveness of sins was available through repentance (1:15).

After the death, resurrection, ascension, and the outpouring of the Holy Spirit on the day of Pentecost, these aspects were incorporated into the proclamation of the gospel of God to form "the gospel of Jesus Christ the Son of God" (Acts 2:14–40; 3:11–4:22; 10:34–43). Joseph Thayer intimates that,

> After the death of Christ the term τὸ εὐαγγέλιον comprises also the preaching of (concerning) Jesus Christ as having suffered death on the cross to procure eternal salvation for men in the kingdom of God, but as restored to life and exalted to the right hand of God in heaven, thence to return in majesty to consummate the kingdom of God; so that it may be more briefly defined as *the glad tidings of salvation through Christ; the proclamation of the grace of God manifested and pledged in Christ*.[30]

After the apostolic epoch, the change to the referent of the term "gospel" was not in the scope of content of the proclamation. Rather, the books that narrated various biographical aspects of Jesus Christ were designated "the Gospels." Inadvertently, this designation invites a perception that proclamation of the oral gospel in the times of Jesus and the apostles entailed narrating the biographical episodes in the daily itinerary of Jesus Christ. This change had and continues to have serious ramifications to the study of the Markan text. Labelling the books by the four evangelists as "gospel" imposes a hermeneutical presupposition that, a priori, one is dealing with the gospel in textual form.

Some studies on the books that are now labelled the Gospels are premised on a general supposition that they were sourced from multiple written sources.[31] This view does not take into account the fact that eyewitnesses to the Christ event were a reliable source for the writers of these texts (Luke 1:1–4). What is certain though is that there was an oral gospel that was being proclaimed as a continuum of the "gospel of God" (1:14) which Mark calls

---

30. Thayer, *Thayer's Greek-English Lexicon*, 257.

31. Dockey, *Holman Bible Handbook*, 542, "The three canonical gospels drew their material from an earlier, more primitive gospel that has not been preserved, probably written in Aramaic. An alternative view is that Mark was the first gospel which was the foundation of Matthew and Luke."

"the gospel of Jesus Christ the Son of God" (1:1). However, there appears to be a dearth of studies on the relationship between the then extant oral gospel and the written texts. Extant research, which is rather old, is mainly on the transition from oral tradition to written gospels – such as works by Martin Dibelius, Graham Stanton, Werner H. Kelber and Helmut Koester,[32] which suppose that the written texts are a transcription of the oral gospel.

Orality[33] as an emerging trend in biblical studies has recently attracted some interest. However, it has been approached from the supposition that texts were written to be read aloud as oral presentations. Though the existence of an oral gospel before the gospel texts were written has been acknowledged, the independence of the oral gospel from the gospel texts has not been acknowledged. Similarly, the significance of the written texts on the audience response to the oral gospel has not been studied. Studies by Kelber and Dewey, and the group of scholars that have researched orality in the canonical gospels, have concerned themselves with the aural nature of the written canonical gospels,[34] that is, "a text intended to be heard, not read."[35]

The need to explore the relationship between the written texts and the oral gospel that was outside and independent of the Markan text is the concern of this work. The issue under scrutiny is whether the common oral tradition about Jesus Christ was synonymous with the oral gospel about Jesus Christ that was being proclaimed by the various preachers and missionaries in the first century? A multiplicity of the synoptic texts supports the postulation that reminiscences of the apostles could have been as many as the apostles were willing to write, but the gospel was one. This assertion puts a distinction between the oral gospel and the different reminiscences of which the four canonical texts' by Matthew, Mark, Luke, and John were important parts.

Joel B. Green tries to reconcile the four Gospels and the one gospel by postulating that the gospel is one but in multiple perspectives that "complement

---

32. These writers have been variously cited in this book.

33. Orality is understood to be the study of the nature of the oral medium of transmitting the gospel. It has also been understood as the study of how the written texts were written in order to have them read to audiences as if they were direct oral presentations from the author.

34. Kelber, Dewey, and Hearon have all explored the orality of the gospel texts from the supposition that they were written to be recited orally. See Kelber, *Oral and the Written Gospel*, 17; Dewey, "Mark as Aural Narrative," 47.

35. Dewey, "Mark as Aural Narrative," 47.

one another."³⁶ Green is hereby suggesting that the gospel is a narration of Jesus's life and ministry as opposed to the proclamation of the nature and significance of the salvific episode to its heirs. Furthermore, if Mark was the major source of both Matthew and Luke, it cannot be said that they are different views of the same gospel. They can only be different ways of narrating episodes within the Christ event as rhetorical fodder to eliminate different exigencies in rhetorical situations of different audiences. However, these audiences were hearing only one orally and festally³⁷ proclaimed gospel.

Arguably, the texts by the four evangelists, Mark, Matthew, Luke, and John, are narrations about the Jesus of history. The oral gospel proclaimed the Christ of faith. This gospel is explicitly expressed in the Markan text as "the gospel of Jesus Christ the Son of God" (1:1), in Matthew it is presented as what Jesus had taught his disciples and that which he commissioned them to preach to the whole world (Matt 28:20), in Luke it is referred to as the word that had been taught Theophilus (Luke 1:2–4) and in John 21:30 it is referred to as that which makes people believe that Jesus is the Christ the Son of God and in believing they may have life in his name. Actually, the four evangelists, in different ways that are dictated by their social-cultural and literary backgrounds, and the rhetorical situation of their audiences, are endeavoring to show that the Christ of their faith, as explicated in the oral gospel, is actually the Jesus of history and the Christ of Scripture.

2.3.4 Gospel during the Apostolic Period

The apostolic period is taken to be the time from Pentecost to the time of the demise of the last apostle who is presumed to be John. However, the period of the apostles and the time of the patristic fathers overlap showing that there was occasion for smooth succession between these important epochs. As such, a study of this era would illuminate the traditions that were bequeathed the patristic fathers by the apostles of the Lord and especially in the usage of the term εὐαγγέλιον.

Stanton rightly posits, "Sociolinguists would surely be fascinated by one of the most startling developments in the linguistic usage of the first Christians.

---

36. Green, *How to Read the Gospels and Acts*, 28.
37. Ritual proclamation of the gospel in this study is taken to be a proclamation of the gospel through eating the Lord's Supper according to 1 Cor 11:26.

In the earliest post-Easter decades, τὸ εὐαγγέλιον referred to the oral proclamation of the nature and significance of the death and resurrection of Jesus, not to a written account of the story of Jesus."[38] Paradoxically, by the mid-second century, the same word had mutated to refer to the books about the life and times of Jesus Christ. No doubt a study of post-resurrection transmission of the reference to the word gospel sheds light and directs New Testament biblical studies. This is because the development of ευαγγελίζομαι from an oral proclamation into a purely hermeneutical exercise, which is the current engagement, was an important turning point in understanding the relationship between the text and the oral gospel. It also illuminates the relationship between the oral gospel and the Markan text and shows that the text was a paraenesis in that it exhorted its readers to respond in faith and obedience to the oral gospel.

Post-Pentecost proclamation

Peter's first sermon in Acts 2:14–40 shows that preaching of the gospel incorporated an introduction of Jesus as both the scripturally promised Messiah and Lord (Acts 22–36). The rhetorical devices of citing Old Testament and the miracles that Jesus performed were aimed at establishing the plausibility of the gospel message by anchoring it on Old Testament scriptural promises, and to show that God affirmed the messiahship of Jesus by performing miracles, signs, and wonders through him and in his name (Acts 2:22). The last item in the gospel message was a call to repentance and baptism in the name of Jesus Christ.

The sermon in Acts 3:11–4:22 follows the same pattern: an introduction of the man Jesus, scriptural support that he was indeed the promised Messiah through attestation by miracles that were performed by both Jesus and the apostles, through the name of Jesus, and finally a call to the audience to respond favorably by believing the gospel. Stephen's sermon in Acts 7:2–53 also relied on Scripture to prove that Jesus was the promised Messiah. The last of Peter's recorded sermon in 10:34–43 follows the same outline. The pattern and content of these sermons show that preaching the gospel entailed an introduction declaring that Jesus was the Messiah, a proof that he was indeed the Messiah by citing relevant Old Testament texts and by extolling

---

38. Stanton, *Jesus and Gospel*, 52.

the wonderful deeds of Jesus, and finally a call to the audience to respond in faith and trust in Jesus and his work on the cross.

Francois Bovon refers to the New Testament books that are labelled Gospels as "windows through which the post-Easter life of the apostles and Churches can be seen."[39] This supposition suggests that the writing of these texts was influenced by the need to eliminate the exigencies of the rhetorical situation of the church and the apostles. As such, these texts were rhetorical communications. A. J. Bellinzoni refers to εὐαγγελιόν as "the saving work of God revealed in Jesus and still alive in the life of the early Church."[40] In other words, Bellinzoni sees the salvific work as an existential and continuous work that was mediated through oral proclamation of the gospel message. Both Bovon and Bellinzoni's suppositions suggest that the gospel message was outside and independent of the texts. Thus, the churches came to designate the writings of the apostles as Gospels long after the oral gospel had established itself as the only bona fide gospel. The method of proclamation was oral and festal in the celebration of the Lord's Supper. Eusebius supports the orality of proclamation by asserting that:

> Those who were divine and most truly worthy of God, and I am speaking of Christ's apostles, having been utterly purified in their life, and having been adorned in their souls with all virtue, being unskilled in speech, nevertheless having confidence in the divine and wonderworking power that had been given to them from the saviour, while they neither knew how, nor attempted to, to represent the lessons of their teacher with subtle and artistic words, but using only the proof of the divine Spirit who was working in them, and the miracle-working power of Christ that was being carried out through them, they were proclaiming the knowledge of the kingdom of heaven to all the inhabited world, caring little for attention to writing books.[41]

Eusebius's postulation suggests that the gospel was a Holy Spirit inspired oral proclamation.

---

39. Bovon, "Canonical Structure of Gospel," 520.

40. Bellinzoni, *Sayings of Jesus*, 3.

41. Whitacre, *Patristic Greek Reader*, 232. This excerpt is quoted from Eusebius and Ecclesiastical History and Life of Constantine, Ecclesiastical History 3.24.3.

Furthermore, Martin Dibelius asserts,

> All the observations and conclusions which we can put forward, in fact, prove that the primitive Christian missionaries did not relate the life of Jesus, but proclaimed the salvation which had come about in Jesus Christ. What they narrated was secondary to this proclamation, was intended to confirm it and found it . . . the material of tradition gave objectivity to the preaching of salvation; it explained, expanded, and, in accordance therewith was either introduced into the preaching, or related at its close.[42]

As such he positions the *Sitz im Leben* of much of the gospel material in the early preaching of the church. That is, the content of the text was used as fodder for the kerygma. Similarly, Marshal is of the view that "it is likely that no disparity was seen between the kerygma and the 'history' of Jesus; the latter would be used to illustrate and give content to the former."[43] Marshall's conclusion that "it is notoriously difficult to proceed further than this and to find actual examples of the connection between the *kerygma* and the gospel tradition"[44] is a critical beginning point in this study. Whereas it is agreeable that it is difficult to find examples of direct connection between the kerygma and the gospel tradition this work supposes and argues that material from the oral tradition about the life and times of Jesus, as written in the Markan text, was used to catalyze audience response to the kerygma.

Narrating the Christ event as an episode within the once anticipated eschatological promises and prophecies in the Hebrew Scripture imbues oral traditions – the stories about episodes in the Christ event which inhered in the individual memories of the eyewitnesses and the collective church witness – with rhetorical and speech act efficacy. As such, narrating these episodes was used to urge belief in the oral gospel that was premised on the redemptive work of Jesus on the cross. E. M. Cornelius posits, "the gospel of Mark is viewed as narrative literature; a story with its own narrative world, characterization and point of view and it is assumed that the narrator not only reports, but comments and evaluates in order to create a story which has to

---

42. Dibelius, *From Tradition to Gospel*, 15.
43. Marshall, *Luke*, 49.
44. Marshall, 49.

convince the reader by the way it is told."[45] Consequently, Mark's rhetorical devices and the inherent speech acts suggest that the text was used to exhort the readers to respond to the oral gospel.

Later, as the people and institutions that were repositories of the oral traditions about Jesus became extinct – by reason of the death of eyewitnesses of Jesus and the calamitous destruction of Jerusalem wherein the mother church in which the institutional memory of the life and deeds of Jesus inhered – these writings became the only source of information to validate the oral gospel message (Luke 1:1–4). Because of the enhanced value of these written texts, they eventually eclipsed the oral gospel as the bona fide gospel. Again, it is not lost to any observer that these changes occurred at a time when these texts were under serious scrutiny by critics like Marcion, who according to Koester had already designated his "revised version of Luke 'εὐαγγέλιον,'"[46] and a need to ring-fence them against attacks by Marcion and other heretics may have contributed to their being labelled the Gospels according to the individual writer. Under the circumstances, this was an inevitable step. However, this paradigmatic change and its implications to hermeneutics of these texts should be acknowledged and accounted for in every interpretative enterprise of the books that are currently labelled the Gospels.

Gospel in performance of ordinances

The thesis fronted and argued in this section is that the Lord's Supper was an aspect of the gospel proclamation. Whereas the oral gospel was a proclamation to both the church and the world, taking part in the Lord's Supper was, exclusively, a proclamation among the believers for the purpose of perpetuating and inculcating the teachings of the gospel in the life and psyche of the believers. Whereas the Markan text was a witness of the episodes in the Christ event in order to highlight the person and ethos of Jesus, the ordinance of the Lord's Supper embodied and interpreted the meaning and significance of Christ's incarnation and passion to humanity's redemption in view of his second coming and final judgment.

By setting the inauguration of the Lord's Supper in the context of the Passover feast, and by extension the history of salvation, in his use of the

---

45. Cornelius, "Rhetorical Function(s)," 58.
46. Koester, "From the Kerygma-Gospel," 376.

participial phrase Καὶ ἐσθιόντων αὐτῶν ("And as they were eating") in Mark 14:22, Mark was able to show the propitiatory, sacrificial and vicarious aspects of Christ's incarnation and passion. Therefore, it is plausible to argue that by the time of writing the Markan text, the gospel was being propagated in the church and to the rest of the world through oral proclamation. It was also inculcated in the life and psyche of the believers through administration of the ordinances.

As such, it can be said with good reason that the mighty acts of God, which include but are not limited to his redemptive and providential acts, were preserved for remembrance, teaching and edification not only in written Scripture and oral form but also in the celebration of the ordained feasts of the redeemed community (Exod 12:14). In celebrating, God's people would not only remember but reflectively enliven his grace acts of redemption and provision. As shown in the "hymns of the Hallel (Ps. 113–118),"[47] the celebrations were conducted in a way that would draw the participants to relationship, reverence, worship, thanksgiving, and obedience to God. As such, ordained feasts were functionally *paraklectic* in that they edified the participant. They celebrated God's creative acts in the Sabbath (Exod 20:8–11), redemptive acts in the Passover (Exod 12:14), and his provision in Pentecost (Exod 34:22). Thus, ordained feasts were not merely moments to indulge in eating and drinking but solemn moments of reflection and worship. They were means of enlivening and perpetuating God's word and revelation throughout successive generations. According to Ryken, Wilhoit, and Longman, "feasts are not just parties, but celebrations of God's goodness towards his people. Feasts provide occasion of fellowship with one another and with the Lord and to remember and celebrate what wonderful things God had done."[48]

As a component of Jesus's speech imperatives, partaking in ordinances, serves a purpose greater than mere joyous celebration. They are, just like parables and Bible narratives, communication tools of the revealed truth about God, his will, his gracious acts, his relationship with man, and his demands on the believing community. They are part of the sacred history of the people's experience of their God. Ordained feasts keep an aspect of history

---

47. Keener, *Matthew*, 369.
48. Ryken, Wilhoit, and Longman III, *Dictionary of Biblical Imagery*, 278.

alive as the people reminisce on the wonderful works of God that also have an anticipatory and hope inspiring aspect.

The physical preservation of the deeds and words of Jesus's redemptive work through papyri were prone to destruction. Similarly, literary ability was limited to a select class (1 Cor 1:26). James Jeffers intimates, "Rome offered no formal technical education – vocational schools, no applied fields. Its education system would have seemed very impractical to the lower classes even if they could have afforded it, but the lower classes could afford little or no formal education."[49] As such, there was no better way of preserving and propagating the gospel of redemption from sin through the work of Jesus on the cross than the old, tested and tried method of embedding it into the psyche of the individual and into the community's culture through oral witnessing of the gospel and administration of the ordinances of baptism and the Lord's Supper.

John Bright has postulated that

> even in more recent times, in societies where writing materials are scarce and the rate of illiteracy high, whole bodies of traditional literature are known to have been passed down for generations, even centuries, by word of mouth. Even when the material has been given written form, oral tradition does not necessarily leave off, but may continue to function side by side with the written tradition, the latter serving as a control upon the former but not as a substitute for it.[50]

Furthermore, in the literary tradition of the Jews, "they placed great emphasis on oral transmission as the main education medium."[51] Thus, though the New Testament ordinances depict God's acts of grace, they are not themselves sources or avenues of transmitting grace as is commonly thought but rather, they mainly serve as metaphorical symbols to remind, urge and exhort the believer not only to worship God but to reminisce, preserve and communicate the gospel.

---

49. Jeffers, *Greco-Roman World*, 256.
50. Bright, *History of Israel*, 71.
51. Guthrie, *New Testament Introduction*, 140.

An examination of the two New Testament ordinances shows that they are markers of defining moments of God's gracious intervention in the life of the individual and community. They actually represent and retell all the aspects of the redemption story. Whereas baptism signifies the believer's death to sin and newness of life in righteousness (Rom 6:3–4), the Lord's Supper reminiscences and confesses the believer's fidelity to Jesus and his work on the cross. It also calls upon the celebrant to live a life worthy of the price paid for his redemption (1 Cor 5:7–8). These ordinances can aptly be regarded as the gospel about Jesus Christ, however, it is not written on tablets of stone or papyri, but in the performance of the baptismal act and in the festal celebration of the Lord's Supper.

Celebrating the Lord's Supper, as also is in all other holy feasts of the Old Testament, speaks to the celebrant, with a language deeper and more lasting than either parable or idiom. It is complementary to the preaching of the gospel by word of mouth. Philo, a contemporary of Jesus and Paul equates food to "the word of the Lord, like dew, surrounding the whole soul in a circle, and allowing no portion of it to be without its share of itself."[52] As such, the meal in the Lord's Supper is a metaphorical symbol[53] that reminds the believer of their dependence on the work of Jesus on the cross. It is the word of God in a festal symbol and, as such, it is a metaphor. David H. Aaron refers to such metaphors as "semiotic structures other than those exclusively linguistic, such as ritual acts, iconography, even music cognition, to name just a few."[54] In fact, the major Christian doctrines are ably and powerfully embedded in the celebration of the Lord's Supper. Just as the Passover communicated God's redeeming love and established the basis of his covenant relationship with Israel in a better way than any written text could have done, the New Testament's ordinance of the Lord's Supper is a feast that proclaims the redemptive work of Christ on the cross (1 Cor 11:23–26).

Just as any reflection on the word edifies, so also partaking the Lord's Supper. It teaches the doctrines of God, Christ, *ecclesia*,[55] sin and salvation

---

52. Philo, *Works of Philo*, 69.

53. Ian Paul, "Metaphor," 507, says that all language about "imagery" or "symbol" in Scripture is in fact referring to metaphor.

54. Aaron, *Biblical Ambiguities*, 3.

55. In reference to 1 Cor 11:27–30, Carson (*Faith of the Vatican*, 160), says that "one of the reasons for the institution of the Lord's Supper was that this unity [*Church's unity*] should

through a single feast. Christ did not write any scriptural text, but the establishment of ordinances of baptism and the Lord's Supper amounted to packaging the whole gospel message and a priori ordaining its mode of propagation to successive generations through administration of baptism and celebrating the Lord's Supper. They embody the salvific episode, its profession and proclamation. Whereas Scripture witnesses the salvific episode, administration of baptism and partaking in the Lord's Supper deconstructs and interprets the salvific episode for greater understanding and inculcation in the cultural fabric of the Christians and the church of all ages.

Gospel in the Pauline epistles

Paul has used the term εὐαγγέλιον extensively. A. B. Luter has posited that "since *euangelion* is found in all the traditional Pauline letters except Titus, it should be considered a central feature of the apostle's vocabulary."[56] Paul's understanding of the gospel is summed up in his statement that:

> Christ died for our sins in accordance with the Scriptures, that he was buried, that he was raised on the third day in accordance with the Scriptures, and that he appeared to Cephas and then to the twelve. Then he appeared to more than five hundred brothers at one time, most of whom are still alive, though some of them have fallen asleep. Then he appeared to James, then to all the apostles. Last of all, as to one untimely born, he appeared also to me (1 Cor 15:3–8).

This text shows that post-Pentecost oral gospel consisted of a proclamation that Jesus had died for the sins of the world. This was validated by Old Testament citation, eyewitness testimonies to the Christ event that included his resurrection from the dead to support that declaration.

Most of Paul's letters were written to audiences who had heard him or others preach the gospel orally. The relationship between his referent of the term εὐαγγέλιον and his letters shows that he understood the gospel to be outside and independent of his letters. His letters directed and exhorted his audience to both believe and practice the performative demands and obligations of a

---

be declared in the loving fellowship gathered at the Lord's Table."

56. Luter, "Gospel," 369.

gospel that they had heard before receipt of the text. Thus, Paul and his audience's referent of the term εὐαγγέλιον was the proclamation of the incarnation, death, resurrection, and ascension of Christ in addition to their soteriological significance. This perspective agrees with the Markan referent of the term εὐαγγέλιον in Mark 1:1. This shows that during the time of Paul, the word gospel referenced the oral proclamation of the incarnation of Jesus and the soteriological significance of his death and resurrection.

2.4 Effect of the Destruction of Jerusalem on the Term "Gospel"

Bauckham notes that "after the resurrection, it was the Jerusalem Church, under the leadership of the Twelve and later James the Lord's brother, that became the mother Church of the whole Christian movement."[57] Evidently, the church in Antioch referred the dispute between the Judaizers with Paul and Barnabas to the church in Jerusalem for arbitration (Acts 15:1–29). However, the destruction of Jerusalem and the killing of James, the brother of Jesus and the first bishop of the Jerusalem church (Acts 15:13–21), by the religious establishment[58] must have had a profound effect on the Jesus movement.

Eusebius reports that "the whole body of the Church at Jerusalem, having been commanded by a divine revelation, given to men of approved piety there before the war, removed from the city, and dwelt at a certain town beyond the Jordan, called Pella."[59] S. G. F. Brandon argues that "the Jerusalem Church fell together with the Jewish nation in the catastrophe of A.D. 70 because that Church in its principles and the loyalties of its members was essentially one with the nation."[60] Either way, Jerusalem's important position as a custodian of the Jesus movement's institutional memory and as a point of recourse and reference was lost.

Burnett Hillman Streeter says, "Till its destruction, A.D. 70, Jerusalem was the natural capital of Christianity – with Caesarea and Antioch as subordinate centers. After the fall of Jerusalem, Antioch, Ephesus and Rome

---

57. Bauckham, *Jesus and the Eyewitnesses*, 298.
58. *Antiq.* 20.9.1. Josephus places James's death at around 61 CE after the death of Festus the procurator and before his successor, Albinus, took over. Josephus, *Works of Flavius Josephus*.
59. Eusebius, *Ecclesiastical History*, 75.
60. Brandon, *Fall of Jerusalem*, 180.

are for a hundred years centers of more or equal importance. After that the influence of Rome steadily increases, while Alexandria steps into the place once held by Ephesus."[61] Evidently, these catastrophic happenings must have had a profound impact on the church in Jerusalem. The history of the church, its ecclesiastical and compositional traditions, which were mainly oral and domiciled collectively in the memories of the apostles and other eyewitnesses, must have been lost during this tumultuous period of the Christian church in Jerusalem.

As suggested by the letter of Clement to the Corinthians later in the first century,[62] this role slowly moved to Rome, albeit minus the movement's primitive memory. This move had serious consequences to the practice of faith.[63] W. Jaeger states that, "although Paul's insistence on faith remains unchanged in Clement's epistle, the special emphasis is on good works . . . A whole system of Christian virtues is already emerging from Clement's important historical document; its concept of Christianity is closer to Stoic morality than to the Spirit of St. Paul and his letter to the Romans."[64] This shift must have hastened making the movement's memory even hazier and as such creating room for newer concepts of faith and terminologies to emerge.

Consequently, it is arguable that the destruction of Jerusalem hastened the inculturation of the church into a more hellenized church. Again, it can be deduced that whereas the books by the apostles and their acquaintances acquired greater importance in validating the oral gospel message during the time of the apostles, after the destruction of Jerusalem and demise of the apostles, these books assumed a more reverenced position as Scripture to be used in catechetical instruction and church worship. However, they were being held by the different audiences to whom they had been addressed by the different writers. Archaeological discoveries show that the different manuscripts had traction in different locations.[65] Whereas this changed view of what constitutes the gospel message had a positive implication in that it precipitated the production of a canon of the Christian Scripture and hence a

---

61. Streeter, *Primitive Church*, 31.
62. Unnik, "So-Called First Epistle of Clement," 117–118.
63. Jaeger, "Early Christianity," 107.
64. Jaeger, 107.
65. Greenlee, *Introduction to New Testament*, 53.

control and limiting instrument to proliferation of heretical and unorthodox teachings, the change should be noted in the process of interpretation of the texts in order to ward off instances of anachronistic reading of word referents in the patristic milieu into their referents in apostolic milieu.

According to Young, the second-century Christianity sought to show that it "fulfils all that has gone before in Greek philosophy, as well as the inspired predictions of the Hebrew prophets, and involves a 'school-like' teaching and learning process more than religious activity as then understood."[66] Contrariwise, in the apostolic era, faith and practice of the demands of the gospel were more of a religious activity than a "school-like" teaching and learning process. In contrasting the second-century Christian endeavor with the Christian endeavor in the apostolic times, Young says, "what we have here are exhortations to living according to the precepts of Scripture and Jesus the teacher, alongside narratives typologically shaped to provide prophecy and precedent, and material which intends to explain and justify the ways in which Christians differentiated themselves from both Jews and Greeks."[67] Young's exposé explains the changes that should be accounted for in understanding the development of the term "gospel" from its referent in the time of Jesus to its referent in the patristic times.

By the time Jerusalem stabilized as a center of Christianity after the devastating revolt of 65–70 CE and the 135 CE Bar-Kochba revolt, it was more of a hellenized Christianity devoid of the historical role that it had once played as a custodian of the history and primitive traditions of the Jesus movement. Streeter avers, "Between the original Jewish Christian Church of Jerusalem and the purely Gentile Church of the city re-founded there (with the name Aelia) after A.D. 135, there was a complete breach of continuity."[68] Devoid of a center that claimed custodianship of the movement's primitive oral tradition, faith, and praxis, it is understandable that the only connection between the movement and its roots were the books that had been written and sent to different local churches by the apostles and their associates. With this development, preaching and worship tradition transitioned from the oral proclamation of the gospel and celebration of the ordinances to hermeneutics

---

66. Young, "Christian Teaching," 103.
67. Young, 103.
68. Streeter, *Primitive Church*, 29.

of the books of both the Old and New Testaments. This time around, the texts were not read to validate the salvific episode and urge faith in the oral gospel but as the only form of gospel.

Notwithstanding these changes, in the process of interpreting these texts, the transmission history of important terminologies like "εὐαγγέλιον" from the time of Jesus to the time of the patristic fathers should be probed and its hermeneutical implications accounted for in order to avoid reading back the views of the patristic milieu as views of the apostolic milieu. Wright notes that "a later writer recording an earlier division may well project backwards an anachronistic understanding of that division."[69] This study notes that the Markan text has so far been read and interpreted within the understanding of the term "εὐαγγέλιον" that prevailed in the patristic milieu with the consequence that the oral gospel as an independent dialogue partner with both the Markan text and the audience has been eclipsed, of course, with serious hermeneutical implications.

Young suggests that the New Testament texts should not "be approached as 'works' in their own right, but as data, material evidence for a historical project which is other than reading the texts."[70] Therefore, Young sees the text as supporting a historical project that existed outside of the written texts. This work identifies this historical project as the oral gospel that was outside and independent of the text. His position supports the argument that gospel in the apostolic milieu was oral in proclamation, ritual in administration of the ordinances, practical in worship, and works of service. To properly and effectively interpret these New Testament texts, scholarship must break through the veil of presuppositions consequent of the changes that took place during the developmental history of the designation of apostolic writings as the gospels.

2.5 Gospel in the Time of the Church Fathers

This section investigates the referential changes that happened during the transmission history of the term "gospel" from the time of Jesus to the time of the church fathers. It also probes the historical development of the purpose

---

69. Wright, *New Testament and the People of God*, 346.
70. Young, "Christian Teaching," 103.

of the Markan text from being seen as a paraenetic treatise to being perceived as a repository of the life and deeds of Christ.

2.5.1 Gospel in the Time of Clement of Rome

1 Clement is one of the earliest extant epistles outside the canonical writings. Its contents can shed light on how the successors to the apostles viewed the writings that are now labelled the New Testament. In their comments on the writings of the apostolic fathers, Andrew Gregory and Christopher Tuckett intimate that:

> Some texts appear to include frequent references to Old Testament, sometimes with the introduction formula "it is written," but there are few examples of such explicitly acknowledged from the writings of the New Testament to be found in the Apostolic Fathers. Ignatius, Polycarp, and the author of 1 *Clement* each appeals explicitly to Paul. But no other individuals whose names are associated with the New Testament are appealed to as authorities whose teaching and/or writings may be used to resolve contemporary issues or debates.[71]

This shows that during the times of the apostolic fathers and especially Clement of Rome, the books that are now designated as the Gospels had not gained universal acclaim as Scripture and therefore, they could not have been regarded as gospels in his time. Similarly, though the writers of the *Didache* (8:2; 11:3; 15:3), and 2 Clement 8:5 allude to materials appearing in the books currently labelled the Gospels, the implicit nature of the allusions suggests that the writers may have appealed rather to the extant common traditions about the life and times of Jesus and his teachings which are currently labelled oral traditions.[72] As such, they may not have been privy to these texts.

Koester says,

> In the first one and half centuries, "Scripture" i.e., authoritative writing comprised exclusively what was later called the Old Testament. Any additional authority referred to in order

---

71. Gregory and Tuckett, "Reflections on Method," 68, quoted in Lindemann, "Paul in the Writings," 28.

72. Holmes, *Apostolic Fathers*, 132–138, 334–344.

to underline the legitimacy of the Christian message and the teaching of the Church was present in a variety of traditions which were still undefined. Sometimes these were transmitted orally sometimes in written form. Such authorities could be called "the sayings of the Lord," usually transmitted orally. But even the quotations of 2 *Clement*, although drawn from a written source, are still introduced as words of the Lord, just as Justin (*1 Apology* 15–17) introduces the teachings of the gospels as "what Jesus said" and not as quotation from a book.[73]

This shows that long after the writing of the Markan text, which according to Koester was written to underline the legitimacy of the Christian message, the Markan text was being referred to as the sayings of the Lord and not a gospel. The corpus of the oral gospel may not have been defined into a systematic handbook canon. However, it was not amorphous. Its bounds were defined by the Old Testament and the instructions of the Lord which were in the repository of the apostles' memory.

2.5.2 Gospel in the Time of Papias Bishop of Hierapolis

Papias was a contemporary of Polycarp, who lived between 70–155 CE, and John the elder, who some say was John the apostle.[74] As such, he happens to be one of the earliest church fathers and, from the claims in his writings, he can be adjudged to be the best link between the apostolic milieu and the patristic milieu. Unfortunately, none of his writings have survived in manuscript form. However, Eusebius, the earliest church historian has passed on citations from some of Papias's writings. Papias is reported by Eusebius to have written five volumes which bear the title "*Interpretation of the Lord's Declarations.*"[75] Eusebius is the major source of Papias's writings which can illumine understanding of the transmission of the term gospel.

According to the second fragment of Papias,

> John the presbyter also said this, "Mark being the interpreter of Peter, whatsoever he recorded he wrote with great accuracy,

---

73. Koester, *Ancient Christian Gospels*, 31.
74. Fragments of Papias 1:1 accessed via BibleWorks.
75. Eusebius, *Ecclesiastical History*, 113.

but not, however, in the order in which it was spoken or done by our Lord, for he neither heard nor followed our Lord, but as before said, he was in company with Peter, who gave him such instructions as was necessary, but not to give a history of our Lord's discourses."[76]

The text's lack of order, against expectations in a historical or biographical treatise, has continued to vex interpreters of the Markan text to this very day. Informed by K. L. Schmidt, Burridge agreeably avers, "The Markan text is a collection of units of oral tradition, loosely strung together by the Gospel writer."[77]

Papias is also reported to have put more weight on oral information from those who were acquaintances of the apostles of the Lord than on written records. He posits, "For I did not think that information from books would profit me as much as information from a living and abiding voice."[78] This suggests that during his time, the oral gospel and oral tradition regarding the life of Jesus were more prevalent and that he preferred them more than the written texts. In conclusion, it appears that the books labelled Gospels had not acquired such lofty label as gospel of Jesus Christ in Papias time as they acquired in later years, otherwise he would have relied more on their accounts than on oral information.

2.5.3 Marcion's Understanding of Gospel

Koester is of the view that Marcion was the first person to designate his revised edition of Luke as the εὐαγγέλιον. He avers,

> There is no evidence that anyone before Marcion called a gospel writing εὐαγγέλιον. But all reports about Marcion agree that he called his revised edition of Luke "εὐαγγέλιον". This is the first instance in which a Christian used the term as a title of a written document. Marcion introduced this novel usage in conscious protest against the still undefined and mostly oral traditions to

---

76. Eusebius, 115.

77. Burridge, "Who Writes, Why, and For Whom?," 102; Schmidt, "Die Stellung der Evangelien," 127.

78. Holmes, *Apostolic Fathers*, 735.

which the Churches of his day referred as their dominical and apostolic authority.[79]

As earlier posited, the need to ring-fence the orthodox written texts against mutilation by such heretics as Marcion was most likely the reason for designating them τὸ εὐαγγέλιον. As such, when the rest of Christianity embraced the written texts as the Gospels, the oral gospel was sidelined as the one and only gospel.

2.5.4 Gospel in the Time of Justin Martyr

Justin Martyr lived "during the time when Christian oral and written tradition still existed side by side."[80] However, he preferred referring to these texts as ἀπομνημονύματα των ἀποστόλων "(memoirs of the Apostles)."[81] Craig D. Allert posits that "Justin made reference to the memoirs in one concentrated section of the *Dialogue* a total of 13 times."[82] Evans posits, "memoirs" (απομνημονύματα) "were current at the time for the narration of the life, deeds or teachings of a prominent person."[83] In his dialogue with Trypho, Justin Martyr appears shy to refer to the books by the apostles and their acquaintances as the Gospels. This explains why he would describe these memoirs as "which are also called gospels"[84] while Trypho refers to them as "the so-called gospels."[85] Such expressions show that, in Justin Martyr's milieu, the written texts by Matthew, Mark, Luke, and John had not been widely acknowledged as Gospels. Koester avers,

> While Marcion revised the Gospel of Luke in order to eliminate all references to the Law and the Prophets, Justin did not hesitate to revise the texts of Matthew and Luke in order to establish an even closer verbal agreement between the prophecies of the Greek Bible and the record of their fulfillment. As records of this nature, the gospels are, indeed a fountain of the

---

79. Koester, "From Kerygma-Gospel," 376.
80. Allert, *Revelation, Truth, Canon*, 187.
81. Stanton, *Jesus and Gospel*, 101.
82. Allert, *Revelation, Truth, Canon*, 100.
83. Evans, "New Testament in the Making," 270.
84. Allert, *Revelation, Truth, Canon*, 193.
85. Allert, 193.

truth of the Christian beliefs and they substantiate the validity of the Christian kerygma. That this is the case is not related to their "kerygmatic" character or structure. Rather Justin sees the gospels as reliable historical records. As the testimony of true divinity is the fulfillment of prophecy, the gospels as reliable records of history provide the evidence for the fulfillment of prophecy in the story of Jesus. The Christian kerygma which proclaims this Jesus is trustworthy divine revelation because it is confirmed by the historical record provided by the gospel.[86]

In this supposition, Koester has shown that the written texts were used to authenticate the oral kerygma as a divine revelation.

2.5.5 Gospel in the Times of Tertullian

Tertullian's response to the production of what Marcion considered as the authentic gospel has a very illuminating statement on his view of the gospel. He says in *Marc.* 4.4.2, "And in the end, is that to be regarded as more faithful to the truth which is later, even after so many and significant works and testimonies to the Christian religion have been produced for the world, which without the truth of the gospel could not have been published."[87] To Tertullian the works of the apostles were and should be a testimony to the Christian religion. He suggests that the written texts were works that testified to a gospel that was outside the texts of the apostles. Tertullian's concept of gospel is described as the rule of faith which was "a guide or standard of right belief whose general content was seen as flowing directly from Christ, through the Apostles and to the Church."[88] As such, to Tertullian, gospel referenced an oral proclamation.

From a reading of the prologue of the Markan text, Martin Hengel supposes that it assumed the title Gospel at its inception.[89] He also notes that "the transference of this title, quite unusual in ancient literature, to the later Gospels including the numerous apocryphal Gospels in the second century, can only meaningfully be explained in the light of the earliest Gospel, that of

---

86. Koester, "From Kerygma-Gospel," 380.
87. *Adv. Marc.* 4.4.2.
88. Allert, *Revelation, Truth, Canon*, 207.
89. Hengel, *Studies in the Gospel of Mark*, 83.

Mark."[90] He has not supported his argument by a probe of the transmission history of the term "gospel." Instead, he has relied on an unsubstantiated supposition that the "gospel" referenced in Mark 1:1 is the content of the Markan text.

Bauckham supports Hengel in his position that using the label "Gospel according to the individual writers" "was the only way that one of the Gospels could have been distinguished from another . . . Again the universality of these ascriptions of authorship and the fact that they seem never to have been disputed indicate that they became established usage as soon as the Gospels were circulating."[91] However, it is noteworthy that in a closely guarded environment, such as was the established church context, it is possible for an issue that has the leader's sanction and protection to acquire universal acclaim without any dispute even though it calls for reconsideration. Bauckham's argument needs re-evaluation outside the limitations and yoke of the presupposition consequent of the second-century labelling of the text as "the Gospel according to Mark."

Certainly, by the time of Irenaeus, the four books had already been labelled the Gospel according to the individual evangelist. However, a study of the development of the referent of the word εὐαγγέλιον from Jesus's milieu to the patristic father's milieu coupled with a grammatical analysis of Mark 1:1 collaborate in showing that by the time when Mark was writing his book, the word εὐαγγέλιον did not refer to either the oral tradition about the life and times of Jesus or their written versions.

2.6 Term "Gospel" in Mark's Text

Willi Marxsen[92] opines that Mark's use of the term εὐαγγέλιον is a confluence of a "conceptual-theological concept, represented by Paul and the kerygmatic-visual, using the so-called material of synoptic tradition."[93] He suggests that

---

90. Hengel, 83.

91. Bauckham, *Jesus and the Eyewitnesses*, 304.

92. Marxsen, *Mark the Evangelist*, 117–150. However, he seems to be controlled by the presupposition that the book is a gospel message, as such, his conclusions are subjective. However, his study is very insightful and a starting point for further studies on the referent to the term gospel in the Markan text.

93. Marxsen, *Mark the Evangelist*, 147. This means that Mark was influenced by Paul's concept of the term and that it was used to refer to the oral tradition.

the gospel referenced in Mark 1:1 constitutes the textual content. He notes that the Markan text "is obviously oriented to the content, but not to the genre of the writings."[94] Though Marxsen has answered his question "how is the gospel's content more closely described?" with the answer that "the καιρος is fulfilled," he has however, under-interpreted the use of καιρος in stating that it is "fulfilled in the proclamation occurring in Mark's time."[95] The fulfilling of time[96] and the coming of Jesus are not synonymous. The coming of Jesus subsists and is an aspect of the fulfilled time. The second coming of Christ and final judgment, which are yet to be fulfilled, are aspects of the same fulfilled time.

Marxsen interprets the term gospel from a reading of Mark 8:35 and 10:29 in which he takes the καὶ joining ἕνεκεν ἐμοῦ and τοῦ εὐαγγελίου as epexegetical.[97] As such ἐμοῦ and εὐαγγέλιον are interpreted as synonymous. In such a scenario, gospel becomes a representation of Jesus. Consequently, Marxsen posits that for Mark, "the Lord is present in the gospel."[98] He therefore considers the Markan text to be a "re-presentation of both the crucified Jesus and the exalted king." As such, the text "makes contemporary the one who has come and the one who will come."[99] Consequently, he concludes that "'Gospel' becomes the designation of the book."[100] Marxsen has investigated the synonymy between Jesus and the gospel from a very limited study. Since these two sayings are attributed to Jesus and not to Mark, he should have compared them from their Hebrew and Aramaic source from which the Greek equivalent was translated instead of noting the epexegetical natures of the sayings in Greek. The waw-consecutive in Hebrew would not have constituted an epexegetical relationship.

Use of the noun Ἀρχὴ describes a specific aspect of the oral gospel that Mark was writing about, that is, the salvific episode on which it was premised. However, Marxsen sees the use ἀρχῇ as a pointer to "the point towards which

---

94. Marxsen, 117.

95. Marxsen, 131.

96. The fulfilling of time is taken to be God's act of inaugurating the kingdom of God in his own time.

97. Marxsen, *Mark the Evangelist*, 128.

98. Marxsen, 128.

99. Marxsen, 148.

100. Marxsen, 150.

this event (gospel) is to be traced."¹⁰¹ Whereas Marxsen's point of view is plausible, this book is of the view that ἀρχῇ also referenced the events on which the oral gospel was premised. As such, the term Ἀρχὴ, in Mark 1:1, positions the premise of the oral gospel on a God appointed and sanctioned Christ event just as בְּרֵאשִׁית, in Genesis 1:,1 positions the foundation of creation in God and ἀρχῇ in John1:1 positions the foundation of ὁ λόγος in God. Therefore, Ἀρχὴ should be understood not to be a generating aspect but as referencing the premise on which the subject of his discussion is founded.

The anecdotes that Mark narrated as constituting the events that were foundational to the gospel of Jesus Christ are congruous to the episodes that Peter understood to have been foundational to Jesus's ministry (Acts 10:36–43). Peter points out that the beginning of Jesus's ministry was premised on God's anointing Jesus with the Holy Spirit and power, his miraculous works of healing those who were under the power of the devil (Acts 10:38) and the fact that God affirmed him to be Lord by resurrecting him from the dead. Mark's anecdotes seem to be emphasizing Jesus's anointing with the Holy Spirit (1:2–13), his miraculous deeds (1:14–8:36) and his passion and resurrection (8:36–16:20). Patterning his book in semblance with Peter's sermon suggests that Mark wanted to demonstrate that the gospel that was being preached conformed to the pattern of the gospel that was being preached by the apostles.

2.6.1 Reference of the Term "Gospel" in Mark 1:1

The major supposition that defines and directs this research is that the gospel under reference in Mark 1:1 was an oral gospel that was outside and independent of the Markan text. In a context where preaching of the gospel was considered to be divinely enabled through the Holy Spirit, it would not be difficult to understand the aura that the oral kerygma attracted (Acts 1:8). In such a scenario, it would not be unheard-of to write a paraenetic treatise exhorting the audience to hearken to a divinely inspired oral gospel. Stanton agrees with this position in his statement that "For Mark, το εὐαγγέλιον is the proclaimed message about Jesus Christ . . . Whether του εὐαγγελίου is taken as a subjective or as an objective genitive, Mark 1:1 refers to 'proclamation,' not

---

101. Marxsen, 132.

a written report."[102] This supposition has major hermeneutical implications. Among them is that; the oral gospel is a distinct and independent interlocutor within the matrix of the Markan discourse.

Ever since the time of Marcion and later on Justin Martyr when the designation of the books of Matthew, Mark, Luke and John as the Gospels[103] is first noted, most scholars have adopted the label as implying that the contents of the individual books constitute the contents of the gospel message. Hengel points out that "Before Irenaeus, it is found only twice: once in Justin, *1 Apol.* 66.3. ἐν τοῖς [...] ἀπομνημονευμασιν, ἀ Καλειται εὐαγγέλια and in Apollinaris of Laodicea, in Dindorf (ed.), *Chronicon Paschale ad exemplar Vaticanum* (Bonn: Weber, 18320), 1, pp.13–14. Only Irenaeus, in connection with his 'fourfold Gospel', uses the plural 'the Gospels' a few times."[104] Though, as this work has argued, the syntactical expression in Mark 1:1 supports a contrary opinion, most scholars still hold on to the view that the gospel under reference in Mark 1:1 is the content of the text.

The designation of the writings of the four evangelists Matthew, Mark, Luke, and John as gospels coincided with the apologetic debates of the mid- and late-second century as evidenced by the cited works of Marcion, Justin Martyr, and Irenaeus. Therefore, it is arguable that it was a response to questions on the authenticity of these texts in view of evident differences in their accounts that, according to the prevailing thought, should have constituted one orderly account of the life and times of Jesus Christ. It is apparent that their differences were a matter of concern to the reading community. As such, it is understandable why Tatian had tried to prepare a harmonized

---

102. Stanton, *Jesus and Gospel*, 56.

103. Hengel, "Four Gospels," 13. Hengel posits that, only in Justin do we find a single occurrence of the plural εαγγελια for our four Gospels. Elsewhere he avoids it and prefers to use the formula "reminiscences of the apostles" (14). Koester has argued against Hengel's position and sees Marcion as the first person who conceived of the four books as Gospel. Hengel's position is contrasted by Gregory ("Looking for Luke," 408), who posits that "Debates continue as to when gospels were first called gospels and when the traditional names of the evangelists were associated with each text, but even the bookish Justin Martyr, whose knowledge of Luke seems clear, never refers to it by its traditional title, just as he does not refer to that of any of the other gospels." What is clear is that the books by the four evangelists were explicitly labeled Gospels in the second century CE.

104. Hengel, "Four Gospels," 13–14.

form[105] of the four accounts in his Diatesseron,[106] while Marcion had tried to discriminate some of the accounts as not being authentic.[107]

Bovon notes that "the second century was a century of harmonizing discrepancies between the synoptic gospels."[108] However, it can be argued that those who designated them Gospels and those reading their differences as contradictory accounts of the life and times of Jesus, had not appreciated that the books were not different gospels but different rhetorical communications whose source material is a common tradition. The reason for the differences was that, these narratives were designed and rhetorically embellished to solve extant exigencies of different rhetorical situations of audiences in different locations. The occasions that prompted the writings of the texts ranged from a need for catechetical instructional material for Matthew,[109] setting an orderly account of the Christ event for Luke (Luke 1:3–4), enhancing faith in Jesus as the Christ for John (John 20:31), and catalyzing audience response to the oral gospel for Mark.

Different scholars have taken different positions on whether the gospel referenced in Mark 1:1 is the content of the Markan text. In his support for the gospel referenced in Mark 1:1 being the content of the book of Mark, R. A. Guelich grounds his argument on the historical survey of the Jewish formula for scriptural citation and argues that,

> The citation formula "as has been written by . . .," in 1:2 connects the first sentence with verse 1–15 which becomes the beginning of the gospel and that "if 1:1–15 represents the beginning of the gospel . . . in keeping with Isaiah's promise, then Mark 1:16–16:8 must be the rest of the 'gospel concerning Jesus Messiah Son of God' for which 1:1–15 is 'the beginning.'"[110]

---

105. Ferguson, "Factors Leading to the Selection," 302. On the work of Tatian, Everett Fergusson has argued that "If the four gospels were regarded as Scripture, he would not have treated them so freely as to weave them together into a separate narrative . . . on the other hand why would he have bothered unless the works were considered important?" He concluded that "because they were authoritative, Tatian was concerned enough to do the study involved in reducing the four authorities to one unified account."

106. Kurian, *Nelson's New Christian Dictionary*, 238.

107. Padgett, "Marcion," 706.

108. Bovon, "Reception and Use of the Gospel," 394.

109. France, *Matthew*, 20–21.

110. Guelich, "Gospel of Mark," 513.

Guelich has further supported his argument by noting that Peter's first sermon in Acts 10:34–43 compares well with the Markan text.

However, Guelich has not explored the text from the more plausible presupposition that the gospel referenced in Mark 1:1 was outside and independent of the text. In such a scenario, his argument could still be valid but different questions would have surfaced and hence his conclusion would have been different. Furthermore, in reference to Peter's sermons, Guelich has not considered the fact that the actions of Jesus and the Old Testament quotations and allusions recorded in Acts, just as in the Markan text, are purposely meant to validate the oral gospel message by Peter which is later recorded in Acts 10:42–43. The gospel message that Peter preached was that Jesus "was ordained by God to be judge of the living and the dead . . . through His name, whoever believes in Him will receive remission of sins" (Acts 10:42–43 NKJV).

Guelich's position places serious hermeneutical hurdles to interpretation of the Markan text and is usually the source of the major difficulties associated with the interpretation of the text. It introduces a contradiction between the expected hermeneutical outcomes if the text was considered to be the gospel and the hermeneutical outcome if the legitimate genre of the text, whose identification has been clouded by the limitations and bridle placed by the presupposition consequent of the editorial labelling, is taken into account. As such, the significance and purpose of the book are not easy to identify since the said presupposition limits the questions that interpreters can pose to the text. This situation has been identified and pointed out by Guelich himself in saying,

> Despite numerous attempts to find Mark's purpose in the theological struggles (e.g., Christology) or social circumstances of the early Church (e.g., the fall of Jerusalem), the rather generic character of the story (lacking specific clues about place and date of authorship) and the narrative integrity of the gospel makes such historical and theological reconstruction at best speculative.[111]

---

111. Guelich, "Mark, Gospel of," 783.

Guthrie too takes the gospel referenced in Mark 1:1 to be the contents of the Markan text. He explains the episodic nature of the textual content by noting the large portion dedicated to the passion narratives and posits, "The cross and resurrection were the central features of the Christian gospel. The events and teaching which led up to the cross were preparatory . . . The movement of the narrative is dominated by the passion story, but in Mark's gospel the action is heightened by the relative absence of blocks of teaching material."[112] Guthrie has not explained his supposition in view of lack of an apt conclusion to the resurrection story to give it the prominence he asserts. As such, he cannot ascribe prominence to the passion by the mere volume of material without citing its significance.

Contrariwise, N. Clayton Croy has posited that "every other use of the word *euangelion* in Mark's Gospel can be understood wholly in terms of the first-century meaning of the 'oral proclamation of good news.'"[113] This statement supports the supposition that the gospel referenced in Mark 1:1 was oral and therefore it was outside of the Markan text. Dibelius avers, "even his first expression of his document signifying, if I understand the matter rightly, not his book but the Christian estimate of the story of the Baptist as 'The beginning of the preaching of salvation.'"[114] He sees the gospel of Jesus as being "outside of the Markan gospel."[115] However he considers the referent of the term "gospel" in Mark 1:1 as an amalgam of the sayings of Jesus, which are rarely mentioned in the Markan text. As such, his concept of the gospel of Jesus Christ being outside of the Markan text is based on his understanding that against Matthew, who has explicitly recorded the sayings of Jesus, largely, Mark leaves them outside of the text "to which he refers as opportunity arises."[116]

Most of the reviewed scholars consider the writings of the four evangelists as announcements of the coming of the Saviour into the world and hence a gospel. Although Mark affirms the coming of Jesus Christ, it is incidental rather than the main aim of the text. His discriminative choice of episodes

---

112. Guthrie, *New Testament Introduction*, 65.
113. Croy, *Mutilation of Mark's Gospel*, 131.
114. Dibelius, *From Tradition to Gospel*, 264.
115. Dibelius, 264.
116. Dibelius, 264.

with a bias towards narrating episodes that highlight Jesus's persona suggests that the text is aimed at catalyzing audience response to the oral gospel about Jesus Christ. Moreover, at the background of every narrated episode, there was either the preaching of the gospel, a reference to a need to preach, or a command to preach the gospel (1:1; 8:38; 10:29; 13:10; 14:9; 16:15). As such, before the writing of any of the books referred to as the Gospels, the oral gospel that was commissioned to be preached by Jesus (Matt 28:19, Mark 16:15) and that which is mentioned in the text of Mark 1:1 was being orally preached and continued to be preached by the apostles and those who succeeded them.

Therefore, it was in order for Mark to urge belief and performance of the oral gospel by extolling the ethos of the one on whom it was premised, by connecting it with the fulfilment of the Old Testament Scriptures and promises, by narrating the miracles and wonders that Jesus performed, by a retelling of Jesus's enigmatic parables, and by narrating stories of the passion of Christ. Specifically, the controversy narratives and the parable of the sower were aimed at laying bare the audience's rhetorical situation and the exigencies therein to catalyze a positive response to the oral gospel message.

Argument from Mark's syntax in Mark 1:1

The phrase, Ἀρχὴ τοῦ εὐαγγελίου Ἰησοῦ Χριστοῦ [υἱοῦ θεοῦ] (1:1) identifies the subject of discussion of the Markan text. Ἀρχὴ describes and specifies the aspect of the subject under discussion. Such a phrase that lacks a verb can best be understood by scanning its context. Walhout posits, "The reference or designation of sentence indexicals such as demonstrative pronouns, proper names, certain adverbs, and time indicators can be understood only if we know their context of use; they cannot be understood from the subject and predicate alone."[117] Furthermore, Wolterstorff has also said that sentences considered only in the context of a text are "not enough to determine the noematic content of that act of the discourse."[118] As such, Mark 1:1 can be better understood by reading it within its winder social and religious context.

Walhout further posits that "the sense of a sentence depends also on what speech-action theorists call the illocutionary force of the sentence, that is, the

---

117. Walhout, "Narrative Hermeneutics," 67.
118. Wolterstorff, *Divine Discourse*, 152.

purpose for which the sentence is used."[119] As such, using speech act theory by John R. Searle, Ἀρχὴ τοῦ εὐαγγελίου can be identified as a "speech act of referring."[120] It refers to a specific aspect of the subject under discussion in the text, that is, the beginning of the gospel. As such, it is plausible that Mark's interest was to highlight and stress the salient episodes on which the gospel of Jesus Christ was premised. In essence, the writer is telling the readers, "I am writing to you concerning the episodes on which the gospel was premised." Furthermore, τοῦ εὐαγγελίου is a descriptive genitive describing αρχη.

Gundry asks, "does τοῦ εὐαγγελίου mean 'the good news' as such, as preached, or as written up in Marks gospel?"[121] Again he asks, "Does beginning of the good news of Jesus Christ refer to the subject matter of the whole gospel or to the subject matter only of the first verses?"[122] The grammatical construction of Mark 1:1 establishes that the subject of the text is the beginning of the gospel of Jesus Christ the Son of God. Since a major supposition in this dissertation is that the gospel referenced in Mark 1:1 is outside the Markan text, then the episodes narrated in the book are collectively deemed to constitute the beginning of the gospel.

This work has also argued that the genitive Ἰησοῦ Χριστοῦ [υἱοῦ θεοῦ] is unambiguously an objective genitive describing εὐαγγέλιον as about Jesus Christ. Luter has argued that "if 'gospel of Christ' is taken as an objective genitive, God and Christ are the contents of the gospel message ('the gospel about God/Christ')."[123] Luter's argument suggests that the gospel was a message about God and Christ. Therefore, gospel is a proclamation of the good news of God's fulfillment of the promise to the forefathers to inaugurate his kingdom and its salvific benefits through the work of Jesus Christ on the cross.

Argument from the outline of Mark 1:1–15

Notably, Mark 1:1–5 is structured in a chiasm.

    A. Announcement of the gospel of Jesus Christ 1:1

        B. John comes to the desert 1:2–8

---

119. Walhout, "Narrative Hermeneutics," 67.
120. Searle, *Speech Acts*, 26.
121. Gundry, *Mark*, 29.
122. Gundry, 29.
123. Luter, "Gospel," 370.

C. Jesus baptized by John 1:9–11

B¹. Jesus comes to the desert 1:12–13

A¹. Announcement of the gospel of God 1:14

In her comments on use of chiasm as a rhetorical device, Dewey has postulated that "repetition may be used to indicate emphasis, as a means of retarding action, or as a way of indicating climax."[124] She further posits that "chiasm is an instance of word repetition for rhetorical effect."[125] The chiasm evident in Mark's prologue indicates that Mark's concern is the oral gospel, as highlighted in A and A¹, which Jesus began to preach after his baptism. This shows that the gospel referred to in Mark 1:1 is the same gospel that Jesus began to preach in Mark 1:14. However, its contents continued to expand as futurist aspects of the eschatological kingdom of God continued to happen. For example, the death and resurrection of Jesus Christ, which had not yet happened by the time of Jesus's earthly ministry, was later on proclaimed as part of the gospel.

Another chiasmic structure in the pericope running from Mark 3:12–6:56 presents the same results.

A. Jesus appoints the Twelve to preach the gospel 3:12–19.

B. More miracles and the Beelzebub controversy 3:20–30.

C. Teachings on who is his mother and brothers 3:31–35.

C¹. Jesus teaches in parables 4:1–34.

B¹. More miracles and the rejection of Jesus in Nazareth 4:35–5:43.

A¹. Jesus's disciples sent to preach the gospel 6:1–56.

The gospel message was central to the Markan text. Notably, Jesus was the central figure of the oral gospel message. This study's supposition and major hypothesis, that the gospel under reference in Mark 1:1 is the oral gospel that Mark and his contemporaries were preaching, is supported by the text's structure, the genre of the text, textual analysis of the prologue of 1:1, and the etymology of the word εὐαγγέλιον.

---

124. Dewey, *Markan Public Debate*, 32.

125. Dewey, 32.

Argument from textual discourse

Mark mentions the gospel in two different perspectives. First, he mentions the gospel that he and his contemporaries were proclaiming (1:1). Second, he connected this gospel with the gospel that had been preached by Jesus in Mark 1:14 (τὸ εὐαγγέλιον τοῦ θεοῦ), which is also the gospel that Jesus commissioned the disciples to preach in Mark 6:7–13. Though Mark mentions and ascribes importance to the gospel preached by Jesus, he does not endeavor to elaborate its nature, choosing rather to only mention that Jesus preached it with power unlike the teachers of the law. This suggests that the gospel he was referring to was within the knowledge domain of his audience. The difference between τὸ εὐαγγέλιον τοῦ θεοῦ and τὸ εὐαγγέλιον τοῦ Ἰησοῦ χριστοῦ, υἱοῦ τοῦ θεοῦ was that the proclamation of the nature and significance of the death and resurrection of Jesus Christ was added to the former to make the latter.

2.7 Content of the Oral Gospel

Up until the creedal councils and the later church confessions that established the bounds of the Christian faith in the fourth and fifth century CE,[126] the limits of the gospel message had not been definitively set. Moreover, other than the two ordinances of baptism and the Lord's Supper that encapsulated the doctrines about man's newness of life after conversion (Rom 6:4) and the nature and significance of Jesus's person, life, and work on the cross (1 Cor 11:23–26) respectively, albeit in a ritual form, there is no extant record that shows the bounds of the content of the oral gospel message that was being proclaimed by Jesus and his disciples.

Nevertheless, the essential content of the salvific message can be reconstructed by analyzing the nature and significance of the salvific episode which is narrated in the texts. Essentially, the gospel was grounded on the notion that the time of fulfilment of God's promises to Israel's forefathers and that had become their hope (Acts 28:20), had fully come. As such, the essence of the gospel was that, God had taken over the rule over his people and that the once anticipated divine and anointed ruler who was to rule over God's kingdom

---

126. Of these, the Apostles' Creed and the Nicene Creed are the major creedal confessions. The Augsburg Confession (1530), Scots Confession (1560), the Westminster Confession (1647), and the Baptist confession of Faith (1689) are later day confessions that form the matrix of the creedal confessions of the church over the centuries.

(Dan 7:13–14) had already come. By comparing Jesus's birth, deeds, passion, and resurrection with the person and work of the anticipated Messiah, Christians interpreted the historical Jesus to be this anticipated King. As such, they were justified in ascribing to him the title, faith, and worship due to this anointed King. Therefore, to them, the kingdom of God had come. However, it was to be fully consummated at the second coming of the Christ (1 Pet 1:3–5). Moreover, the existential fellowship with God in the Holy Spirit, evidenced in the Spiritual gifts that accompanied them (Mark 16:20; 1 Cor 12:7–11), served to validate the gospel as a truly divine prerogative.

When Paul proclaimed this notion to the Jews in Rome (Acts 28:23), he quoted Old Testament Scriptures to validate his claim, "So when he had appointed him a day, many came to him at his lodging, to whom he explained and solemnly testified of the kingdom of God, persuading them concerning Jesus from both the Law of Moses and the Prophets, from morning to evening" (Acts 28:23 NKJV). Paul's example shows that Old Testament quotations were used to authenticate this profound claim which was the major proclamation of the gospel.

Peter's sermons in Acts 2:28–40; 3:11–26; and 10:34–43, suggest that preaching the gospel involved a proclamation that Jesus was "He who was ordained by God to be the judge of the living and the dead," and that "through His name, whoever believes in Him will receive remission of sins" (Acts 10:43, Mark 16:15–16). Old Testament Scriptures and references to Jesus's deeds and miracles of healing were cited to authenticate these claims. In Acts 20:21, Paul says that his message consisted "testifying both to Jews and to Greeks of repentance towards God and of faith in our Lord Jesus Christ." Wright postulates that the oral gospel, which he calls the rule of faith, emphasized on "the goodness of the creator and creation, the historical reality of the incarnation of the Son, the unity of the old and new covenants and the concreteness of the last things."[127] He further posits that "the appeal to the rule of faith had validity but by Origen's time, it is losing obvious contact with the apostolic kerygma."[128] Wright is suggesting, and rightly so, that the rule of faith was running concurrently with the written texts and that it was orally transmitted.

---

127. Wright, "Creeds, Confessional Forms," 259.
128. Wright, 259.

2.7.1 Pointers to the Oral Gospel in the Markan Text

Though the content of the gospel that Jesus had proclaimed is not explicitly spelt out in the Markan text, the outlay of the oral gospel that Mark and his contemporaries were preaching can be reconstructed from the textual pointers. The text identifies two important aspects of the gospel proclamation: first, affirming that Jesus was the Christ the Son of God (1:1) and second, highlighting the salvific significance of his passion and death on the cross in the Last Supper narratives (14:22–25). These two aspects are pointers as to why the proclamation of the incoming kingdom of God is said to be good news.

Ἀρχὴ τοῦ εὐαγγελίου Ἰησοῦ Χριστοῦ υἱοῦ θεοῦ in Mark 1:1 indicates that the referenced gospel is about Jesus Christ the Son of God. The importance of the affirmation that Jesus was the Christ the Son of God, as an aspect of gospel proclamation, is suggested by the priority of place Mark gave this emphatic statement in his structure. It is also emphasized by Mark's use of Old Testament to ascertain that the Jesus of history, who was also the Christ of faith, was indeed the Christ of Scripture (1:2–15). To emphasize his assertion, he narrated the epiphany of the Holy Spirit and the heavenly witness of the divine voice that declared that Jesus was indeed the Son of God (1:11–12). The benefit that makes the appearance and work of Jesus to be indeed τὸ εὐαγγέλιον was the availability and accessibility of repentance and forgiveness of sins to whoever believes in the gospel (1:14–15).

Mark also highlighted the importance of the gospel in his treatise by narrating the transfiguration episode (9:2–8). He connected Jesus with the Old Testament greats, Moses and Elijah. Here, Mark enjoined God in the gospel proclamation by recording his affirming utterance, "This is my beloved son, listen to him." (9:7 ESV). The transfiguration and appearance of Moses and Elijah affirmed the eschatological proclamation of the gospel that the dead will be raised (13:26–27; 14:25). It also shows that Jesus's prediction in Mark 9:1 was fulfilled after six days. It is significant that Peter referred to this episode in affirming the gospel message that he and his contemporaries were preaching (2 Pet 1:16–21).

Another pointer to the content of the oral gospel message in Mark is seen in the defining moment when Mark is changing his text's concentration from narrating episodes of the miraculous works of Jesus on earth to his salvific work in the passion (8:27–16:8). Whereas Mark portrays Jesus as not being keen on revealing his person during this phase of ministry until in wonder they asked "what manner of man is this?" (4:41 KJV), at the start of the second phase of his ministry Jesus reveals his person to his disciples in Caesarea Philippi by asking them a question the answer to which would no doubt reveal his identity: "Who do men say that I am?" (8:27–31). Through Peter's answer that "You are the Christ" (8:29), Mark highlights that the proclamation that Jesus was the Messiah the son of God was also part of the content of the post-resurrection gospel message.

Another aspect of the gospel proclamation that is suggested by the emphasis in the text is the significance of the first coming and death of Jesus Christ. As has been suggested, Mark ascribes significance to the coming of the Christ by recording the initial proclamation of Jesus that "ὅτι Πεπλήρωται ὁ καιρὸς καὶ ἤγγικεν ἡ βασιλεία τοῦ θεοῦ· μετανοεῖτε καὶ πιστεύετε ἐν τῷ εὐαγγελίῳ" (1:15). The aspect that confers the message about the fulfilment of time, the nearness of the kingdom of God, and the passion of Jesus Christ the honor of being labelled a gospel is its efficacy to engender redemption from sin to those who believe it.

After Jesus revealed himself to the disciples in Caesarea Philippi, he predicted his passion three times (8:31; 9:31; and 10:33). This triad recording of the prediction suggests the importance of the passion of Christ in the proclamation of the gospel. This perspective is reinforced by Mark's narration of the inaugurating episode of the Last Supper. He did not only highlight that the ordinance, which had by then become part of the church's rites, was ordained by Jesus but more significantly, through the words of its inauguration, he ascribed salvific value to the passion of Christ. By setting the passion narrative within the Passover, Mark alluded to the fact that Jesus was the sacrificial lamb of the new covenant thereby ascribing a propitiatory, vicarious, and sacrificial value to the death of Jesus Christ. Consequently, he dignified the death of Jesus that may have been seen as a humiliating scandal in some quarters.

The content of the gospel also entailed an exhortation to praxis of the ethical demands set in the Old Testament as explicated by Jesus in quoting the Hebrew *Shema* (12:29–31). These are the ethics demanded of the new status which is conferred by believing in the gospel. Finally, the oral gospel message must have included a proclamation of the eschatological hope of believers and the final consummation of the kingdom at the parousia (13:26–27).

In summary, although the oral gospel is not directly explicated in the Markan text, it is given as the reason for Jesus's controversy with the Jewish leaders (3:1-6). It was also preserved and transmitted in the inauguration and perpetual celebrations of the ordinances of baptism and the Lord's Supper (Matt 28:19, Luke 22:19, 1 Cor 11:23-26). Finally, the eschatological hope, which was an important aspect of gospel (Mark 13:26-30, 1 Cor 15:50-54) was enjoined by a proclamation of the soon coming of the glorified Christ.

2.8 Summary: "Gospelness" of the Markan Text

The transmission of the referent of the term "εὐαγγέλιον" over the period between Jesus Christ's milieu and the patristic milieu can be explained in terms of interlocking referents. The first referent was the oral gospel that was proclaimed by Jesus and his disciples which Mark referred to as "τὸ εὐαγγέλιον τοῦ θεοῦ" (1:14). The content of this gospel was the proclamation ὅτι Πεπλήρωται ὁ καιρὸς καὶ ἤγγικεν ἡ βασιλεία τοῦ θεοῦ· μετανοεῖτε καὶ πιστεύετε ἐν τῷ εὐαγγελίῳ (1:15). The moral demands of the gospel were also part of the proclamation (12:29-31). This proclamation continued until the crucifixion of Jesus. After the passion, resurrection, and the gift of the Holy Spirit on the day of Pentecost, the referent of the term "εὐαγγέλιον" was expanded to include the proclamation of the passion, resurrection, the gift of the Holy Spirit, and their salvific significance (Acts 2:22-40). This amalgam was the gospel that Mark and his contemporaries were proclaiming during and after the time of writing the Markan text. As such, it is the gospel that is referenced in Mark 1:1 as the gospel of Jesus Christ the Son of God.

Alongside the oral proclamation of the gospel, there was an oral tradition of the sayings and deeds of Jesus. This essentially consisted of oral narratives of the episodes and sayings making up the Christ event. It inhered in the collective memory of the eye witnesses of the life and times of Jesus. Williams notes that "the stories and teachings of Jesus that Mark inherited were already basic elements of an early Christian tradition."[129] The oral tradition was a rich repository of information concerning the Christ event from which historians, biographers, preachers and aretalogists could draw for their various communicative needs. According to Dunn, "In an oral culture, tradition – oral tradition – is *communal memory*."[130] He further says

---

129. Williams, *Gospel Against Parables*, 38.
130. Dunn, *New Perspective on Jesus*, 121.

A group's tradition is the means by which the group affirms and celebrates what is important about its origins and about its past. So the alternative is to envisage little groups of disciples and sympathizers, their identity as a group given by their shared response to Jesus himself or to one of his disciples/apostles – little groups who met regularly to share the memories and the traditions that bound them together, for elders or teachers to tell again stories of Jesus and to expound afresh and elaborate his teachings.[131]

However, with the passage of time, the memory of the Christ event was bound to become hazy in the minds of the eyewitnesses. As such, written stories on the episodes of the Christ event, which were then referred to as the reminiscence of the apostles,[132] become the only reference material for narratives about various aspects of the Christ event.

Agreeably, Dunn notes that "the tradition Mark drew upon continued to circulate in oral communication and was known more widely than the gospel itself."[133] However, Dunn has not captured an obvious difference between the oral tradition, which consisted of information concerning the deeds and sayings that consisted the life and times of Jesus Christ, as it existed in the memories of the eyewitnesses and the oral gospel proclamation which consisted of a divinely inspired interpretation of the nature and significance of the Christ event (Acts 2:4; 4:8; 4:29; 4:31). Nonetheless, Dunn has rightly said that Mark drew from an oral tradition.

The oral gospel, kerygma, which also drew its affirming information from the oral tradition and Old Testament Scripture, was different in form and content from the oral tradition that inhered in the memories of the eyewitnesses and the Markan text. The oral tradition was historical and biographical in nature and inhered in the memory of eyewitnesses to the Christ event. The oral gospel was a proclamation summoning the audience to faith in Jesus. The Markan text was hortatory, catalyzing audience response to the

---

131. Dunn, 121.
132. Loveday, "What is a Gospel?," 21.
133. Dunn, *New Perspective on Jesus*, 122.

oral gospel. Whereas the Markan text was more localized,[134] the oral gospel was a universal phenomenon. This suggests that the Markan text existed to serve the purpose of the oral gospel.

The individual and institutional memories are temporary aspects. The demise of the eyewitnesses of the salvific episode and destruction of Jerusalem must have had the effect of raising the profile of the texts on the Christ event to a reverenced status and hence their later consideration as part of Scripture. They became the immortalized memory of the Christ event. The second-century referent of the word εὐαγγελίον as the written texts must have been incidental. The Spirit inspired gospel proclamation as described by Papias[135] must have waned after the death of the apostles giving way to the written texts on the life and times of Jesus to assume the elevated title of εὐαγγελίον. Richard Norris, Jr., has posited that the four books designated Gospels "came to be described as Gospels 'according to' Mark, Matthew, John and Luke only in the second century (*see Irenaeus, AH 3.1.1*)."[136] A consolidation of all the writings of the apostles on the Christ event and other teachings into a corpus that would direct faith and practice must have become an acute need.

The presupposition consequent of designating the Markan text as "the Gospel according to Mark" by the late-second-century fathers and its later inclusion as part of the canon of Scripture had the effect of completely eclipsing the oral gospel as an independent interlocutor with the Markan audience. The change of referent of the term εὐαγγέλιον from an oral gospel that was outside and independent of the text to written texts introduced a paradigm shift in the way the gospel was proclaimed. There was a shift from oral proclamation to exegesis of the newly canonized texts. Burridge concurs and says that "such linking of the content of early Christian preaching with narratives about Jesus' ministry, death and resurrection changed the word's [εὐαγγέλιον] use."[137] Lately, the word gospel has also acquired the referent of a literary genre. However, of exegetical importance, these changes and their implications should be accounted for in the study and interpretation of the New Testament texts which were labelled the Gospels.

---

134. Localization is premised on the fact that the text was addressed to a specific audience. Mark is said to have been written in Rome, see English, *Message of Mark*, 22.

135. Eusebius, *Ecclesiastical History*, 3.24.3.

136. Norris, "Apostolic and Sub-Apostolic Writings," 16.

137. Burridge, *What are the Gospels?*, 187.

Marshall credits Mark with "expanding the original meaning to include the whole historical ministry of Jesus."[138] He further says, "Mark's intention is to suggest equivalence between the preaching of Jesus and that of the Church."[139] However, Mark's referent to the word εὐαγγελίον could not reference a meaning that was unknown in his milieu. Marshall has transferred the patristic outlook to the apostolic milieu. He has not explained how Mark invented a new usage of the word εὐαγγέλιον from its well-established referent in his milieu. The most plausible explanation is that Mark understood εὐαγγέλιον in the same way that it was understood in his milieu. Koester has rightly stated that these texts are "indeed, the foundations of the truth of the Christian beliefs and they substantiate the validity of the Christian kerygma."[140]

After the demise of the apostles and their contemporaries, the only recourse of the believers to the witness about Jesus and his deeds was in gleaning the writings of the apostles. It is plausible that this recourse to the writings of the apostles resulted to a changed concept of the reference of εὐαγγέλιον from the oral gospel to the written texts about Jesus Christ. The view that the writings of the apostles were hortatory messages urging adherence to the oral gospel changed into a view that they were the actual gospels. Koester intimates that,

> the evidence of all extant sources from the first and early second centuries show that εὐαγγέλιον is always and everywhere understood as the proclamation of the saving message about Jesus Christ or the coming of the kingdom. There is no indication that such understanding of the term gradually developed into a designation of written documents as "gospels." Not one of the authors of a gospel writing understands his work as a "written gospel," nor do the authors of the Gospels of Mark, Matthew, Thomas, and John even reveal any consciousness that they are producing works of the same literary genre that is representative of the εὐαγγέλιον, i.e., the proclamation of and about Jesus Christ.[141]

---

138. Marshall, *Faith as a Theme*, 45.
139. Marshall, 45.
140. Koester, "From the Kerygma-Gospel," 380.
141. Koester, 380–381.

Strangely, a view that there were four-fold written form of the one gospel[142] was adopted in the full knowledge that the entire New Testament witnesses only one gospel which is expressed in the New Testament texts in singular form (1:1, 14–15; 8:35; 10:29; 13:10; 14:9; 16:15). The preaching of Peter (Acts 10:36–41) shows that notwithstanding the presence of the stories about the Christ event, the oral gospel, as commanded by Jesus was that they "preach to the people and to testify that he is the one appointed by God to be judge of the living and the dead. [And that] To him all the prophets bear witness that everyone who believes in him receives forgiveness of sins through his name" (Act 10:42–43 ESV). Overall, the purpose of the text was to catalyze audience response to the oral gospel that was outside and independent of the text. As such, the best designation of the Markan text that is in sync with its purpose would have been, "An Apology for the Gospel of Jesus Christ."

---

142. Koester, 381.

CHAPTER 3

Contextual, Structural, and Form Analysis

3.1 Introduction

There is a direct correlation between the context in which a literary work is produced and its purpose and meaning. Context supplies the rhetorical situation, the literary and language conventions, the presupposition pool of the author and readers, and worldviews that contribute to the nature of a literary composition. Structure, on the other hand, is the architecture of a text. It determines the arrangement and flow of the content. Form analysis studies the literary type of the text. In this study, form analysis probes the rhetorical situation and genre of the text. In a literary production like the Markan text, which does not explicitly suggest its geographical, historical, and cultural setting, an analysis of the context, structure, and form does provide leads as to the reasons for the literary and rhetorical choices of the author.

Explicit historical information that would help in locating the dating of the Markan text is lacking. Nevertheless, an approximate dating can be applied by locating the text within the context of the writings of his contemporaries. Similarly, the text's occasion and purpose are determinable by analyzing its implied rhetorical situation from the suggested exigence which the text, as a rhetorical communication, seeks to eliminate. The rhetorical situation and its exigence are also useful in profiling the behavior of the implied audience. As such, this section analyzes the text's context, structure, form, rhetorical situation, genre, and purpose.

3.2 Socio-Religious Context of the Markan Text

Since the first half of the second century, external evidence in the writings of Papias[1], has identified John Mark, the companion of Paul and Barnabas on their first missionary journey (Acts 13:5) and who was in Rome with Paul (Col 4:10; 2 Tim 4:11; Phlm 24), as the author of the Markan text. As such, it may be dated contemporaneously with Paul's epistles.

It has been argued in some quarters that Mark was written in a context of great State persecution. Alan Cole posits, "Mark's gospel, with its probable background in Rome, seems to have been aimed at preparing Christians, whether at Rome or elsewhere, for future persecution. It does this by telling of Christ's suffering and how he had foretold similar suffering for his followers."[2] This supposition is premised on the notion that "Mark has much to say about the importance of disciples following the 'road to the cross' walked by our Lord."[3] However, the exigences explicated in the parable of the sower, that is, preaching the gospel as represented by the sower who sowed his seed without any hindrance, temptations by Satan, desire for riches, could not subsist simultaneously in a state of political persecution.

Moreover, incidents in Acts (16:19–23; 19:24–41; 21:27–32) suggest that the biggest threat and opposition to the preaching of the gospel in the days of Paul and Barnabas was more from the Jewish religious leaders than from the political establishment. Needham concurs, "In the days of the apostles, the authorities of the Roman empire were generally friendly or at least neutral towards the Jesus movement. Opposition and persecution came mainly from the unbelieving Jews, and sometimes from ordinary pagan Gentiles (Acts 19:21–41), but not usually from government officials."[4] This suggests that the dating of the Markan text can be placed at a time before the first recorded state-sponsored persecution during the reign of Emperor Nero in 64 CE.[5]

The political authorities within the Roman Empire considered Christianity to have been one of the renewal groups within Judaism. Only religious activities that would foment sedition and riots were viewed as threats to the

---

1. Holmes, *Apostolic Fathers*, 759.
2. Cole, "Mark," 947.
3. Carson, Moo, and Morris, *Introduction to the New Testament*, 98.
4. Needham, *2000 Years of Christ's Power*, 49.
5. Needham, 49.

Empire and as such, they were quelled expeditiously (Acts 19:35–41). The reason given by Josephus why Herod executed John the Baptist was that "he feared lest the great influence John had over the people might put it into his power and inclination to raise a rebellion (for they seemed ready to do anything he should advise)."[6]

If the Markan text was written during the persecution by Emperor Nero, then the political context would be considered to have impacted the writing of his text. However, other than the episode when Jesus urged his disciples to take up their crosses daily and follow him (8:34, 10:21) and the suggestion in the parable of the sower that persecution was one of the reasons for Jesus's audience's poor response to the oral gospel (4:17), there is complete lack of mention, hint, or literary bent suggesting state persecution as the occasion of the writing of the Markan text. The religious persecution in Acts that is evident up to the wee years of Paul's incarceration in Rome around 62 CE is a more likely context in which the text was written. Gundry says, "But a theology of suffering does not pervade the gospel."[7] This diminishes the argument that the major purpose of the Markan text was to encourage the audience who were facing political persecution. In any case, the apostolic interpretation of the cross has been anachronistically read into Jesus's interpretation. The apostles interpreted the cross in the context of the passion of Jesus. On the other hand, Jesus interpreted it as a symbol of his disciple's persecution in the hands of the Jewish religious leaders for their faith and for preaching the gospel (13:9–13).

The issue that greatly impacted the growth of the Jesus movement well into the second half of the first century was opposition by the Jews in Jerusalem and the Diaspora (Acts 4:1–22; 5:17–42; 6:8—7:60; 9:1–2, 23; 14:19; 17:5–9, 13; 18:12–17; 21:26–36) by reason of their differing religious views. Even so, the jurisdiction of the Sanhedrin did not extend beyond Jewish Palestine. Thus, the gospel was not overly impeded by the imperial powers in Mark's milieu. Nevertheless, just as it was opposed by the Jews in the days of Jesus Christ, so was it also opposed in the apostolic milieu by the Temple and Synagogue establishments, the Diaspora Jews, and the Gentiles who had their indigenous religions (Acts 4:1–3; 16:16–19; 17:16–23; 19:11–20; 19:23–27).

---

6. Josephus, *Works of Flavius Josephus*, 581.
7. Gundry, *Mark*, 1024.

Evangelization of societies having deeply entrenched indigenous religious beliefs and world views has to contend with the general opposition related to peoples' aversion to religious change.

As recorded in Acts, Mark's milieu was marked by zealous preaching by the apostles and other leaders of the Christian movement (Acts 2:24; 3:12; 6:8; 8:5; 18:26). This scenario presented two important exigencies that can be considered as having occasioned the writing of the Markan text. First, the Markan community, which included his audience and contemporaries in ministry, needed to be exhorted to embrace and maintain an enhanced level of response to the gospel, church ministry, and mission. Second, the burgeoning oral gospel proclamation needed to be founded on a verifiable historical episode. Otherwise – as the distance in the geographical space from Jerusalem and the time from the salvific episode increased in the progression of history – the oral gospel risked being mythologized for lack of a historical phenomenon on which it is premised, and consequently its belief value would wane. It is arguable that these needs prompted Mark to write the Markan text in order to (1) catalyze audience response to the gospel, authenticate the gospel, and spur church ministry and missions, and (2) ward off any likelihood of mythologizing the salvific episode on which the oral gospel was premised.

Myth can be defined as "a tale to be conveyed and to be verified by someone else than the act of telling it. A myth that can be proved or verified by something outside of the living oral or written religious tradition is not really a myth."[8] As such, Mark's text moved the oral gospel from the "unprovable" to "provable" thereby protecting it from being mythologized. According to Eliade, "Contrasted with *logos* and later, with *historia*, *mythos* came in the end to denote 'what cannot really exist.' Judaeo-Christianity put the stamp of 'falsehood' and 'illusion' on whatever was not justified or validated by the two Testaments."[9] In this understanding, the Markan text's narratives were used to validate the oral gospel message by premising it on a scripturally anticipated episode which had been fulfilled in the Christ event.

Wiesel argues that, "to say that 'it's only a myth' means it is not serious. It is 'history' means it is permanent, triumphant, and eternal."[10] Informed

---

8. Gadamer, "Religious and Poetical Speaking," 92.
9. Eliade, *Myth and Reality*, 2.
10. Wiesel, "Myth and History," 21.

by Wiesel's supposition, it is arguable that, anchoring the oral gospel on the person and work of the historical Jesus, who is shown to have the approval of God by the author's enumeration of the miracles that God performed through him, effectively authenticated the gospel about him. The Markan text also served the purpose of immortalizing the salvific episode thereby perpetuating the salvific gospel.

3.2.1 The Christ Event as a Setting and Context of the Markan Stories

Scholars have labelled the life and times of Jesus that are his deeds, passion, resurrection, ascension, and second coming, as the Christ event. It was foretold and anticipated in the Torah, the Writings, and the Prophets. Particularly, Genesis 49:8–10 foretold that the sceptre shall not depart from Judah, nor a lawgiver from between his feet, until שִׁילֹה (Shiloh) comes; Deuteronomy 18:15 foretold that a prophet like Moses would come; Psalm 110:1 refers to the coming one as the Lord who sits at the right hand of the Lord until his enemies are made his footstool. Isaiah 9:6 identifies him as the Son who will be given and on whom the government will be upon his shoulders, whose name will be the Wonderful Counsellor, Mighty God, Everlasting Father and Prince of Peace; while Isaiah 42–53 hails him as the Servant of the Lord. Indeed, Isaiah 53:1–12 shows that the chief purpose of the Servant of the Lord is to be a vicarious atonement for the sins of humanity.

Both Jesus and the New Testament writers describe the fulfilment of this time and episode in such lofty phrases as "The time is fulfilled" (Mark 1:15), "When the fullness of time had come" (Gal 4:4), and "the fullness of the times" (Eph 1:10). The life, deeds, and passion of Jesus compare very well with the person and work of the anticipated Christ. As such, the Christ event was presumed to be an episode that fulfilled the eschatological expectation of the anticipated king and kingdom of God. This view of the Christ event is a presupposition that impacts the interpretation of stories about Jesus and the gospel that is premised on his person and work.

Arguably, the coming of Jesus, his work on earth, his death and resurrection were the episodes on which the proclamation of the gospel of Jesus Christ the Son of God was premised. Therefore, during the post ascension period, every single episode within the Christ event had value to authenticate specific aspects of the gospel. The virgin birth proclaimed his divinity (Matt 1:23), his baptism affirmed his divine sonship (Mark 1:11), his miracles proved that he was a man sent from God for no one can perform such miracles if God is not with him (John 3:2), and his death purchased the redemption of the world (John 3:16). It was therefore an act of rhetorical genius to catalyze response to the salvific message by narrating anecdotes within the Christ event. As such, Old Testament quotations, miracle anecdotes, parable stories, conflict stories, passion stories, and resurrection narratives are apt rhetorical devices that Mark used to catalyze audience response to the oral gospel. In agreement with Papias, these episodes need not be written in their chronological order to fulfil their purpose. Their function as enhancers of the persona of Jesus and hence believability in the oral gospel about him is arguably the overriding appeal factor for their being chosen as rhetorical devices.

3.3 Structure of the Markan Text

A section of scholarship considers the Markan text to be lacking literary sophistry. Dewey's statement that "the gospel though one third shorter than either Matthew or Luke, tends to be wordy . . . and is frequently pleonastic. The style is simple, with preference for the connective καὶ and the use of the historic present, and occasionally crude and harsh,"[11] captures this perception very well. Peter G. Bolt, borrowing from K. L. Schmidt says that the Markan text's structure can be identified as "pearls and string in which units of tradition were strung together by a loose geographical and temporal framework."[12] Similarly, in his study of Luke's use of Mark, Yamada argues, "it is likely that Luke recognizes Mark's gospel as 'a series of notes' without rhetorical order and embellishments when it is handed over to him."[13] However, Mark's lack of sophistry in Greek language does not imply that he had inferior literary and rhetorical skills. This work has argued that the structure of the Markan text was deliberately organized to meet its rhetorical purpose.

Though living in a culture that was biased towards Greco-Roman literary expression, to a large extent, "Mark used Hebrew literary method with its

---

11. Dewey, *Markan Public Debate*, 19.
12. Bolt, "Mark's Gospel," 393.
13. Yamada, "Preface to the Lukan Writings," 168.

rhetorical expressions."[14] Nevertheless, by coincidence or design, his structure and style show some aspects that conform to Greco-Roman style. Greco-Roman rhetoric is identifiable in how the material is arranged. He starts with an apt introduction followed by a body with a fitting, though disputed, conclusion. Dewey's suggestion that the Markan text lacks literary sophistry does not appreciate that it is not intended to be an orderly account of biographical episodes in Jesus's life per se but a rhetorical communication that was intended to supply rhetorical fodder to catalyze his reader's response to the oral gospel.

Phillips has identified the type of rhetoric in the Markan text as "natural eloquence."[15] As such, its literary composition is not expected to conform to purely Greco-Roman literary rhetorical forms. As is noticeable in the frequent use of the connective καὶ and use of the historic present, the Markan composition shows remarkable reliance on Hebrew rhetoric. Therefore, it would not yield much to analyze the text's rhetorical structure using purely Greco-Roman rhetorical conventions. Its literary form and structure may be a result of Mark's double Greco-Roman and Hebrew literary heritage. Moreover, as Watson has postulated, "Even if a NT writer had not been formally educated, rhetorical practice was everywhere and its forms would have been familiar. Much of Jewish and Greco-Roman rhetorical practice was shaped by the needs of oral culture."[16] Mary Ann Beavis notes:

> It is not inconceivable that our evangelist, with his strange blend of literary awkwardness and ingenuity, was educated in Greek and Jewish schools, and even that early in his career he was the disciple of some first century rabbi. The gospel with its mixture of Greco-Roman and Jewish thought-forms is the kind of literary production we might expect from a Jewish scribe with some training in Greek.[17]

Arguably, the Markan structure was influenced by the need to cluster similar themes in one section of the book in order to intensify the effect of the stories on the audience in a similar way as parallelism would. Similarly, he also

---

14. This supposition has been argued in section 1.9.8.
15. Lund, *Chiasmus in the New Testament*, 8.
16. Watson, "Rhetoric, Rhetorical Criticism," 1041.
17. Beavis, *Mark's Audience*, 40.

narrated episodes that highlight the divine persona of Jesus in the first half of the text to lead his audience into a predetermined interpretation that the passion episode was propitiatory, sacrificial and vicarious.

Clustering similar stories in one section of the book to intensify the affective effect on his audience affirms that the Markan text is a well-planned literary production. The introduction, body, and conclusion show a well-planned *inventio*, which is normally an aspect of Greco-Roman rhetoric. However, in form and purpose, Hebrew rhetoric is the major bulwark of the text.

3.3.1 Outline of the Markan Text

1. Prologue (1:1–13)
    A. Introduction (1:1)
        i. Scriptural proof for the oral gospel (1:2–3)
        ii. Fulfilment of Scripture in John's ministry (1:4–8)
        iii. Christ revealed in Jesus's baptism (1:9)
        iv. Holy Spirit descends on Jesus (1:10)
        v. God affirms Jesus as His Son (1:11)
        vi. Spirit leads Jesus into the desert to be tempted by the Devil (1:12–13)
2. Jesus's Preaching and Miracle Ministry in and around Galilee (1:14–9:50)
    A. Introduction (1:14–15)
    B. Calling of First Disciples (1:16–20)
    C. Initial Preaching and Miracle Ministry in Galilee (1:21–3:12)
        i. Teaching and miracle ministry (1:21–1:45)
    D. Jesus's Controversy with the Jews (2:1–3:35)
        i. Jesus accused of blasphemy (2:1:12)
        ii. Eating with sinners (2:13–17)
        iii. Jesus and fasting (2:18–22)
        iv. Sabbath controversy (2:23–3:12)
        v. Jesus appoints the twelve apostles (3:13–19)
        vi. Jesus accused of having Beelzebub (3:20–3:30)
        vii. Jesus's mother and brothers (3:31–35)
    E. Teachings in Parables (4:1–34)
        i. Parable of the sower (4:1–20)
        ii. Parables as the lamp on a stand (4:21–25)

     iii. Parable of growing seeds (4:26–29)
     iv. Parable of the mustard seed (4:29–34)
   F. More Miracle Stories (4:35–5:43)
     i. Jesus calms the storm 4:35–41)
     ii. Healing of demon possessed (5:1–20)
     iii. Healing of the sick girl and woman (5:21–43)
     iv. Unbelief in Jesus's home (6:1–6)
     v. Jesus sends out the twelve (6:7–13)
     vi. Herod's reaction to Jesus's teaching and miracle ministry (6:14–29)
     vii. Jesus feeds five thousand people (6:30–44)
     viii. Jesus walks on the water (6:45–52)
     ix. Jesus heals and teaches at Gennesaret (6:53–7:23)
     x. Healing of Syro-Phoenecian woman's daughter (7:24–30)
     xi. Healing of a deaf and mute man (7:31–37)
     xii. Jesus feeds four thousand people (8:1–9)
     xiii. Jesus teaches in Dalmanutha (8:10–21)
     xiv. Healing of a blind man at Bethsaida (8:22–26)
3. Peter's Confession of Christ (8:27–30)
4. Jesus Predicts His Death (8:31–38)
5. The Transfiguration (9:1–13)
6. More Teachings and Miracles (9:14–50)
   A. Healing of Boy with an Evil Spirit (9:14–29)
   B. Exlusive Teachings to the Disciples (9:30–50)
7. Jesus's Teaching Ministry in Perea and Judaea (10:1–13:37)
   A. Teaching on Divorce (10:1–12)
   B. Teaching on Little Children (10:13–16)
   C. Rich Young Man's Querry (10:17–31)
8. Jesus Talks about his Death (10:32–34)
9. James and John's Request to Sit at Right and Left of Jesus (10:35–45)
10. Healing of Blind Bartimaeus (10:46–52)
11. Triumphal Entry into Jerusalem (11:1–11)
12. Jesus Cleanses the Temple (11:12–19)
13. Jesus Curses the Fig Tree (11:20–26)

14. Jesus's Controversy with the Jews in Jerusalem (11:27–12:34)
    A. Jesus's Authority Questioned (11:27–33)
    B. Jesus's Rebukes Jews through Parable of the Tenants (12:1–12)
    C. Jesus Tested in Regard to Paying Taxes (12:13–17)
    D. Question on Marriage at the Resurrection (12:18–27)
    E. Jesus's Position on the Greatest Commandment (12:28–34)
15. Further Teachings (12:35–13:37)
    A. Jesus's Teaching on the Person of the Christ (12:35–40)
    B. Jesus's Teaching on Offerings (12:41–44)
    C. Jesus's Teaching on Signs of the End of the Age (13:1–37).
16. The Passion Narratives (14:1–16:8).
    A. Jesus is Annointed at Bethany (14:1–11)
    B. The Last Supper Narratives (14:12–26)
    C. Retreat to the Mount of Olives (14:27–52)
        i. Jesus predicts Peter's denial (14:27–31)
        ii. Jesus prays in Gethsemane (14:32–42)
        iii. Jesus's betrayal and arrest (14:43–52)
    D. Jesus Before the Sanhedrin (14:53–72)
        i. Trial before Sanhedrin (14:53–65)
        ii. Peter disowns Jesus (14:66–72)
    E. Jesus Before Pilate (15:1–15)
    F. Jesus's Sentence (15:16–47)
        i. Soldiers mock Jesus (15:16–20)
        ii. The crucifixion of Jesus (15:21–32)
        iii. The death of Jesus (15:32–41)
        iv. The burrial of Jesus (15:42–47)
17. The Ressurection of Jesus (16:1–8)
    A. The Empty Grave (16:1–8)
18. Appearance to the Disciples (16:9–20)
    A. Appearance to Mary Magdalene and Two Other Disciples (16:9–13)
    B. Appearance to the Eleven (16:14–20)
        i. Jesus castigates his disciples for lack of faith (16:14)
        ii. Jesus commissions the disciple (16:15–18)
19. Ascension (16:19–20)

Observations from the outline

The prologue runs from 1:1–13. The subject of the text is the "beginning of the gospel." Old Testament quotations from Exodus 23:20 and Malachi 3:1 are used as proof texts to show that the beginning of the gospel conformed to prophecies concerning the Christ event and that Jesus was the anticipated messiah who was to deliver and lead humanity, in a way similar to the Exodus experience, to full emancipation from captivity in sin. Citing Isaiah 40:3 followed by a narration of John's ministry (1:4–9) shows that Mark interpreted the anticipated messenger who would herald the messiah as John the Baptist.

However, the main subject of the prologue is neither Jesus's nor John's ministries; it is the beginning of the gospel of Jesus Christ the Son of God. Actually, Mark 1:4–9 shows that the forerunning ministry of John the Baptist fulfilled Isaiah's prophecy quoted in Mark 1:2–3. It shows that the Jesus of the gospel proclamation is indeed the Christ who was promised in Scripture.

Mark used the portrait of John's humble persona and mission as an amplifying foil of the superior persona and mission of Jesus. Arguably, the story of John the Baptist (1:4–9) plus the Old Testament citations in Mark 1:2–3 have been used to authenticate the Christ event on which the oral gospel of Jesus Christ the Son of God was premised. In other words, the gospel referenced in Mark 1:1 is premised on the Christ event, which, in turn, is authenticated by John's Scripture-authenticated forerunning ministry (1:4–9). This shows that Mark interpreted John's forerunning ministry as a fulfilment of Old Testament Scripture. His intention was to support his assertion in 1:1 that Jesus was the Christ, the Son of God.

Over and above the religious view that the Christ event occurred at a time when the anticipated eschatological kingdom of God was to be fulfilled, the introduction of Mark's preaching ministry (1:14–15) shows that Jesus's proclamation of the gospel was the major context in which his miracles, his controversies with the Jewish religious leaders, and the passion took place. As such, these episodes are better interpreted within the context of Jesus's oral proclamation of the gospel.

Broadly, Mark 1:14–13:37 narrates the preaching and miracle ministry of Jesus. Specifically, Mark 1:14–5:43 comprises a cluster of miracle stories which are set within and around Galilee. This cluster of miracles stories has been identified as a rhetorical formation that was aimed at evoking greater awe in the person of Jesus.

The other important section that is also set within the context of Jesus's preaching and miracle stories is the narrative of the controversy between Jesus and the Jewish religious elite and especially those from Jerusalem (2:1–3:45). The controversy with the religious leaders is shown to have resulted from the Jewish religious leaders' distaste for Jesus's superior teachings that were accompanied by performance of miracles. These teachings challenged the prevailing hypocrisy and lifeless legalism that characterized the religious life and ministry of the Jewish leaders (2:1–12; 3:1–6). In return, they explained his miracles as having being aided "by the ruler of demons" (3:22).

Yet another section that is critical to this study is the parable of the sower (4:1–12). Jesus employed it to entreat his disapproving audience to respond to the word of God and at the same time warn them of the consequences of their obduracy. He painted a vivid portrait of his audience's wanting rhetorical situation with a parabolic description of its exigence of obduracy and lukewarm response towards the word of God. Mark retold this parable and the parable of the ungrateful servants in Mark 12:1–12 as mirror portraits of his audience's rhetorical situation in order to provoke them to abhor their obduracy and at the same time to urge them to aspire for the equally portrayed norm of optimal fruitfulness.

The other section that is critical to this study is the passion story (14:1–15:47). This study has identified the passion narrative as a major rhetorical device that Mark used to convict and convince his readers concerning the truth value of the oral gospel. Within the passion story is the excursus on the inauguration of the ordinance of the Last Supper (14:1–26). This study has argued that the institution of the Lord's Supper is a summary of the oral gospel proclamation packaged in a festal ordinance. The Old Testament fulfilment in Christ, his preaching about the kingdom of God, his grace and compassion that were revealed in the healing miracles, and the passion that was foreboded by the controversies with the religious elite are brought together as one teaching in the institution and perpetuation of the ordinance of the Lord's Supper. Interpreting the ordinance of the Lord's Supper many years later, Paul says, "For as often as you eat this bread and drink this cup, you proclaim the Lord's death till He comes" (1 Cor 11:26).

The final section, the resurrection narrative, runs from Mark 16:1–14. Part of the resurrection narrative and epilogue (16:9–20) is disputed by a majority of scholars though it "is present in the vast number of witnesses, including A C D K X W Δ Θ Π Ψ 099 0112 f^{13} 28 33 *al.*"[18] However, it is absent in what are considered to be the major and old manuscripts – the Codex Sinaiticus, Codex Vaticanus, and codex Alexandrinus. An investigation to verify its authenticity and therefore the need to include or exclude it as part of the Markan text is outside the scope of this study. However, a closure to the debate on the merits and demerits of expunging or retaining the portion in the cannon of Scripture should be, as currently is, held in abeyance awaiting further research by future researchers.

Summary of the outline

The outline suggests that the text's subject is the beginning of the gospel of Jesus Christ the Son of God. It is the gospel that Jesus was proclaiming (1:15), that which he sent his disciples to preach in the towns and villages of Galilee (6:7–13), that which he finally commissioned his disciples to preach to the whole world (16:15–18), and that which Mark and his contemporaries were preaching by the time of writing the text (1:1). The prologue was aimed at premising the oral gospel on the foundation of the Torah and the Prophets as shown in the Old Testament quotations in the prologue (1:2–3).

The outline also shows that Mark deliberately structured the text into clusters of anecdotes having similar themes. To achieve coherency, he deliberately narrated episodes with the same geographical setting in unified clusters. This structure appears to be a deliberate rhetorical tool that was aimed at engendering greater response to the oral gospel.

The three most noticeable geographical settings are Galilee and its environs, Perea, and finally Jerusalem. Most of the miracle stories have their setting in Galilee and its environs. Jesus's major teachings and the passion narratives have their setting in Jerusalem. A comparison of the text with the Johannine text, which records multiple visits to Jerusalem (John 2:13; 5:1; 7:10; 10:22), suggests that Mark was not overly interested in the chronological ordering of events. Rather, he was interested in their rhetorical value to engender his readers' response to the oral gospel.

---

18. Metzger, *Textual Commentary*, 124.

The outline also suggests that the disputed verses (16:9–20) were written in due consideration of the structure and purpose of the Markan text. Mark 16:15–20 seems to be an apt epilogue for the entire text. It ties up the prologue (1:1–13) and the body (1:14–16:8) into a single coherent whole. Therefore, a rhetorical reading and interpretation of the text summons the reader to look positively into the disputed epilogue.

After its first mention in the prologue, the overarching theme of the gospel of Jesus Christ the Son of God is alluded to throughout the text. Jesus preaches it powerfully throughout his life in and around Galilee, Perea, and in Jerusalem where he was finally crucified. After he rose from the dead, he commissioned the disciples to preach it to the whole world (16:15–16). Arguably, the Markan text is a book about the salvific episode on which the oral and ritual proclamation of gospel was premised.

The clustering of similar episodes in the same sections of the outline shows that Mark was more interested in the rhetorical value of the episodes than in narrating them for their biographical value. The outline does not show a smooth flowing narrative. Instead, as Schmidt noted, the Markan text's structure can be described as "pearls strung on a string."[19] This is a brilliant observation which should be analyzed and explained in light of the text's context, structure, purpose, and genre. This exposé has identified the so-called pearls as the rhetorical devices of Old Testament quotations, miracle stories, stories of the controversies between Jesus and the Jewish religious leaders, parables, and the passion story.

3.4 Contextual Structure of the Markan Text

According to Dewey, the stories in the Markan text are structured in a "concentric manner."[20] She has also identified the interlocking characteristic of the different stories. In addition to the interlocking nature of stories in the text, a contextual structure is also evident. It is a build up from R. T. France's description of Mark as "a master at the narrative art of 'sandwiching' one

---

19. Schmidt, "Die Stellung der Evangelien," 50–134.
20. Dewey, *Markan Public Debate*, 1.

story or scene within another. It is also variously described as interpolation, intercalation, dovetailing, and framing."[21]

Observably, the Markan text is structured in the form of contextual strata whereby narratives of episodes within the same theme are set within the contexts of their occasioning episodes. The overriding contextual stratum in which all the episodes in the text are set is the kingdom of God, which had been promised in Scripture and which had finally been fulfilled (1:15). Within the context of the kingdom of God, all other thematic episodes find their context, form, purpose, and being. The oral proclamation of the gospel is set as the major happening within the context of the kingdom of God. Much as the proclamation of the gospel finds its context in the kingdom of God, it has also been made and positioned to be the context within which other stories are narrated. The proclamation of the gospel will come to a close at the parousia (Matt 24:14; Mark 13:10).

Jesus's miracle stories are set within the context of gospel proclamation. Both the gospel proclamation and the miracle episodes form the context in which Jesus's controversy with the Jewish religious leaders (3:22) are narrated. The parables are retold in the context of the controversy episodes. Finally, the passion episode, which is a build up of Jesus's controversies with the Jewish leaders, is narrated within the context of the controversy episode. The passion episode is narrated as the highpoint of the Christ event. In summary, the episodes narrated in the Markan text are structured in such a way that episodes within the same theme are narrated within the contexts of the episodes in which they are generated. As such the textual structure forms layers of contextual strata.[22]

A graphic representation of this contextual structure is shown here below. Noticeably, the strata representing both the kingdom of God and the oral proclamation of the gospel are open ended. This shows the eternal nature of the kingdom of God. Daniel 7:14 says, "His dominion is an everlasting

---

21. France, *Gospel of Mark*, 18.

22. The fulfilled time and the anticipated Christ event are the overarching context in which the proclamation of the gospel happened. The fulfilled time and proclamation of the gospel are open ended. They transcend generations to the parousia. The miracle stories, controversy stories, passion, and resurrection stories narrate past episodes within the life and times of Jesus. They are structured within the context of gospel proclamation. Whereas gospel proclamation is the context within which miracles were performed, stories of Jesus's controversies and passion are set within the context of gospel proclamation and miracle stories.

dominion which will not pass away and his kingdom is one that shall not be destroyed." (ESV). It also shows that the proclamation of the gospel will continue until the parousia. According to Matthew 24:14, "And this gospel of the kingdom will be preached in all the world as a witness to all nations, and then the end will come." The miracles, controversies, and the passion are episodes that happened once in history. However, their impact in engendering faith in Jesus and the gospel that is premised on his passion endures until the parousia. This structure is an excellent Markan innovation. It appears to have been employed for the pragmatic purpose of directing the reader in locating the major themes and in understanding the meaning and purpose of the text.

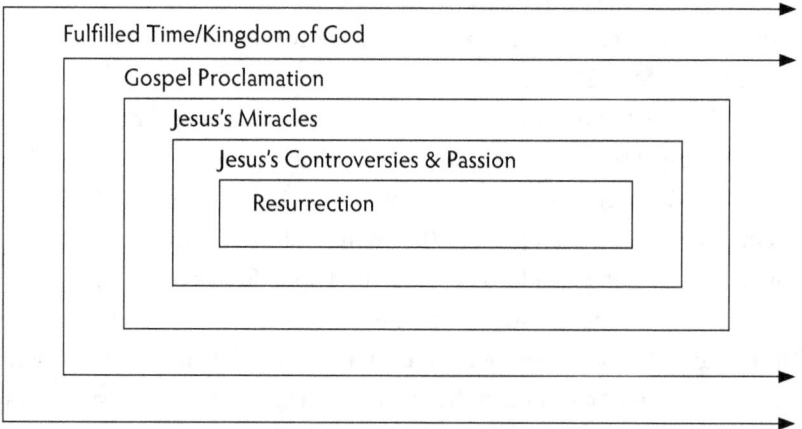

Figure 1. Contextual Structure of the Markan Text.

3.4.1 Observations from the Contextual Strata of the Markan Text

The oral and ritual gospel proclamation was a function within the fulfilled time when the kingdom of God was to appear (1:14–15). Both the kingdom and the proclamation of the gospel are contexts that are external to the text.[23] That is, the kingdom is a spiritual dominion that was, is, and is to come. The proclamation of the gospel predated the text and existed within and after

---

23. The kingdom of God and the gospel proclamation exist outside and independent of the text.

the writing of the text. As such, it was outside and independent of the text. The Markan text was written within the context of the kingdom of God and the proclamation of the oral gospel. To borrow the words of Bauckham, this means that "the text of Mark was entirely pliable to the uses to which it was put in Mark's kerygmatic and paraenetic practices, that is, the proclamation of the gospel and its instructions to believers in the Christian ways."[24]

The structure also supports the view that Jesus's controversy with the Jewish religious leaders was instigated by their distaste of Jesus's proclamation of the gospel and his performance of miracles, which were the context in which the controversy occurred (2:6–7). However, Wright's position, which seems to legitimize the actions of Jesus's opponents, is that "it was precisely Jesus' eschatological programme which led him into opposition with a good many of his contemporaries, and which finally steered him towards the actions which provoked his death."[25] Wright's position suggests that the death of Jesus was not divinely sanctioned. The text's structure and style reveal a well-thought-out rhetorically embellished treatise.

The advantage of identifying Mark's contextual structure is that, more than showing how the literary units are related to one another, it illuminates the contexts within which the narrated episodes happened. The benefit is that it enhances the reading appeal and narrows the range of textual meanings and purposes to the most probable.

3.5 Jesus's Retold Parables as Portraits of the Text's Occasion

This section argues that Mark retold the parable of the sower (4:1–12) and the parable of the wicked tenants (12:1–12) to describe the rhetorical situation that prompted the writing of the Markan text. The Markan parables can be categorized into two divisions: the Galilee parable stories and the Jerusalem parable stories. The supposition that guides this section is that on the one hand, at the compositional stage, the parable of the sower is a portrait of the rhetorical situation of Jesus's audience. It describes their levels of response to the proclamation of the "gospel of God" (1:15). Keener's commentary on

---

24. Bauckham, *Jesus and the Eyewitnesses*, 278.
25. Wright, *Jesus and the Victory of God*, 383.

the parable of the sower in Matthew 13:3–23 notes, "that the parables address his people's acceptance or rejection of the kingdom message follows from the context: Jesus speaks parables *that same day* that he has confronted Pharisaic opposition (Matt 12:24–45) and offered a culturally offensive statement about his family (12:46–50)."[26]

However, on the other hand, at the narrative level, the retold parable of the sower is a mirror of the rhetorical situation of author's audience. Just as Jesus was preaching to his audience, Mark also wrote with a target audience in mind. As such, Mark was not a disinterested preserver of traditions for the sake of it. In an analysis of the mirroring function of parables in Luke, David B. Gowler notes, "Parables become, on the narrative level, indirect presentations of character traits of the Lucan Pharisees."[27] Mary Ann Tolbert aptly illumines how a later retelling of a story can represent a similar audience or otherwise in averring,

> Many literary works generate a *Nachleben*; later authors borrow, revise, adapt, or are heavily influenced by the plots, characters, episodes, and speeches of their predecessors. When the *Nachleben* becomes totally conventionalized or stereotypical, it begins to function as a commonplace or topos. That later writers depend on earlier material presents no difficulty; the problem arises in using later adaptations to interpret the earlier work. It is certainly possible that a later use of material will be in basic harmony and continuity with its earlier formulation. It is also possible, and perhaps more probable, that it will not be. Later generation of writers, living in different historical and cultural contexts, addressing different audiences from different social settings may employ the plot, characters, or design of an earlier story for the same purpose and goal as the earlier author *or oral narrator* [italics mine], but it may be more likely that the purpose, goal, and intention will be different to fit changed circumstances, genre or viewpoint.[28]

---

26. Keener, *Matthew*, 235.
27. Gowler, *What Are They Saying?*, 36–37.
28. Tolbert, *Sowing the Gospels*, 27–28.

Though Jesus's parables were certainly oral, Tolbert's supposition indeed explains how Mark applied the parable of the sower in his context (4:1–12). Retelling of a story or parable involves a refocusing of their themes and motifs thereby giving them a fresh functional focus. As such, it is arguable that Mark used Jesus's portrait of his audience in the parable of the sower to mirror his own audience's rhetorical situation.

Moreover, Jesus told this parable in the context of serious opposition by the teachers of the law and the presence of his disciples who were, more often than not, slow to understand his gospel message. The retold parables should therefore be interpreted within their literary, social, and religious contexts. In their response to Jesus's preaching, the teachers of the law were at the extreme end of the spectrum that describes his obdurate audience – the seed that fell on the foot paths – while on the other extreme end were some of his disciples who, at times, were optimally fruitful. Jesus's composition and telling of parables was a reaction to his audience's response to the gospel message in which he castigated the obdurate for their hardness of heart, exhorted the lukewarm to strive to greater responsiveness, and encouraged the optimally responsive to maintain their responsiveness to the oral gospel message.

Similarly, the parable of the wicked servants describes the generational attitude of Jerusalemites against the prophets of Israel which at that time included their intention to kill Jesus – the Son of the Landlord (12:1–12). According to Craig L. Blomberg, the parable of the wicked servants "so closely matches the history of Israel's leaders' antagonism to God's prophets, and finally to Christ, that many commentators admit that the parable as it stands is allegorical."[29] The question that directs this line of enquiry is this: Why would Mark use the portrait of the response of Jesus's audience to the gospel to mirror his own audience's response to the gospel? The aspect that invited Mark to retell the parable of the sower and the parable of the unfaithful tenants to his audience is the rhetorical and mimetic efficacy, to urge adherence to the gospel, which is inherent in retelling these parables.

Since the dating of the Markan text has not been precisely established for lack of unassailable internal and external evidence, the political context cannot be precisely ascertained. Therefore, the most rewarding way of establishing the occasion of the text is to reconstruct its implied rhetorical situation.

---

29. Blomberg, *Interpreting the Parables*, 17.

This is achievable through a probe of the text as a rhetorical communication that consists of, in this respect, Old Testament quotations, miracle stories, controversy narratives, the parable of the sower, and the passion narratives as rhetorical devices. The assumption is that a rhetorical communication is occasioned by the need to eliminate an exigence in a wanting rhetorical situation. A study of Jesus's controversies with the Synagogue and Temple establishments, the parable of the sower (4:1–12), and the parable of the wicked tenants (12:1–12) shows that Mark used the portrait of Jesus's audience's rhetorical situation, that is portrayed through retelling these parables, to mirror his own audience's rhetorical situation and its exigence of obduracy and lukewarm response to the gospel. Klyne Snodgrass agreeably notes, "In some cases . . . parables are indeed a mirror held up to the nation or society as a whole."[30] In this way, Mark confronts his audience with the damning reality of their obdurate and lukewarm response towards the gospel.

3.5.1 The Parable of the Sower as a Portrait of the Markan Audience

Discussions on the purpose of the parable of the sower have elicited diverse views. A common line of argument is that the aim of this parable is to contrast between insiders and outsiders to Jesus's circle of believers. From this argument, two streams emerge. The first one is represented by Morna D. Hooker's argument that

> Mark shares the fundamental Jewish conviction that God is at work both in historical event and in people, whose actions are ultimately the result of his decree . . . If men and women had refused to accept Jesus, then it must have been the will of God that this should happen. In spite of people trying to soften Jesus' words, there can be no doubt that this was his meaning.[31]

Hooker maintains that the obduracy exhibited by the Jews was predestined and worked out by God. The second argument, which counters the first, postulates that the argument that the obduracy exhibited by the Jewish religious

---

30. Snodgrass, "Reading and Overreading the Parables," 65.
31. Hooker, "Mark's Parables," 90.

leaders was predestined by God is contradictory to the core ministry of Jesus Christ and as such, it cannot be sustained.

John R. Donahue offers an interesting but plausible explanation of the reason for Jesus's use of this parable. He argues that the ones outside Jesus's circle are determined by belief and unbelief and not by predetermined divine fiat. He bases his argument by showing that, at one time, the relatives of Jesus were once considered to be outsiders to the circle of Jesus (3:31) while the crowd about him were inside. Arguing that in both Mark 4:10 and Mark 3:31 there is the same juxtaposition of people round Jesus contrasted with outsiders, he then concludes that, "the distinction between those around Jesus and those outside is not between called disciples and the crowd, nor is it between Jews and Christians but it is a distinction between those who will understand the true meaning of discipleship and those who will not."[32] David Garland takes a similar position and posits that the difference between outsiders and insiders is that "the outsiders simply do not regard what he [Jesus] says to be critical enough to bother joining the disciples around Jesus in order to receive illumination."[33]

Vernon Robbins notes that the parable of the sower describes the subculture of what Jesus's followers ought to subscribe to. He avers, "This, then, is an alternative sub-cultural discourse among some early followers of Jesus."[34] He sees the parable as descriptive of a cultural situation. Specifically, he sees the parables in Mark 4:1–34 as "Gnostic manipulationist since not anyone is able to understand this discourse."[35] He surmises by saying, "this discourse does not give prominence to a 'thaumaturgic' response to the world but to a 'Gnostic manipulationist' response where one seeks full life by pondering and celebrating the mysterious ways God works in the world."[36] While Robbins is right in positing that parables describe a cultural situation, he has neither explained how Mark 4:1–34 represents Gnostic manipulation nor how one may attain full life by pondering and celebrating the mysterious ways of God's works in the world. These differing views show the varied positions

---

32. Donahue, *Gospel in Parable*, 43–44.
33. Garland, *Mark*, 160.
34. Robbins, *Tapestry of Early Christian Discourse*, 172.
35. Robbins, 171.
36. Robbins, 171.

that scholars have espoused. This study suggests that the parable is rather a paradoxical narration embedded with rhetorical efficacy to both indict and at the same time entreat Mark's audience to respond positively to the oral gospel.

Boucher rightly posits, "The parable has two historical settings. Mark tells of Jesus' preaching to a Jewish audience, and so the 'word' is Jesus' proclamation of the coming kingdom (cf. 2:2); but Mark himself is addressing his own readers, and so the 'word' is the Church's proclamation of the Christian message (cf. Lk 1:2; Acts 4:4; 1 Cor 1:18)."[37] Following Boucher's plausible postulation, a need to probe the nexus between Mark's portrait of the rhetorical situation of the audience of Jesus and the rhetorical situation of the audience of Mark arises.

The rhetorical situation that prompted Jesus to tell the parable of the sower was similar to the rhetorical situation that prompted Mark to retell the same parable. While proclaiming the gospel in Rome (Acts 28:26–27), Paul quoted the same Old Testament admonition (Isa 6:9–10) as Jesus had quoted after telling the parable of the sower (4:12). Paul quoted this admonition to the Jews who had showed a similar attitude towards his gospel message as the audience of Jesus had earlier shown. Mark, who was certainly Paul's contemporary, possibly in the same location and time, must have also faced similar obduracy as Jesus and Paul had earlier faced. The barriers that impeded the response of Jesus's audience to the gospel could mirror the barriers that impeded the response of the audiences of Paul and Mark. As such, the rhetorical situations of Jesus's audience, Mark's audience, and Paul's audience could be portrayed using the same parable – the parable of the sower (4:1–12).[38] Under the circumstances, the parable of the sower, that no doubt portrayed Jesus's audience's obduracy and lukewarm response to the gospel of God, was retold to mirror the rhetorical situation of Mark's audience.

This work has identified the parable of the sower as programmatic for the study of the Markan text. The allegorical nature of the parable, in which it represents realities outside the text in which it occurs, makes it a good

---

37. Boucher, *Mysterious Parable*, 42.

38. Whereas it is explicit in Acts 28 that Paul preached in Rome, implicit textual and external evidence shows that Mark wrote his text from Rome (1 Pet 5:13). Translation of Aramaic expressions (3:17; 5:41; 7:34; 14:36; 15:34) and Greek to Latin (12:42; 15:16) suggests a Roman audience. Papias suggests that Mark was Peter's interpreter, perhaps in Rome (Eusebius, *Church History*, 3.39.15).

medium of vividly mirroring the audience's rhetorical situation. It is endowed with rhetorical efficacy to prick the audience's conscience in regard to their unbelief and at the same time to exhort the believers to greater responsiveness towards the gospel. Leland Ryken notes, "Parables are an invitation and even a trap to move a listener or reader to take sides for or against the characters in a story. By confronting the audience with an obvious contrast, a parable of Jesus tends to polarize the hearers."[39] In reference to the Markan parable of the sower, Boucher has aptly explained that

> with artful skill, the author has delineated the psychological disposition of various hearers who by their state of mind are led to one or another kind of action of a moral order. The author has done this in such a way that the description of each kind of hearer in the interpretation is quite suited to the description of each kind of soil in the parable.[40]

Mark aims to confront his audience with God's demand for attention and obedience to the oral gospel. In seeing the portrait of their exigence in the parable, Mark's audience are not only pricked but are also provoked to reflect and respond to the demands of the oral gospel.

Robert W. Funk terms this type of narrative as "mimesis."[41] He intimates that, in mimesis

> the narrator transports the listener or reader, by means of words to a specific time and place with participants present, and allows him or her to look on and listen in . . . The narrator achieves this effect by bringing the scene into focus and by invoking the readers' senses directly. The words of the text re-present the actions in such a way as to give the impression that they are recurring before the reader's eyes and ears.[42]

By a careful choice of words, Mark is urging a faith walk from obduracy to optimal fruitfulness. Robert H. Stein has postulated that parables "create

---

39. Ryken, *Read the Bible as Literature*, 141–142.
40. Boucher, *Mysterious Parable*, 50.
41. Funk, *Poetics of Biblical Narrative*, 134.
42. Funk, 135.

meaning by forcing the reader to participate in the parabolic event."[43] The parable of the sower provokes the reader to desire to participate in solving the exigence of obduracy so as to attain optimal fruitfulness in response to the oral gospel.

The parable of the sower shows that obduracy, as a result of Satan's temptations, was a barrier and threat to response towards the gospel. This scenario is portrayed as seeds that fell on the paths and the birds of the air ate them up. Jesus likened the birds to Satan who covertly makes the hearers to be irresponsive to the word of God. The parable also shows that persecution consequent of faith in the gospel was a part of contextual threat to faith and praxis of the demands of the gospel message. This is portrayed as the sun that scorches the seedlings that were not well rooted in deep soils. Persecution can be construed as an external cause of obduracy. A third contextual threat which is revealed in the parable is the desire for riches. Jesus likened such threats and inhibitors to faith and fruitfulness to thorns that chokes believers and prevents them from being optimally fruitful in their knowledge of the word of God. T. E. Schmidt says, "the instruction of John the Baptist to tax collectors (Lk 3:12–13) and the restitution pledge of Zacchaeus (Lk 19:8) are consistent with this tendency towards fraud."[44]

According to Jeffers, within the Greco-Roman world,

> groups with some natural social affinity such as wool workers or veterans, who didn't have their own professional associations, would set up a religious one. By adopting a patron deity they took advantage of a loophole in law and registered themselves as a club whose primary purpose was religious, even though the social pleasures of the monthly meetings were probably more important to most members.[45]

People who may have been in such professional guilds may have found it harder to leave them and the inherent benefits they derived to become Christians. This exposé shows that Jesus's audience was a mix of people who believed in him and those who were vehemently opposed to him. To each,

---

43. Stein, "Genre of the Parables," 35.
44. Schmidt, "Taxation," 1165.
45. Jeffers, *Greco-Roman World*, 75.

he had a message either of exhortation or warning. The single message in the parable of the sower served to address the whole spectrum of Jesus's audience. The challenge is how to develop a single rhetorical message that speaks to a rhetorical situation with such diametrically opposed exigences. An even greater challenge is how to interpret such a message when it is in the form of a parable. As such, Mark's ability to retell the parable of the sower as a portrait to mirror his audience's rhetorical situation in order to catalyze audience response to the oral gospel reveals his remarkable prowess as an author and rhetor.

The parable of the sower and indeed the other Markan parables portray the exigence that occasioned the writing of the Markan text.[46] It is comparable to the song of the vineyard in Isaiah 5:1–7. This explains Jesus's quotation of Isaiah 6:9–10 in explaining the meaning of the parable of the sower (4:10–12).[47] The hardness of heart that the Jewish religious leaders had shown towards Jesus and his message is portrayed as being comparable to the hardness of heart by Judah in Isaiah 5–6.

Ben Witherington has captured an interesting but very plausible view concerning the occasion of the parable of the sower. He notes that "the exigence that the parable seems to be dealing with is the discouragement a sower (read proclaimer or persuader) faces when so many do not, or do not for long, respond positively to the message implanted in their minds."[48] In view of this perception he postulates that "the historical situation addressed is that Mark's audience faces a world that is in large measure unreceptive to the gospel. Mark must persuade this audience to continue to share the gospel in spite of this fact."[49] To Witherington, therefore, Mark retold the parable to encourage his contemporaries not to slacken in proclaiming the gospel.

Witherington's position is laudable. However, he has not explained the effect of the parable on Mark's audience. Jesus's parable, no doubt, spoke to

---

46. The use of the conjunction Καὶ in Mark 4:21 shows that the pericope about the lamp (Mark 4:22–25) is a further exposition that the teaching in the parable of the sower is too important to be hidden to the ones it is meant to illuminate the meaning of the gospel. The rest of the parables about the scattered seed and the mustard seed are describing the context in which the kingdom of God was being established and how it will finally overcome the exigencies therein.

47. This position is argued more comprehensively in chapter 5, section 5.5.

48. Witherington, *Gospel of Mark*, 162.

49. Witherington, 162.

both the disciples and the crowd, which included both believers and unbelievers. As such, the parable portrayed the rhetorical situation of both the disciples as proclaimers and the rest of the audience as hearers. However, to Mark's audience who were to be majorly impacted not by the parable but by the oral gospel, the retelling of the parable of the sower was biased towards addressing his audience than his co-workers. In any case, the context does not exhibit an exigence of lack of forwardness in proclaiming the gospel.

In summary, Mark retold the parable to portray and confront his audience's obduracy and lukewarm response towards the oral gospel. Hooker captures the connection between this parable and Mark's preaching ministry in his observation that,

> The fact that each of these parables is placed immediately after a direct challenge by the Jerusalem religious authorities concerning the nature of Jesus' authority – the parable of the sower after the challenges recounted in 3:20–35; the parable of the vineyard and the wicked tenants after that of 11:27–33 – suggests that Mark regarded both of them as allegories of Israel's response to and rejection of Jesus. Taken together, they encapsulate the whole story of his ministry.[50]

3.6 Purpose of the Markan Text

According to H. N. Roskam, "Mark's interest in writing was presumed to have been historical and biographical, and his main objective is to preserve the tradition about the historical Jesus."[51] D. A. Carson and Douglas Moo have suggested that "Mark wants to help his readers understand who Jesus is and what real discipleship involves."[52] They argue that "a record of Jesus' deeds was becoming a great need in Mark's day, as the original witnesses, such as Peter were beginning to pass from the scene."[53] However, as has been observed, the absence of the nativity narratives in the Markan text weakens the argument that suggests that the purpose of Mark was to write a repository of the life

---

50. Hooker, "Mark's Parables," 89.
51. Roskam, *Purpose of the Gospel*, 3.
52. Carson, Moo and Morris, *Introduction to the New Testament*, 101.
53. Carson, Moo and Morris, 101.

and times of Jesus Christ. The nativity narrative, which must have been part of the Christian community's oral tradition by the time Mark was writing his text, is so fundamental to Christology. Anybody writing a christological repository of the life and deeds of Jesus would be hard pressed to explain why he would not consider these details as important to his purpose though they must have been known to the author as shown in the details about Jesus's family in Mark 6:1–5.

The purpose of the Markan text is not explicitly stated in the text. It can only be deduced by an examination of its overarching subject and *leitmotiv*. Mark 1:1 indicates that the subject is the beginning of the gospel of Jesus Christ. As a pointer to the reference of the term "gospel" in Mark 1:1, Donahue and Harrington aver, "The distinctive use of *euangelion* is found in the Pauline writings where the term appears over sixty times as a virtual recapitulation of the Christ-event; that is the meaning of the life, death, and resurrection/exaltation of Jesus."[54] Consequently, according to Donahue's exposé, Mark falls short of being a Gospel since it does not include an interpretation of Jesus's miracles, death, and resurrection.

Reference to the beginning of the gospel in Mark 1:1 points to an episode or episodes that were foundational to the gospel of Jesus Christ. These episodes were situated in the past of the time of writing the Markan text and hence the use of the phrase Ἀρχὴ τοῦ εὐαγγελίου. It also connotes a continuation of the soteriological impact of the episode through proclamation of the gospel to the time of writing the text and beyond. Particularly, the episode under reference was the fulfilment of the time when God was to usher his kingdom and the Christ into the world just as he had promised Israel's forefathers according to the Old Testament (Gen 12:1–3; 49:10; Isa 7:14; 9:6–7). Mark's quotation of Old Testament was aimed at showing that the Jesus of history and faith was indeed the Christ of the Old Testament prophecies and promises. Highlighting the exalted person and work of Jesus showed that he was indeed a man sent from God.

Therefore, the purpose of the Markan text was to validate that Jesus was the Christ so as to consequently enhance believability in the oral gospel that was premised on his person and work on the cross. According to Witherington, the purpose of the Markan text was "to instruct as a supplement to such

---

54. Donahue and Harrington, *Gospel of Mark*, 14.

proclamation."⁵⁵ However, lack of a substantive record of what Jesus had taught disallows the argument that Mark was in any way supplementing the oral gospel. The choice of the text's rhetorical devices of miracle stories, Old Testament quotations, and the passion narratives shows a bias towards narratives that ground the oral gospel on a God-sanctioned historical episode. Numinous power was thought to be vested only in God. Any other person who could perform supernatural signs was thought to be sent by God (John 3:2).

Another major purpose of the Markan text was to urge a faith shift among the audiences who may have been followers of the Pharisees, the scribes and the Sadducees. This is shown by Mark's depiction of Jesus as one who taught as one having power and not as the scribes (1:22). He also narrates controversies between Jesus and these sects' leaders which depict Jesus's teaching as more dependable than the teachings of the Pharisees and the scribes (2:16–17). The Sadducees are also depicted as having a doctrine that is based on lack of knowledge of the word of God (12:24). This demeaning of the teachings of the chief Jewish sects and their teachers in contrast to the elevated ethos and teachings of Christ acts as a subtle foil and rhetorical device calling hearers from other alternative beliefs to faith in the gospel of Jesus Christ the Son of God.

Furthermore, the eruption of God into the world through the incarnation (Matt 2:1–12) and Pentecost events (Acts 2:1–4) was not just a historical event that is encoded in Scripture for reflection, edification, exemplification, and motivation. It was an inaugural phenomenon of an enduring relationship between humanity and their God as both Immanuel (Matt 1:23) and παράκλητος (John 14:15–17; 15:26). However, the compilation of the Christian canon has been interpreted in some quarters as the end of an existential relationship between God and man where interaction between man and the divine is not only mediated through Scripture but also through a real presence of God through the Holy Spirit. It is presumed that man should thereafter seek God not by appealing to his ever-abiding real presence but through interpretation of Scripture. The initial kerygma and *Didache*, which involved witnessing of what the disciple's had seen, heard, and experienced through their interaction with the risen Jesus, was replaced by hermeneutics of texts about what he

---

55. Donahue and Harrington, 11.

did in history. As such, miracles and charismatic experiences are construed as being a first-century phenomenon that has since ceased.

A divide has thus been created between faith by being led and experiencing the daily presence and work of God and the faith by reading Scripture. Leroy Huizenga laments this dichotomy and longingly quips, "the semiotic matrix within which the New Testament writers lived and had their being was not merely Scripture qua Scripture, but rather the entire cultural encyclopaedia."[56] By this he means that Christian faith was not only epistemological but also an affective relationship between man and God that permeated every facet of the Christian's being. For the Markan community, it was a cultural and religious encyclopaedia of the early Christian tradition which included and not limited to a Spirit led life, kerygma, administration of ordinances and Christian ethics in both personal and corporate lives. The Markan text was calling its readers to an enhanced response to this religious encyclopaedia that was embodied in the words of the oral gospel and in the administration of the ordinances of baptism and the Lord's Supper.

It was to this semiotic matrix, within which Mark lived and had his being, that he was urging his audience to respond to and abide in. This semiotic matrix was shaped by the proclaimed and ritual gospel. Witherington presses this point more forcefully in saying, "the author is a partisan and is unashamedly trying to convict and convince his audience about a particular point of view."[57]

In summary, Mark's aim was to draw his audience into faith by affirming the divine foundation of the oral gospel without which its "gospelness" would be in question. Jesus himself supports this point of view in saying, "You search the Scriptures because you think that in them you have eternal life; and it is they that bear witness about me, yet you refuse to come to me that you may have life" (John 5:39–40 ESV). This supposition is in line with Walhout's assertion that "texts are used by readers in various ways one of which is to confirm and challenge our beliefs."[58] An implicit achievement, that may not have been part of his core aim, was to avert any possibility of mythologizing the salvific episode or worse still consigning it to mere folklore as exemplified by the New Testament pseudepigraphic writings in the second century CE.

---

56. Huizenga, *New Isaac*, 61.
57. Witherington, *Gospel of Mark*, 11.
58. Walhout, "Narrative Hermeneutics," 90.

This aim is achieved, albeit incidentally, by immortalizing the salvific gospel by grounding it on a historical and undeniable reality of the then Scripture and the Christ event.

3.7 Literary Genre of the Markan Text

Rene Wellek and Austin Warren have defined genre as "a grouping of literary works based, theoretically, upon both outer form (specifically meter or structure) and also upon inner form (attitude, tone, purpose – more crudely subject and audience)."[59] In this understanding, the genre of a literary work can be ascertained by probing its outer and inner forms. Burridge avers that "proper identification of the genre of a certain work is necessary before we can undertake a rhetorical analysis."[60] The importance of identifying the literary genre of biblical texts in the hermeneutical process is also emphasized by Stanton who states that, "if we make a mistake about the literary genre of the gospels, interpretation will be skewed or even misguided. A decision about the genre of a work and the discovery of its meaning are inextricably inter-related; different types of text require different types of interpretation."[61] Emphasizing on the importance of genre identification, Nyende avers that "the identification of a text's rhetorical genre is critical in helping the rhetoric critic to understand and unlock its *inventio*, since rhetorical analysis presumes that rhetoric follows the logic of its genre."[62]

Identification of the genres of the books labelled Gospels is problematic. Though they share a common "oral tradition"[63] for their source material, they are different in form, structure, and purpose. As such, their genre can better be identified by probing their form, structure, and purpose as opposed to a comparative analysis with other writings from different geographical, historical and religio-cultural milieus. For any comparative analysis with other writings to yield helpful conclusions, it ought to compare writings in the same milieu, similar contexts, form and purpose. An analysis of the Markan

---

59. Wellek and Warren, *Theory of Literature*, 219.
60. Burridge, "Gospels and Acts," 507.
61. Stanton, *Jesus and the Gospel*, 192.
62. Nyende, "Hebrew Exegesis," PhD Seminar, author's notes.
63. Tradition in this sense is a shared immediate history of the Christ event which was being orally transmitted for epistemological purposes.

text's genre should consider reviewing similar religious literature and more so hortatory literature in evangelistic and conversionist religious contexts.

The Markan text has been adjudged by a large section of scholars as being either a biographical or historical genre. However, none of the genres that have been suggested for the Markan text has received unanimous acclaim. Vines says, "Contemporary research into the genre of the gospel has reached a stalemate."[64] As such, the question of the Markan genre is open for further investigation. The presupposition that the Markan text is a "Gospel according to Mark" can, in a way, misdirect identification of its genre. It eclipses the obvious observation that, before, within, and after the writing of the text, there was an oral gospel that was outside and independent of the text. As such, a need to probe the connection between the written text and the oral gospel has not been identified. Consequently, a priori, the text is adjudged a biography of Jesus, that is, a record of the life and times of Jesus instead of an amalgam of rhetorical anecdotes of episodes on which the oral gospel of Jesus Christ was premised. These two different subjects, the anecdotes of the episodes on which the oral gospel is premised and the oral gospel itself, are at times confused to be one and the same subject. Compounding the problem further, whereas the subject of the text is the "beginning of the gospel" the subject of the gospel is the person of Jesus and the significance of his work on the cross. Consequently, a text that highlights the exalted persona of Jesus for the purpose of validating the oral gospel can mistakenly be labelled a gospel or even a biography of Jesus.

In discriminating against considering the literary genre of the Markan text as historiography, Witherington says, "When the telltale signs of a historical monograph are looked for, they seem to be almost entirely lacking. For example, Mark shows no real interest in synchronisms with the events of the larger Roman world, unlike what we find from time to time in Luke-Acts."[65] As such, he discounts the possibility of identifying the Markan genre as historiography. He regards the Markan genre as biography.

It is widely held as axiomatic that the genre of the Markan text and the rest of the books labelled Gospel is βιοι. As such, the best approach to further the discussion would be to first compare the nature of the Markan text with

---

64. Vines, *Problem of Markan Genre*, 2.
65. Witherington, *Gospel of Mark*, 3.

definite biographical and historical genres like Matthew and Luke respectively. Questions that could push the argument forward are these: is the Markan text made of sub-narratives with definable plots, common in an undisputed genre like Matthew, Luke, or even Genesis? Does Mark construct the anecdotes in the text with the aim of teaching through exemplification or to reveal christological aspects through the characterization and the development of the plot of the story like John? Is the Markan text composed of anecdotes that serve to highlight the exalted persona of Jesus? Since different genres serve different purposes, answers to these questions would definitely illuminate and narrow the alternative considerations of the literary genre to the most probable.

According to Vines, Mark "focuses on the life and activities of a single individual in a rough chronological framework."[66] He seems to support this study's supposition that the narratives of these activities are joined to the whole by the common purpose which they serve, that is, to enhance the belief value of Jesus and the gospel about him. Moreover, the Markan narratives are not aimed at exemplifying Christian living or revealing christological aspects. Jesus's miracles cannot be copied while the disciples are not portrayed in any enviable picture. They are portrayed as people who do not understand things about the kingdom of God. Jesus is the only Markan character who receives unreserved acclaim. Mark highlights the magnitude of the issues that were solved by Jesus's miracles. This suggests that miracle stories were narrated to draw attention to the fact that Jesus had extraordinary numinous power and as such, he was indeed the Christ (John 3:2).

Vines says, "The contents of Mark, with its themes of Jesus' divine commission and his role as the eschatological Son of Man, exceeds the generic limitations of Greco-Roman biography."[67] In agreement with Vines, this study notes that Mark overly concentrated on Jesus's career and completely obscured his social and family ties. A biography would have probed aspects of Jesus's relationship with his family and social contacts. Lack of these elements discriminates it from having been primarily written for biographical purposes unless one wants to see it as Jesus's itinerary in Galilee, on the road to and in Jerusalem. Rather, this discriminative choice of narratives, which exalt the person of Jesus, suggests that they were chosen for their rhetorical

---

66. Vines, *Problem of Markan Genre*, 22.
67. Vines, 12.

value in enhancing the ethos of Jesus and hence the belief value in the oral gospel about him.

Stein posits, "While not fitting the modern-day genre of biography in that it omits the first thirty-plus years of Jesus' life; it fits the general form of Greco-Roman biography of his days."[68] Stein's position has not probed the possible position that the Markan text could have been written as a Hebrew paraenesis. It is directed by his supposition that Mark's aim was to write a Gospel[69] about Jesus Christ. He adds that the "evangelist wants his readers to wrestle with the question 'Who then is this man that even the winds and the sea obey him?' (4:41)."[70] However, Stein has not wrestled with why Mark purposely omitted Christ's nativity though the details form a very significant aspect of answering the question that he has posed. Inclusion of the nativity narratives would have connected Jesus Christ to the Old Testament law and prophets that "testify about him" (John 5:39). It would also have affirmed Christ's incarnation through his virgin birth. Why would anybody writing a historical or biographical narrative on Jesus leave out such an important record of his life without offering an explanation? Mark's omission of this important period of Jesus's life suggests that he was not purposely writing either a biography or history of Jesus Christ.

Stanton notes, "The gospels are now widely considered to be a sub-set of the broad ancient literary genre of βιοι, biographies. Even if the evangelists were largely ignorant of the tradition of Greek and Roman βιοι, that is how the gospels were received and listened to in the first decades after their composition."[71] By saying that the evangelists were ignorant of the tradition of Greek and Roman βιοι, Stanton's statement presents an irreconcilable disharmony between the intended genre of the Markan text and the genre that the readers' perceived it to be. Stanton's argument seems to have been forced to support a position taken a priori.

---

68. Stein, *Mark*, 20.

69. The exotic references of the term εὐαγγέλιον as a genre or a written text eclipses the understanding in Mark's milieu that gospel was the kerygma – announcement that God had finally fulfilled his promise and had ushered his kingdom in the coming of Jesus.

70. Stein, *Mark*, 21.

71. Stanton, *Jesus and the Gospel*, 192.

In rooting for βιοι, Burridge argues that "like most Greco Roman βιοι, Mark and Mathew include the name of their subject at the very start."[72] This study notes that whereas Matthew's subject is explicitly Jesus Christ, Mark's subject is "the beginning of the gospel," that is, the episodes on which the gospel about Jesus Christ was premised. It however appreciates that the significance of Jesus and his work to humanity's redemption is the major subject of the proclamation of the oral gospel. As such, validating the oral gospel is accomplished by a validation of Jesus's historicity and messiahship. Nevertheless, the oral gospel and the biographical information about Jesus are not synonymous topics in the text.

Burridge's argument that a statistical analysis of the Markan text shows that a substantial number of verbs in the Markan text have Jesus as their subject may not be a viable point of argument to support his claims. In any case, the works of Jesus are the bulwark of the subject of the main topic of the Markan text – the beginning of the gospel of Jesus Christ the Son of God. To argue for the validity of the oral gospel is tantamount to arguing for the historicity and messiahship of Jesus but the difference in the subjects of the two arguments should be noted. As such, Burridge's conclusion is inevitable in the event that the acts and work of Jesus are used to validate his messiahship, him being the subject of proclamation of the oral gospel.

Again, as Burridge's statistics show[73] the Markan text was biased towards recording episodes that reveal Jesus's exalted persona rather than Christology or his relationships with the religious leaders, the political leaders, or his social contacts. Each of the text's narrated episodes has a paraenetic value in exhorting the Markan audience to respond to the oral gospel. The Old Testament quotations authenticate it, the miracle stories exalt Jesus to affirm it, Jesus's teachings urge its belief and performance, and the passion story affirms it. This is more in harmony with paraenesis than biography. Markan paraenesis depends on aspects of historiography and biography; hence the struggle to authoritatively identify the Markan genre. However, it is undeniable that, as it stands, the text contains aspects of historiography and biography. Nevertheless, these aspects are made to serve a paraenetic purpose, that is, to catalyze reader-response to the oral gospel about Jesus.

---

72. Burridge, *What Are the Gospels?*, 189.
73. Burridge, 192.

In his study of the Markan genre, Burridge has compared the Markan text with Greco-Roman biographies. It is not within the scope of this study to review Burridge's in-depth research findings. Against Burridge's argument, this study argues that Mark, being a Hebrew and a native of Jerusalem, and a Jew from a relatively well to do family (Acts 12:12), would have been more acquainted with Hebrew literary forms than Greco-Roman forms. Actually, other than sharing political jurisdiction and an unenforced influence from Greco-Roman literary forms, there are no other significant commonalities on which a comparative analysis can be established. As such comparing the Markan literary genre with literary works of Xenophon or even Plutarch narrows the scope of analysis to just comparing the texts on the basis of both literary works being within the same political jurisdiction.

Moreover, it has not been established that the education system in Palestine had integrated the Greco-Roman system which studied the great Greco-Roman philosophers, poets and rhetoricians. Among the works that were very influential in the Greco-Roman literary world were the "poetry of Homer, the history of Herodotus, the medicine of Hippocrates, the mathematics of Archimedes, the drama of Sophocles and Aeschylus, and the philosophy of Plato and Aristotle."[74] Paul, who was Mark's contemporary, studied under Gamaliel, a great Hebrew scholar from Jerusalem (Acts 22:3). Furthermore, the milieus in which these Greco-Roman literary works and the New Testament writings were written are separated by a period of over a century. It should be recognized that though Christianity was expediently transmitted in Greek to its varied peoples, it had very strong religio-cultural ties with Judaism with which it shared a common worldview and Scripture. As such, while not denying that the Markan text inevitably shows some reliance on aspects of Greco-Roman literary conventions, it compares more with Genesis and other Jewish literary works.

Comparatively, Mark wrote to an audience that was going through a similar transition as Moses's audience. While Moses's audience was struggling to keep the Mosaic covenant by reason of their past association with their host's culture and religion in Egypt, Mark's audience was equally struggling to keep faith and praxis of the gospel under a new covenant by reason of other competing religions like Judaism (Acts 15:1) and social pressures in a bullish

---

74. Packer and Tenney, *Illustrated Manners and Customs*, 346.

Greco-Roman culture. Moses used stories from his community's sacred history as a rhetorical device to urge his audience to adhere to an extant reality – the Sinaitic covenant. Similarly, Mark was using his faith community's sacred history to root the oral gospel on an authentic historical reality – the Christ event – in order to urge his audience to believe and adhere to its teachings.

The rhetorical situation of the Markan audience and the rhetorical situation of the Genesis audience are comparable. The prevailing exigences in both rhetorical situations are obduracy towards the word of the covenant in Genesis and the oral gospel message in the Markan text. Genesis' occasion is failure of the Exodus audience to keep the Sinaitic covenant that was evidenced by their making and worshipping the golden calf (Exod 32:7–9). Similarly, the Markan text's occasion is the audience's obduracy and lukewarm response to the gospel about Jesus Christ as mirrored in the retold parable of the sower (4:1–12).

Second, Genesis was written at a time of constituting a new community, Israel, as a nation and people of God through the Mosaic covenant (Exod 19:5–6; Deut 7:6). Similarly, the Markan text was written at a time of constituting a new community, the church. The genre and literary conventions of the Markan text are also comparable to works of Josephus. Josephus records both the community's sacred history and extant happenings "as an explanation of the Jews for the Romans, and perhaps in an attempt to redeem his reputation."[75] As such, a search for the Markan genre ought to analyze such literary works that are similar to the Markan context and more so religious treatises that Mark was certainly acquainted with.

Furthermore, a comparison of the Markan text with literary works that may have been close to his cultural and religious orientation, that is, the Old Testament texts, points to the primary direction and area of study in the search for the Markan genre. In agreement with this observation, Vines avers, "As the numerous citations and allusions to the Old Testament attest, the gospel's only overt literary dependencies are to the Jewish writings."[76] The Markan text was intended to found the oral gospel on his community's belief pillars, that is, their inherited Scripture and God. Structurally, Mark clustered similar episodes together to intensify their affective effect on his audience.

---

75. Josephus, *Works of Flavius Josephus*, Introduction, vii.
76. Vines, *Problem of Markan Genre*, 28–29.

A comparison with the other synoptic texts shows that the Markan episodes are not narrated in a strict chronological order as befits historiography or biography. Whereas John records Jesus as having visited Jerusalem for the Jewish feasts three times, John 2:13; 7:10; 11:55, Mark records only one visit. As such, rhetorical expediency, which is an aspect of paraenesis, as opposed to chronology, which is an aspect of historical and biographic writings, was the main criteria in the arrangement of the material.

Markedly, the Markan text is a persuasive discourse. The subject of the Markan text is "the beginning of the gospel of Jesus Christ" whereas the subject of the oral gospel is "Jesus Christ and the significance of his work on the cross." The subject of the text should not however be confused with the subject of the oral gospel. The following are the main areas of concentration in discussing the beginning of the gospel. First, Mark's grounding of the oral gospel on the community's Scripture. In this respect, he wanted to show that the Christ event was fulfilment of prophecy and God's promises to the patriarchs. Mark also wanted to support the oral gospel's proclamation that Jesus was indeed the Christ the Son of God. He accomplished this by quoting Old Testament Scripture that anticipated the coming of the Messiah (1:2-3).

Second, Mark was also interested in showing that the gospel was founded on a phenomenon that was sanctioned by God. Mark's miracle stories suggest that Mark was after showing that Jesus was a man from God (John 3:2). The importance of connecting Jesus with the divine and thereby founding the gospel on God is emphasized by Mark's narration of the only two theophanic utterances by God in testifying about Jesus. One was during Jesus's baptism (1:11) when God testified that Jesus was his Son. The other similar occurrence was on the mount of transfiguration in which God testified that Jesus was his Son and urged the disciples to hearken to his word, the gospel of God (Mark 9:2-8; 1:14-15).

The text is too biased towards showing Jesus's likeable and compassionate demeanor in opposition to the cold legalism of the Jewish religious leaders, Christ's miracles to highlight Jesus as being a man sent from God (John 3:1-2), and the passion as a sacrificial and vicarious episode to merit being considered a historical or biographical treatise. In comparison to Greco-Roman genres, it comes close to aretalogy – a genre that records deeds of great and famous persons. Moreover, the main deeds that Mark recorded as having been done by Jesus were not narrated as mimetic exemplifiers as are biographical and historical narratives. They are more biased towards highlighting Jesus's persona.

If Mark's aim was christological, he would not have missed to highlight Jesus's nativity which underscores his immaculate conception and hence his deity. There is definitely an element of Christology that can be discerned from a written record on Christ's work but omitting his nativity, which shows significant aspects of his identity, disallows this argument. Mark's purpose was to affirm the oral gospel by commending the persona and work of Jesus, on whom it was premised, so as to convince and convict the audience concerning its truth and belief value. Theissen says, and plausibly so, "The whole of Mark's gospel pushes towards acclamation, towards recognition of Jesus' true status."[77]

In summary, in identifying the genre of the Markan text, this study has taken into account its function of urging audience response to the oral gospel. The oral gospel has also been identified as an independent interlocutor within the matrix of the Markan discourse. The text undoubtedly contains biographical material and looked at independently it can be adjudged as either historical or biographical. However, considering its intended exhortation for the purpose of catalyzing audience response to the oral gospel, its genre is more identifiable with paraenesis.

Most of the studies on the genre of the Markan text are based on a lexical study coupled with a comparison with Greco-Roman texts without taking into account its purpose. The choice of the genre in which to write a text can be informed by the purpose for which the text is intended to serve. In view of the narratives on the life and times of Jesus in the Markan text, it is not surprising to adjudge it a biography or a historical treatise. Inevitably, the rhetorical efficacy that convinces the audience concerning the belief value of the oral gospel draws its effectiveness from biographical and historical information about Jesus. Furthermore, the paraenetic efficacy of the Markan text rests in efficiently matching the Jesus of history, who became the Christ of faith, with the Christ of the Old Testament promises and prophecy. As such, elements of biography and historiography would always be noticed in a paraenetic treatise like the Markan text. To argue for paraenesis is thus to strongly argue for biography and to argue for biography is to argue for historiography. Moreover, in the Markan text, biographical and historical information has

---

77. Theissen, *Miracle Stories*, 212.

been employed to serve a paraenetic purpose. In consideration of the text's relationship with the audience and the oral gospel, the certain genre of the Markan text is paraenesis.

Theissen has described the Markan text as an "'aretalogical gospel composition' based on the realization of motifs of secrecy and acclamation."[78] He avers, "In its treatment of the past the transcendent pre-history is missing, and for the future only the parousia could complete the mythical history. The only finished structure is the aretalogical tension of miraculous event, secrecy and acclamation; mythical anticipations intensify this tension, but are not its course."[79] Comparatively, the Markan text's use of narratives from his community's immediate history, its occasion, form, and purpose are similar to the Genesis' use of its audience's history, its occasion, form, and purpose. In consideration of the texts' occasion, form, and purpose, the genre can be adjudged to be more of Hebrew paraenesis in the similitude of the Genesis account than Greek aretalogy.

M. J. Wilkins says, "Paraenesis is the instructional model in which ethical counsel and moral education were provided in a pattern of exhortation applied to practical problems or issues of living."[80] Since this study argues that the Markan text exhorts its readers to eliminate their exigence of obduracy and lukewarm response to the gospel and at the same time exhorts those responding to be more forward in their response, then it can be adjudged a paraenesis. However, against the form critics, who argued that paraenesis is a genre, recent scholarship has questioned whether it should be so considered. The argument against considering paraenesis a genre is supported by an etymological study of the word paraenesis.

However, it is rather limiting to confine the word paraenesis to only stand for its referent in antiquity. The term should be allowed to encompass growth, in time, in hortatory methods. It should also incorporate hortatory forms in diverse language conventions. Some see paraenesis as serving a social function and others see it as a rhetorical device. Indeed, paraenesis serves a social function of exhorting audiences to perform a social function. At the same

---

78. Theissen, 215.
79. Theissen, 217.
80. Wilkins, "Teaching, Paraenesis," 1157.

time, it can act as a rhetorical device. The Markan text's function of catalyzing reader-response to the oral gospel is indeed a social and rhetorical function.

David Aune defines genre as "a group of texts that exhibit a coherent and recurring configuration of literary features involving form . . . content, and function."[81] In line with Aune's definition, paraenesis is distinguishable as a literary form with a literary configuration that is deliberately skewed to perform the function of exhortation. As such and in line with Aune's definition, it is plausible to designate paraenesis a genre.

3.8 Summary

Internal and external evidence do not provide explicit dating and historical positioning of the text. However, by analyzing the rhetorical situation of the primary audience, it is possible to identify the profile of the audience, the occasion and the social religious context in which the Markan treatise was written.

The audience has been profiled as a people who were obdurate and lukewarm towards the oral gospel. A small percentage was optimally responding to the oral gospel. Similarly, the occasion can be identified as a need to eliminate the exigence of obduracy and lukewarm stance towards the oral gospel as portrayed in the retold parable of the sower (4:1–12).

A unique contribution to biblical studies in the contextual, structural, and form analysis is the identification of a stratification of the themes in the text. Identification of this thematic stratification is useful in identifying the context in which the episodes that are narrated in the text occurred.

---

81. Aune, *New Testament*, 13.

CHAPTER 4

Matrix of Interlocutors in the Markan Text

4.1 Introduction

This section probes the discourse between the Markan text and its implied interlocutors. It also probes its impact on its reader's response to the oral gospel. First, it identifies the explicit and implicit[1] interlocutors that communicate through the textual discourse. Second, it pairs the interlocutors that dialogue at various stages in the discourse. Third, it analyzes the nature and function of each of these interlocutor relationships.

This probe helps in tracking "who is doing what and to whom as well as provide an indication of how the events relate to one another."[2] Consequently, it makes it possible to unpack the flow of both the direct and indirect communication and to pinpoint the cognitive and affective impact of the discourse on the reader.

In this study, discourse is understood to be the explicit and implicit communicative transactions between the interlocutors within the entire matrix of the Markan discourse. According to Gillian Brown and George Yule, "Language used in such a situation is primarily 'message oriented.'"[3] As

---

1. "Implicit" in this case stands for strategic communication that is resultant of perlocutionary acts in the text; an example is the effects of being awed by hearing about the great miracles that Jesus performed.
2. Runge, *Discourse Grammar*, 6.
3. Brown and Yule, *Discourse Analysis*, 2.

such, this probe employs discourse analysis. It is complemented by rhetorical analysis. Terrance R. Wardlaw describes discourse analysis as "the analysis of language and its use beyond the sentence, including the analysis of language situated in its social context. Discourse can be described as a unit of speech (either oral or written) treated by interlocutors as a complete utterance."[4] According to Reed, it involves "probing a text and its interaction with the interlocutors and also the relationship between the interlocutors through the text."[5]

Generally, discourse analysis is aimed at analyzing the texts with a view to elucidate, locate and appropriate meaning. In the process, other objectives are also met. A textual analysis achieves understanding of the components from the smallest unit of the discourse – the word to the entire text as a discourse. The contribution of each interlocutor to encoding and decoding the message is also analyzed. Finally, the various contexts that contribute to the production and interpretation of the text are also analyzed. Discourse analysis aims at facilitation of understanding a text, its production, its interaction and effect on the interlocutors, its relationship with the social context, and finally its meaning.

Discourse analysis can reconcile and stabilize the notion of the locus of meaning within the matrix of a discourse. Whereas the traditional view has been that meaning inheres in the author, today's opinion is that it inheres in the reader. However, discourse analysis shows that elucidating meaning involves a probe of "each and every participant in the communicative process."[6] It has brought in a sobering notion that meaning inheres in "an abstract space between hearers, speakers and text – jointly produced."[7]

4.2 Subject of Discussion in the Markan Text

The syntagmatic relation of Ἀρχὴ with εὐαγγέλιον in Mark 1:1 suggests that the function of the Markan text is to provide information that would help the audience reminisce on the episode or episodes, in history, on which the

---

4. Wardlaw, "Discourse Analysis," 268.
5. Reed, "Discourse Analysis," 203.
6. Wardlaw, "Discourse Analysis," 271.
7. Wardlaw, 275.

gospel about Jesus Christ was premised. Over two decades separated the time between Jesus's ascension and the writing of the Markan text. As such, a written record of the nature of the salvific episode on which the oral gospel proclamation was premised had affirming value. Historical records have intrinsic rhetorical efficacy to validate information that is presumed to be premised on such episodes in history.

According to Wallace, Ἀρχὴ in the phrase Ἀρχὴ τοῦ εὐαγγελίου Ἰησοῦ Χριστοῦ [υἱοῦ θεοῦ] is a nominative absolute.[8] He avers that, "a nominative absolute does not occur in a sentence, but only in titles, salutations, and other introductory phrases."[9] As such, whether Ἀρχὴ is used as a title or an introductory phrase, it suggests that the subject of the Markan text is "the beginning of the gospel." Ἀρχὴ in relation to εὐαγγελίου, in a way, limits the discussion to a particular aspect concerning the gospel, that is, the premise on which it is founded. Thayer describes it as "that from which the gospel history took its beginning."[10]

Εὐαγγελίου in relation to Ἀρχὴ in this introductory phrase is a descriptive genitive. Ἰησοῦ Χριστοῦ in relation to εὐαγγέλιον suggests that Ἰησοῦ Χριστοῦ is an objective genitive. As such, εὐαγγελίου Ἰησοῦ Χριστοῦ denotes the gospel about Jesus Christ and the topic under discussion in the Markan text is "the beginning of the gospel." The subject of the gospel is the significance of Jesus Christ and his work on the cross to the redemption of humanity. Since the text was written at a time when the church was proclaiming and professing the gospel orally and semiotically – through administration of the ordinances that were bequeathed the church by Jesus Christ – then the gospel referenced in Mark 1:1 is, to a large degree of probability, the gospel that Mark and his contemporaries, who included the apostle Peter, were proclaiming. As such, it was outside and independent of the Markan text. Therefore, use of Ἀρχὴ suggests that the Markan text is a reminiscence of the episodes on which the oral gospel was premised.

Snodgrass posits, "The gospel of Jesus Christ, i.e., the gospel Jesus preached, is quite different from the gospel about Jesus which the early

---

8. Wallace, *Greek Grammar*, 49.
9. Wallace, 50.
10. Thayer, *Thayer's Greek-English Lexicon*, 76.

Church preached."¹¹ He supports his position by saying that "the Church's gospel is rightly summarized as the proclamation of the death and resurrection of Jesus."¹² However, it is arguable that the gospel that the early church preached encapsulated the gospel that Jesus and his disciples were preaching, that is, τὸ εὐαγγέλιον τοῦ θεοῦ (1:14–15; 6:7–13). It is the gospel that Jesus commissioned his disciples to preach to the whole world (Mark 16:15–18; Acts 1:8). Therefore, the Markan text's topic of discussion affirms and validates an oral gospel that was a going concern by the time of writing the text.

The Markan text is composed of stories of carefully selected episodes within the Christ event and Old Testament quotations. These textual embellishments are employed as rhetorical devices to convince and convict the readers concerning the reliability and belief value of the oral gospel. After Jesus's death and resurrection, stories about his life and work had become part of the Christian community's common tradition (Luke 24:13–24). This tradition inhered in the memories of the eye witnesses to the Christ event and in the community's institutional memory. It was transmitted orally and was a rich repository from which preachers and writers drew information for their kerygmatic, historical, and biographical purposes.

Furthermore, the fact that oral tradition about Jesus Christ and his salvific work on the cross resided in both the individual and collective memory of the community is supported by the nomenclature of the texts that had recorded the episodes in the Christ event as "'Remembrances of the Apostles' (ἀπομνημονύματα τῶν ἀποστόλων)."¹³ The significance of the salvific episode was proclaimed orally as gospel in order to spur faith in Jesus. Its nature and significance were also symbolized and semiotically proclaimed in the practice of the ordinance the Lord's Supper (1 Cor 11:26).

The term ἀπομνημονύματα has also been translated as "memoirs." This suggests that there could have been some witnesses to the life and works of Jesus who may have recorded them as they happened. However, lack of a single surviving manuscript of such memoirs, in view of their importance, tilts plausibility to only noetic remembrances. This affirms that tradition resided in the individual and community's collective memory. It can therefore

---

11. Snodgrass, "Gospel of Jesus," 31.
12. Snodgrass, 31.
13. Koester, "From Kerygma-Gospel," 377.

be argued that, even after the writing of the New Testament texts, the oral gospel, the oral tradition, and the texts by the four evangelists thrived simultaneously. This supposition is supported by Holmes in observing, "Even after the gospels were written, oral traditions continued to circulate and to influence the written text; and oral tradition was often more valued than written material in a cultural setting that relied upon and trusted memory far more than is customary today."[14]

The identification of anecdotes in the Markan text as rhetorical devices is founded on the supposition that rhetoric is a purposeful embellishment of oral and written communication with efficacious language formations that enhance audience-buy-in value of the proposition being fronted or supported by the text. Notably, rhetoric is employed in the Markan text as a tool to enhance the belief value of the oral gospel. Since rhetorical devices under consideration are not embellished in the oral gospel but in the text, then, their efficacy in impacting audience response towards the oral gospel is affective and catalytic. Voicing a contrary view, Hengel posits that "what is narrated is for Mark *euangelion* which wishes to convey saving faith in Jesus as Messiah and Son of God."[15] Whereas it is plausible to posit that εὐαγγέλιον wishes to convey saving faith in Jesus as Messiah, Hengel's view, that ascribes sacramental value to the stories in the Markan text, has not explained how the saving faith is conveyed.

In his discussion on textual analysis and the complexities of the actions that attend the formation of a text, Walhout says that "the various actions that go into the forming of a text provide a pattern for distinguishing the kinds or levels of analysis that are relevant to interpretation."[16] He further avers that "although we cannot separate these concerns, many controversies occur because interpreters conflate them."[17] Walhout understands and therefore cautions interpreters on the problems inherent in trying to interpret a textual communication within a labyrinth of its interlocutors without first delineating its inherent interlocutor relationships.

---

14. Holmes, *Apostolic Fathers*, 723.
15. Hengel, "Eye-Witness Memory," 70.
16. Walhout, "Narrative Hermeneutics," 85.
17. Walhout, 86.

4.3 Interlocutors within the Matrix of the Markan Discourse

This section discusses the nature and significance of the explicit and implicit interlocutors within the matrix of the Markan discourse. The aim is to disentangle the labyrinth of the different interlocutors and rhetorical devices that participate in the Markan discourse.

According to Young, communication theory arrives at the situation whereby "author, text and reader constitute a triangle, and no hermeneutic is adequate which does not pay attention to each."[18] However, the discourse flow illustrated in figure 2 below shows that the Markan text communicates with the reader through two implicit interlocutors. First, a mimetic world that mirrors the audience's rhetorical situation, which is portrayed by the controversy narratives and the parable of the sower; and second, the episodic rhetorical devices of Old Testament quotations, miracle stories, and the passion story. Moreover, the audience were already hearing an oral gospel that was circulating before, during, and after the writing of the Markan text. As such, four interlocutors are involved and each of the four (the anecdotal rhetorical devices, the mimetic world of the text, the audience, and the oral gospel) are distinct interlocutors in the discourse. This delineation enables the audience, as Young says, "to enter into a critical and dialogical reading"[19] of the text.

4.3.1 The Markan Text

Arguably, the Markan text is aimed at awakening the audience to their wanting rhetorical situation and to provoke a desire to eliminate its inherent exigence. This work has argued that Mark used the rhetorical devices of Old Testament quotations, miracle stories, and passion narrative to draw the attention of his readers, who were also audiences to the oral gospel, to the elevated ethos, person, and salvific work of Jesus so as to enhance the belief value in the oral gospel which was premised on his person and work on the cross. It has also argued that he describes the rhetorical situation of Jesus's audience using narratives of the controversy between Jesus and the Jewish religious leaders. The exigence that prompted the writing of the text is graphically

---

18. Young, "Towards a Hermeneutic," 107.
19. Young, 107.

portrayed by retelling the parable of the sower (4:1–12) and the parable of the wicked tenants (12:1–11).

Jesus employed the parable of the sower as a rhetorical communication to eliminate the exigence in his audience's rhetorical situation. Later, Mark retold the parable to mirror the rhetorical situation of his audience as well as the expected faith shift from obduracy to optimal responsiveness to the oral gospel. Furthermore, this mirror portrait accentuates the grim picture of his audience's obstinacy thereby evoking its abhorrence and, correspondingly, aspiration to shift to faith and obedience to the oral gospel. Funk describes this type of narrative as "a scene in which events are enacted, much as they are in the performance of a stage drama."[20] As such, the reader becomes a participant in the ensuing drama.

Rhetorical devices in the Markan text

The rhetorical devices of Old Testament quotations, miracle stories and passion narratives are particularly aimed at showing that the Jesus of history and faith is the Christ of Old Testament prophecy and promises. His mighty works, which are highlighted in the miracle stories, show that he was approved by God (John 3:1–2). His death on the cross, which was foreboded in his words during the inauguration of the Last Supper, shows that he had offered his life as a vicarious and propitiatory sacrifice for the redemption of humankind.

This study is biased towards analyzing the relationship between the various interlocutors within the matrix of the Markan discourse. It is different from the study by Robert M. Fowler who has also analyzed the Markan text through discourse analysis.[21] His focus is on the text's syntax such as its use of statements of intent and statements of purpose which helped Mark to push his argument forward. Its point of departure from Fowler's method, and hence its unique contribution, is the consideration that Markan text is a

---

20. Funk, *Poetics of Biblical Narrative*, 134.
21. Fowler, *Let the Reader Understand*, 43. Fowler describes his method as a "shift away from the story of the Gospel narrative to the discourse of the narrative – the characters, events, and settings within the narrative." He says that he is "reckoning adequately with the discourse level or the rhetoric of the narrative – the ways in which the language attempts to weave its spell over the reader."

discourse that was aimed at affectively catalyzing reader-response to the oral gospel that was outside and independent of the text.

Ryken posits, "Literature, in short, is *affective* not cool and detached."[22] Since, as has been argued, the Markan text is an affective treatise, it presents more of evocative than argumentative rhetoric. Therefore, in this study one of the parameters by which a literary formation or anecdote is deemed to be a rhetorical device is the identification of its affective efficacy to urge the audience to faith and praxis of the oral gospel's demands. In this category are foils, highlights of the elevated ethos of Jesus, founding the gospel on the faith matrix of the community, and aligning the oral gospel with the scriptural promises and prophecies in the Old Testament. These rhetorical devices are embellishments that are more common in the Old Testament narratives as opposed to the argumentative and logical rhetorical presentation that is more common in the New Testament Epistles.

By delineating and analyzing the relationship between the interlocutors in the Markan discourse, it becomes clear that the Markan text has a well thought-out *inventio*. Heath defines *inventio* as "the discovery of the resources for discursive persuasion latent in any given rhetorical problem."[23] It employs select anecdotes that amplify and anchor the oral gospel on the belief matrix of the community. The purpose is to enhance the truth and belief value of the oral gospel. Such anchoring acquires its rhetorical efficacy in the fact that it is based on "what, presumably, author and audience agree to be the criterion for authentication of such claims, Israel's Scripture,"[24] which had, by then, been adopted as the church's Scripture. A text, such as the Markan text, that is largely composed of anecdotal rhetorical devices for persuasive purposes, demonstrates the writer's literary acumen.

Marion C. Moeser's definition of anecdote aptly captures this study's understanding of an anecdote. She avers that an anecdote is:

> A brief narrative, either oral or written, describing an incident, including its setting, which involves one or more persons and which focuses on an action, saying, or dialogue; the function of an anecdote is to entertain, instruct, relate an historical incident,

---

22. Ryken, *Read the Bible as Literature*, 15.
23. Heath, "Invention," 89.
24. Hanson, *Endangered Promises*, 108.

characterize a person, or authoritatively legitimate a specific opinion, a specific practice, or a broader view of reality.[25]

Though the anecdotes narrated in the Markan text are said, and rightly so, to be disjointed and not forming a systematic narrative, they do however work in tandem to fulfil a common purpose. As such, Mark's purpose is to authoritatively legitimate the oral gospel with the aim of convincing the readers that it was worthy of their faith. In a rhetorical formation that does not rely on argumentation, such as the Markan text, the rhetorical anecdotes need not be ordered chronologically to fulfil their rhetorical purpose. They could be arranged differently and still fulfil their paraenetic purpose. However, they need to be rhetorically and affectively efficacious to evoke belief and action.

Rhetorical situation of Jesus's audience

The parable of the sower (4:1–12) and the parable of the wicked tenants (12:1–11) are rhetorical communications that Jesus employed to eliminate exigencies in his varied audiences' rhetorical situations. The retold parable of the sower acts as a mimetic portrait of the exigence in the rhetorical situation of Jesus's audience which ranged from extreme obduracy, lukewarm, thirty-fold or sixty-fold, to optimal responsiveness to the word of God.

W. Randolph Tate describes the interaction between the mimetic world and the real world by saying, "While the text may be formal in design and does not replicate reality, it does mirror it in the complexity of the design . . . Mimetic critics also claim that characterization, setting, plot, and action in literature invite a comparison with life as we experience it outside the text."[26] Therefore, it acts as "a stimuli to the reader's senses."[27]

Mark employed the mimetic portrait of the exigence in the rhetorical situation of the audience of Jesus to mirror the rhetorical situation and the exigence of his audience. He retold the parable of the sower to evoke disdain towards obduracy of his audience and, paradoxically, to provoke them to aspire for optimal response to the oral gospel. Upon reading the text, Mark's audience is stimulated to believe and live according to the dictates of the oral gospel in the real world.

---

25. Moeser, *Anecdote in Mark*, 20–21.
26. Tate, *Biblical Interpretation*, 335.
27. Tate, 149.

Rhetorical situation of Jesus's audience as a mirror medium

The concept of "*Sitz im Leben* Jesu[28] (situation in the life of Jesus)"[29] that was conceived by the form critics, is an important starting point in discussing the rhetorical situation of Jesus's audience. The form critics conceived the concept of *Sitz im Leben* to help them match the different forms in the text to their original usage in the oral kerygma. Because of an understandable interest in Mark's theology in the early twentieth century, most scholars led by "W. Wrede (1856–1906) and Albert Schweitzer together with the form critics, K. L. Schmidt (1891–1956), Martin Dibelius (1891–1947), and R. Bultmann (1884–1976),"[30] were interested in the *Sitz im Leben* of the different forms of the text to illumine the purpose of the different forms such as, miracle stories, controversy stories, parables, passion story, and the sayings of Jesus.

None of the scholars has this far analyzed *Sitz im Leben* Jesu as an indirect interlocutor within the matrix of the Markan discourse and from the point of view that it was used as a portrait to mirror Mark's *Sitz im Leben* and as such, a mimetic interlocutor with the audience. This study identifies *Sitz im Leben* Jesu as the rhetorical situation that prompted Jesus to tell the parable of the sower to eliminate the inherent exigence. Particularly, it was aimed at arousing his audience to aspire to eliminate the exigence of their obduracy towards the gospel of God.

Analysis of the narratives about the controversy between Jesus and the Jewish religious leaders as well as the programmatic parable of the sower (4:1–12)[31] shows that the *Sitz im Leben* within which Jesus was ministering was a spectrum of audience who showed different levels of response to the gospel.[32] Since the Markan text is audience centered, it is plausible to argue that Mark intended to use the portrait of the response of Jesus's audience to the gospel as a mirror medium through which his own audience would see

---

28. Here and elsewhere, the German term *Sitz im Leben* Jesu is used to designate the life settings in the ministry of Jesus that occasioned his miracle and preaching ministry. Fee, *New Testament Exegesis*, 49. Dibelius refers to *Sitz im Leben* as "the historical and social stratum in which precisely these literary forms were developed." Dibelius, *From Tradition to Gospel*, 7.

29. Blomberg, *Interpreting the Parables*, 73. Some scholars refer to the same situation as *Leben Jesu*.

30. Kealy, *Mark's Gospel*, 90–197. Kealy has reviewed the history and trends of the quest for the historical Jesus, the form critics and the redaction critics.

31. See section 3.6.

32. See section 3.5.

their personal responses to the oral gospel. In a way, by retelling the parable of the sower, Mark was reproving his obdurate and lukewarm audience and at the same time commending those who were optimally responsive to the oral gospel. This portrayal is effectual in rebuking the unresponsive audience and at the same time affirming the optimally responsive believer as part of the fruitful Christian community thereby urging greater adherence and commitment to the oral gospel and its demands.

Rhetorical situation of Mark's audience: An interlocutor in the Markan discourse

This study has argued that the Markan text was born out a need to eliminate the exigence in the rhetorical situation of Mark's audience. In addition, it has shown that the portrait of the rhetorical situation of Jesus's audience is the mirror through which *Sitz im Leben* Jesu, as a mimetic world, affectively communicates with the Markan audience. As such, the mirrored portrait of the rhetorical situation of Mark's audience is an implicit interlocutor within the matrix of the Markan discourse.

The idea of conceptualizing the rhetorical situation of Mark's audience as an interlocutor in the Markan discourse is important to the study of the Markan text. It identifies the profile of his primary audience through which the Markan text, as Scripture, mirrors and speaks to his secondary audience. Furthermore, rhetorical situations that are defined by a people's response to the word of God transcend generations. As such, the rhetorical situation of Jesus's audience aptly mirrors the rhetorical situation of Mark's audience and the rhetorical situations of similar secondary audiences. The method aptly identifies the occasion of the Markan text as obduracy and lukewarm response to the oral gospel. This identification is helpful in narrowing the textual analysis and hence estimation of the purpose for which the text was written to the most probable.

The catalytic function of the Markan text

An analysis of the dialogue between the interlocutors within the matrix of the Markan dialogue[33] shows that Mark's concern in writing the text was to catalyze an existing but moribund engagement between his primary audience

---

33. See section 4.4.

and the oral gospel. Thiselton avers that "without such prompting into action, the text remains a closed book."[34] Through retelling the parable of the sower, Mark appealed to human abhorrence for the unsatisfactory and aspiration for absolute good to urge the audience to shun the former and pursue the latter. Instead of addressing his audience using direct speech, Mark chose to tell various anecdotes that are rich in rhetorical efficacy to validate, urge belief and obedience to the demands of the oral gospel.

The text's communicative transaction is mainly accomplished by use of parabolic satire, foils, enhancing belief in Jesus by narrating miracle stories, aesthetic structuring of the text, Old Testament quotations, and by showing the propitiatory and vicarious aspect of the passion episode in narrating Jesus's sayings in the administration of the Last Supper.

Satire is noticeable in Jesus's concluding remarks of the parable of the sower (4:12). By use of this satire, Jesus rebukes his obdurate audience as people with ears but who do not hear and as people having eyes but who do not see. Paradoxically, the said satire is also used to entreat the audience to respond favorably towards the oral gospel.

Highlighting the authoritative proclamation and doctrine of Jesus in contrast to that of the Jewish religious leaders (1:27) was used as a foil to magnify the persona of Jesus. Again, contrasting Jesus's benevolence, love, and compassion with the cold legalism of the religious leaders in the controversy stories (2:1–12; 3:1–6) was also used as a foil to bring to the fore the lofty Christian ethics that were propagated in the oral gospel. Finally, the interpolation of opposition and popularity of Jesus in Mark 2:1–12, which highlights Jesus's compassion when compared to the callous religion of the Jewish leaders, is in all sense a foil that highlights the exalted ethos of Jesus thereby enhancing the belief value in the oral gospel that was premised on his person and work on the cross. Shiner posits, "When the speaker creates a courteous and agreeable persona in his speech, he is able to secure the goodwill of his listeners."[35] Usage of foils highlights Jesus's courteous and agreeable persona thereby securing the goodwill of his audience and hence an enhanced faith in Jesus and the oral gospel about him.

---

34. Thiselton, "Communicative Action and Promise," 152.
35. Shiner, *Proclaiming the Gospel*, 65.

The text also catalyzes audience response by enhancing Jesus's persona through structuring the miracle stories in a form that highlights the power, excellence and appreciation of Jesus as a man sent of God who had numinous power over demons, diseases, nature and even death (1:21–26, 40–42; 4:35–39; 5:40–43). Notably, the problem that calls for the miracle is magnified through mention of the long time the infirmed had lived with the infirmity, the inability of conventional methods to solve the it, and any other issue that would act as a foil to highlight the power and ethos of the miracle worker. Scripture citation was also used as a powerful rhetorical device to premise the oral gospel about Jesus on the community's inherited faith thereby affirming Jesus as the Messiah.

Mark used a chiastic structure in Mark 1–15 and Mark 1:21–7:23. Chiasm highlights the major themes in the text. Notably, miracle stories are clustered in one section of the text (1:21–8:26). Just like parallelism, this kind of structure evokes awe and admiration in the person of Jesus thereby urging the audience to respond positively towards the gospel. Finally, the text is structured in a contextual stratum whereby the eternal kingdom of God is set as the *leitmotiv* and context of the perpetual proclamation of the gospel. The oral proclamation of the gospel is then set as the context in which miracle stories and Jesus's controversies with the Jewish religious leaders. The passion is lastly set within the context of Jesus's controversies with the Jewish religious leaders.[36] The pragmatic benefit of the author's prior identification of the context in which episodes are narrated is in directing the audience to the intended meaning of the text.

The Old Testament quotations in Mark 1:2–3 were used to show that Jesus, who was proclaimed in the oral gospel, was indeed the Christ of Old Testament Scripture.[37] Moreover, the Old Testament allusion in Mark 4:12 was used to entreat the readers to respond to the oral proclamation of the gospel.[38] Finally, by narrating the inauguration of the Lord's Supper, Mark sanitized the death of Jesus which would have otherwise been viewed as a normal human death with no salvific value. Foreboding the passion of Jesus

---

36. This supposition has been argued in chapter 3, section 3.4.

37. This supposition has been argued in chapter 5, section 5.4.1, "Summary of exegetical analysis of Mark 1:1–3."

38. This supposition has been argued in chapter 5.5.4.

with the Last Supper showed that his death was propitiatory, sacrificial, and vicarious. Placing the Lord's Supper in the context of the Passover by use of the participial phrase Καὶ ἐσθιόντων αὐτῶν in the statement Καὶ ἐσθιόντων αὐτῶν λαβὼν ἄρτον εὐλογήσας ἔκλασεν καὶ ἔδωκεν αὐτοῖς καὶ εἶπεν· λάβετε, τοῦτό ἐστιν τὸ σῶμά μου (Mark 14:22 NA28) shows that Mark was interpreting the Last Supper in light of the Passover feast. Paul, a contemporary of Mark, also interpreted the Lord's Supper as a type of Passover (1 Cor 5:7). Accordingly, the passion story was set and narrated in a context that highlighted the soteriological significance of the passion episode. Mark showed that the passion episode was anticipated in Scripture by showing that it was part of the promises that had been fulfilled in the Christ event (8:31; 9:9; 9:31; 10:33; 14:27).

In summary, by reading the rhetorical anecdotes in the text, reflecting on the portrait of their wanting rhetorical situation and its exigence in the mirror of the portrait of Jesus's audience, and being made aware of the enhanced belief value of the gospel through use of foils and satire, Mark's audience is convicted about its unsatisfactory response to the oral gospel, and is thereby aroused to respond to the gospel's demands.

4.3.2 The Audience

The Markan text has not explicitly identified its audience. Agreeably, R. A. Guelich posits, "As with place and date, one cannot specify the audience and occasion for the gospel."[39] However, it is possible to identify the profile of the implied audience by scanning the rhetorical situation and exigence that occasioned the writing of the text. This study argues that the rhetorical situation of Mark's audience is described in the controversy narratives as opposition to Jesus and his teachings. It is further mirrored in the parable of the sower as audience response to the word of God that ranged from sheer obduracy on one extreme to optimal response on the other extreme.

The audience was a mix of an obdurate and lukewarm hearers of the gospel, on one hand and a partially to an optimally responsive audience on the other hand. It is aptly portrayed as walking paths on which the gospel seed could not thrive, rocky shallow soils on which the gospel seedling is scorched by the sun, and soils with thorn bushes which choke the gospel

---

39. Guelich, "Mark, Gospel of," 773.

seedling. Even the few seeds that were productive are portrayed as having yielded dismal fruit of thirty- and sixty-fold with only a paltry few that were optimally productive.

4.3.3 The Oral Gospel

Though the oral gospel is largely a latent theme in the Markan text, it is a key interlocutor in the Markan discourse. Actually, proclamation of the oral gospel is the only motif that runs from the prologue through the episodic anecdotes to the disputed endings (1:14, 38; 6:2, 12, 34; 7:6–23; 10:1; 11:17; 16:15).

As the opening phrase shows, Mark's text is not about Jesus, it is about the beginning of the gospel of Jesus Christ the Son of God. Though important and prominent in both the oral gospel and the text, Jesus is not the main subject of discussion in the Markan text. In the opening phrase, the genitive Ἰησοῦ χριστοῦ is used to identify which gospel's founding episodes are being discussed. However, the person of Jesus and the significance of his salvific death are the subjects of the oral gospel – the salvific message about the nearness of the kingdom of God and the resultant benefits of salvation through repentance and forgiveness of sins (1:15). As such, the most effective way of catalyzing audience response to the oral gospel is to highlight the authoritative teachings, deeds, and the passion of Jesus. This distinction is important for in disregarding it rests the major misunderstanding that obscures identification of the genre, purpose, and meaning of the Markan text.[40]

Orality of the gospel referenced in Mark 1:1

Recent studies on orality of the Markan text have been concerned with investigating the oral form and performance of the written text other than the orality of the gospel that was being proclaimed orally by Mark and his contemporaries. Though it has been acknowledged lately that orality[41] was the main media in which the gospel was transmitted, current trends of research

---

40. Under the presupposition that the text is the Gospel according to Mark, the Markan text is seen as the content of the gospel that the apostles were proclaiming. However, if, as has been argued, the oral gospel was outside and independent of the Markan text, then the text is seen as an interlocutor urging the audience to respond to the oral gospel that was premised on the salvific episodes recorded in the text.

41. Werner H. Kelber and Joanna Dewey are leading scholars in this area of study.

have suggested that gospel performance was a kind of recitation of the written text while texts are seen as "aids to memory."[42] Alternatively, this analysis has explored the orality of the gospel that Mark and his contemporaries were proclaiming orally. This line of study is informed by the understanding that the gospel referenced in Mark 1:1 is an independent interlocutor within the matrix of the Markan discourse.

Often, references to the gospel in the Markan text are prefixed with the narrator's comments: "κηρύσσων" (1:14) "καὶ λέγων" (1:15), "καὶ ἔλεγεν αὐτοῖς" (4:21), "Καὶ ἐξελθόντες ἐκήρυξαν ἵνα μετανοῶσιν" (6:12). Such usage of the verbs of speaking shows that Jesus proclaimed the gospel by word of mouth to a listening audience. Acts also shows that the post-Pentecost proclamation of the gospel was oral. Again, use of the narrator's comments, "ἐπῆρεν τὴν φωνὴν αὐτοῦ καὶ ἀπεφθέγξατο αὐτοῖς" in Peter's sermons in Acts 2:14 and "ἀπεκρίνατο πρὸς τὸν λαόν" in Acts 3:12 (NA28), "Τότε Πέτρος πλησθεὶς πνεύματος ἁγίου εἶπεν πρὸς αὐτούς" in Acts 4:8, "Ἀνοίξας δὲ Πέτρος τὸ στόμα εἶπεν" in Acts 10:34 and "ὁ δὲ ἔφη· Ἄνδρες ἀδελφοὶ καὶ πατέρες, ἀκούσατε" in Stephen's sermon in Acts 7:2 show that oral proclamation was the only method used by the disciples during the formative days of the Christian movement.

Even after the gospel broke geographical and race barriers from its predominantly Jewish origins to the gentile world, it was still orally proclaimed (13:16). Moreover, the prophetic voice plus the mighty post-resurrection miracles were enough proof that Jesus was still present in the church. As such, narrating the miracles and mighty deeds of the pre-resurrection Jesus could not have been the mode of gospel proclamation. Moreover, the stories about the life and times of Jesus were not the content of the oral gospel that the apostles proclaimed. Instead, the apostles were proclaiming the fulfilment of the promise of God to usher his kingdom into the world and the consequent availability of forgiveness of sins to those who would repent (1:15).

The waning of the prophetic voice, pneumatic fervor, and performance of miracles as the gospel expanded its reach necessitated a reminiscence of both the teachings and mighty deeds that Jesus had performed to validate the salvific gospel that was mainly about his divine identity and the significance of his work on the cross. By the late-second century, the written accounts of the life and times of Jesus Christ had completely taken over the title "gospel"

---

42. Kelber, Review of *The Oral Ethos of the Early Church*.

according to the presumed author. Their reading and interpretation to a listening audience was considered to be the proclamation of the gospel. Thus, hermeneutics of the New Testament texts replaced oral proclamation of the salvific significance of the work of Jesus Christ on the cross.

Kelber credits Mark "for the making of the written gospel."[43] It seems that Kelber's postulation constitutes a reading back of the second-century understanding of the reference of the term "gospel" into its reference in the time of writing the Markan text. Kelber also assumes that "gospel" proclamation was the narration of the life and times of Jesus and that it was being transmitted orally before the writing of the memoirs of the apostles – the initial reference of the books labelled Gospels. His study of orality of the Markan text focuses more on the oral form of the text rather than on an oral gospel that was outside and independent of the Markan text. A sub-topic to the study on orality has been fronted by a section of scholars like Dewey, Rhoads, and Horsley, Draper, and Foley.[44]

Marshall notes, "The problem is that we have so little material – outside the gospels themselves – to reconstruct the early preaching."[45] However, much as the problem of reconstructing the early preaching exists, the fact that there was an oral gospel that was outside and independent of the text is internally and externally evidenced. The sermons in Acts are as early as the day of Pentecost and the early missions of the apostles. Papias also intimates that the apostles preached by word of mouth "caring little for attention to writing books."[46] As such, any interpretation of the Markan text should take cognizance of the fact that it was written in a context where there was an oral gospel that was being proclaimed by Mark and his contemporaries. In any case, whereas texts were localized, the oral gospel was universal. Such a presupposition impacts interpretation of the text.

In summary, without disentangling the labyrinth of the interlocutors that participate in the Markan discourse, it becomes extremely difficult to analyze its flow. Consequently, locating the meaning, genre, and purpose of the Markan text is thereby frustrated. A graphical illustration of the interaction

---

43. Kelber, *Oral and the Written Gospel*, 5.

44. Dewey, "Mark as Aural Narrative," 47; Rhoads, *Reading Mark*, 176–201; Horsley, Draper and Foley, *Performing the Gospel*, 11–15.

45. Marshall, *Luke*, 49.

46. Whitacre, *Patristic Greek Reader*, 232.

of the interlocutors in figure 2 illustrates and puts into perspective the discourse flow.

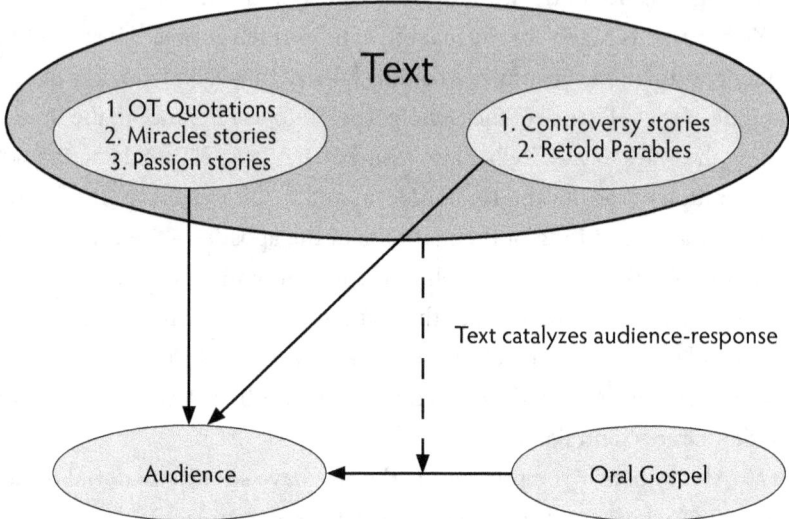

Figure 2. Illustration of Interlocutors in the Markan Text

4.4 Interlocutor Relationships in the Markan Discourse

This section seeks to explain the flow of the Markan discourse. As such, it pairs the interlocutors that are in dialogue within the matrix of the discourse. The aim is to shed light on the nature and impact of the text on audience response towards the oral gospel.

4.4.1 Dialogue between the Audience and the Oral Gospel

The dialogue between Mark's audience and the oral gospel existed long before the introduction of the textual catalyst. The rhetorical situation that is portrayed by the narratives of the controversy between Jesus and the Jewish religious leaders and by the retold parable of the sower portrays an audience that was obdurate and lukewarm in their response to the oral gospel. Therefore, the Markan text is a rhetorical communication that was written to eliminate obduracy of Mark's audience.

The dialogue between Mark's audience and the oral gospel is enhanced and catalyzed by a confluence of two dialogues. The first is between the audience and the text's mimetic world that is portrayed by both the parable of the sower and controversy stories. The second dialogue is between the audience and the rhetorical devices of miracle stories, Old Testament quotations, and the passion story. By extolling the deeds of Jesus, affirming his approval by God, and assigning salvific significance to his death, this dialogue enhances the persona and belief value of Jesus thereby urging the audience to believe in the gospel that was premised on his person and work on the cross.

4.4.2 Dialogue between the Markan Text and the Audience

The prologue of the Markan text introduces its topic of discussion as "Ἀρχὴ τοῦ εὐαγγελίου Ἰησοῦ Χριστοῦ [υἱοῦ θεοῦ]." It therefore draws the attention of the audience to the subject that Mark intends to discuss; that is, the person and salvific episode on which the oral gospel was premised. As such, the text seeks to support the supposition in the introductory phrase that Jesus is the Christ, the Son of God (1:1). The text narrates rhetorical anecdotes that highlight Jesus's persona with a view of impressing upon the implied audience that Jesus, on whose person and work the oral gospel was premised, was indeed the Messiah the Son of God.

Again, by narrating stories of the miracles that God had performed through Jesus, Mark seeks to show that the oral gospel was sanctioned by God. According to John 3:2, no one can perform miracles unless God was with him. Once more, the text highlights the propitiatory nature and salvific significance of the death of Jesus by interpolating the Last Supper and passion narratives and by placing the inauguration of the Last Supper within the context of the Jewish Passover. Thus, by using these rhetorical devices, the Markan text aims at convincing the audience, who were simultaneously hearing the oral gospel, that it was reliable and worthy of their faith.

Application of the Markan text to the secondary audience

Though the Markan text was written to a primary audience in mind, it is applicable in contexts with similar rhetorical situations. The oral and semiotic gospel which was being proclaimed in Mark's milieu continued being proclaimed by word of mouth and through administration of the ordinances of baptism and the Lord's Supper in different geographical locations and historical milieus. The rhetorical devices of the Old Testament quotations, miracle stories, the passion narratives, and the mimetic exemplifiers of the foils in the Markan text and the parable of the sower are rhetorically efficacious in catalyzing its secondary reader's response to the salvific message as much as they did to the primary readers.

Furthermore, as Bitzer has postulated, "Some situations, on the other hand, persist; this is why it is possible to have a body of truly *rhetorical literature* . . . From day to day, year to year, comparable situations occur, prompting comparable responses."[47] Rhetorical situations that are a result of obduracy and lukewarm response to the gospel have a tendency of recurring. As such, they invite the same rhetorical communication as was applicable to the primary audience to eliminate their exigence.

Though Jesus's salvific deeds are not meant to be simulated, his amiable character and grace deeds that are portrayed in the Markan text are mimetic exemplifiers of Christ-like virtues to believers of all ages. Moreover, Jesus's kingdom proclamation (1:14–15) and the salvific message that is represented in the administration of the ordinances of baptism and the Lord's Supper are perpetual proclamations[48] that the Markan text continues to urge and catalyze its readers to respond to.

To quote R. Alan Cole, "In a world where thousands of millions perish for want of Christians to preach the love of God that alone can bring eternal life, and yet where, as well, millions still starve and suffer for want of Christians to show the same love of God in action,"[49] the Markan text's exemplifiers of Jesus Christ's amiable character and grace deeds are an exhortation to Christians of all ages to emulate him. Equally, Mark's mimetic portrait of his audience's rhetorical situation exhorts Christians of all ages to abhor obduracy and lukewarm response to the gospel and to aspire to achieve optimal responsiveness.

---

47. Bitzer, "Rhetorical Situation," 13.

48. This aspect of proclamation has been argued in chapter 2, within section 2.3.4, "Gospel in performance of ordinances."

49. Cole, *Mark*, 47.

4.4.3 Relationship between Rhetorical Situation of the Audience of Jesus and the Rhetorical Situation of the Audience of Mark

The rhetorical situation of Jesus's audience is located in the past of the text. As such it is a passive interlocutor in the matrix of the Markan discourse. However, it is revivified when it is used as a mimetic portrait to mirror the rhetorical situation of Mark's audience.[50] Similarly, both the Galilean and Jerusalem parables are immortalized when they are used to portray and highlight the exigence that prevailed in the rhetorical situation of Mark's audience. The potential affective efficacy upon audience reflection on their rhetorical situation is the factor that spurs the text's perlocutionary effects of urging faith and performance of the oral gospel.

W. S. Vorster illuminates the working of this transaction in his statement:

> In retold form, these stories were used not only for different purposes but also for different messages, depending on new situations. Retelling involves creativity, whether in oral or in written form. It is impossible to tell the "same" story twice. Each telling has its particular context and its unique message. The truth of this statement is confirmed by the retelling of the stories of the Old Testament within the Old Testament, as well as in later Jewish literature. Each time a story or event is retold; it is done for a specific purpose and from a specific point of view. In other words, each account involves creativity. The same applies to oral transmission of history.[51]

Much as Mark's audience were at liberty to interpret Jesus's parable and the teachings embedded therein as reflective of God's kingdom, Vorster's postulation suggests that retold parables were intentioned. They mirror the rhetorical situation of Mark's audience which was in need of change. The Markan text sought to eliminate the exigence in his audience's rhetorical situation through a two-pronged approach.

First, by citing Old Testament Scripture, the Markan text enhanced the belief value of the gospel message by grounding it on his community's faith

---

50. This postulation is argued in chapter 3, section 3.5.
51. Vorster, "Production of the Gospel of Mark," 393.

heritage and by showing that it was sanctioned by God through the miracles that Jesus performed. Such presentation of Jesus's exalted persona enhanced the audience's belief in the gospel that was premised on his person and work on the cross. Second, the Markan text was structured[52] in a rhetorical and contextual framework[53] in which belief was evoked and performance urged. The message was also endowed with rhetorical devices with efficacious speech acts aimed at convincing, convicting, and urging performance of the oral gospel thereby transforming the audience from obdurate to optimally responsive hearers and doers of the oral gospel.

Storytelling as a mode of textual discourse is not unique to Mark. The stories in Genesis provide an apt comparative text.[54] It is arguable that the author of Genesis narrated the stories of creation, flood, and the patriarchs not just to reveal God's workings in history but also to urge Israel to adhere to the covenant stipulations by narrating the consequences of breaching the covenant, as exemplified by Adam, as well as the rewards of fidelity to the covenant, as exemplified by Abraham. Moses's concern seems to have been Israel's obduracy that was shown by their breach of the covenant in backsliding into idol worship (Exod 32:1–8).

Moses used the stories about Adam, Noah, and Abraham as rhetorical devices because of their inherent mimetic and rhetorical efficacy to arouse abhorrence towards Adam's disobedience and admiration towards the obedience of Noah and Abraham thereby urging Israel to believe in God and to keep his covenant. Apparently, this category of writing chooses narratives in which the rhetorical situations of the characters are similar to the rhetorical situation of the author's audience. The choice of the storyline is then structured to produce a mimetic situation that mirrors both the audience's rhetorical situation and its exigence. The rhetorical value of such stories is in their efficacy to evoke conviction to the extent that the writer's own audience are urged to act in order to eliminate the illuminated exigence. In this connection, therefore, the narratives about the patriarchs in Genesis were paraenetic stories addressed to the Exodus pilgrims who had received a similar covenant

---

52. This supposition is argued in chapter 3, section 3.3.
53. This supposition is argued in chapter 3, section 3.4
54. This supposition is argued in chapter 1, sections 1.9.2–1.9.3

and similar promises to the ones received by Adam, Noah, Abraham, and the other patriarchs. As Sailhamer posits:

> Historical narrative is the re-presentation of past events for the purpose of instruction. Two dimensions are always at work in shaping such narratives: (1) the course of the historical event itself and (2) the viewpoint of the author who recounts the events. This dual aspect of historical narratives means that one must look not only at the course of the event in its historical setting but also for the purpose and intention of the author in recounting the event.[55]

The dialogue between the Genesis narrative and Moses's audience is akin to the dialogue between the Markan text and his audience. Delineating and analyzing the nature of the dialogue partners that participate within the matrix of the Genesis discourse – which include the mimetic world of the text, the audience, and the word of the covenant – within the rhetorical situation of obduracy to the covenant stipulations, provides echoes and an interpretative grid to the analysis of the Markan discourse which is similar in these respects.

4.4.4 Relationship between the Markan Text and the Oral Gospel

Mark describes the gospel as about Jesus Christ the Son of God (1:1). This description suggests that its belief value is enhanced by ascertaining that the man Jesus, on whose person and work the oral gospel was premised, was indeed the Christ the Son of God. This work has argued that the Old Testament quotations, the miracle stories, and the passion narratives are used in the text to ascertain that the Jesus of faith was indeed the Christ of the Hebrew Scripture and their eschatological hope. Though the oral gospel is rather latent in the text and that it finds explicit mention only in the beginning of the text as its subject of discussion (1:1), in the local commissioning of the disciples (6:7–12), and in their international commissioning (16:14–18). It is not a passive interlocutor in the matrix of the Markan discourse. Rather, it was actively and progressively dialoguing with the Markan audience. The structure, form, and rhetorical posture of the text suggest that its purpose

---

55. Sailhamer, *Pentateuch as Narrative*, 25.

was to stimulate an unreceptive audience to actively respond in faith to the oral gospel's progressive proclamation.

Since the text's main concern was to urge response to an oral gospel that was being proclaimed to an unresponsive audience by the time of writing the text, then the text acted as a catalyst to the audience's responsiveness to the oral gospel. The text also describes the oral gospel as a portent seed that is planted in the audience. Similarly, the text describes the audience as various types of soils with different levels of sustaining growth of the seeds – the word of God – in the parable of the sower (4:1–12). This description of the audience and the oral gospel using contrasting metaphors of barren versus fertile soils and unproductive versus optimally productive seeds is aimed at provoking the reader to despise the rhetorical situation of barrenness and to aspire for the loftily described norm of fertility and optimal fruitfulness in response to the oral gospel.

4.4.5 Dialogue between the Markan Text, Audience, and Oral Gospel

This study has argued that the stories narrated in the Markan text are used as rhetorical devices to highlight and magnify Jesus's persona. Consequently, they enhanced the belief value in the oral gospel which is premised on Jesus's person and work on the cross. As such, the text acts as a catalyst to its reader's response to the oral gospel. In his discussion on Mark as episodical narratives, Cilliers Breytenbach has described this kind of communication as where "a character is cited directly in her or his speech to another character in the narrative, but where the speech is also directed to the implied reader."[56] This description aptly mirrors the relationship between the Markan text, the audience, and the oral gospel. However, because of the understandable quest for the historical Jesus, most scholars have been more inclined to probe the world of the text.

It is arguable that the purpose of the Markan text was to enlighten Mark's audience on the identity of the historical Jesus or even to record history for posterity. However, the rhetorical and aretalogical shade of the stories narrated suggests that it was written to spur the audience's faith and response to the oral gospel. As internal and external evidence shows, the Markan text may

---

56. Breytenbach, "Gospel of Mark as Episodical," 1–26.

have been written between 50 and 55 CE. Gundry suggests an earlier date in the "fifties or late forties."[57] Thus, Mark's audience were living at a time when a sizeable number of eyewitnesses to the Christ event were still alive and a record of written proof of the Christ event could not have been an urgent need. 1 Corinthians 15:6 records that by the time Paul wrote to the Corinthian church, a good number of the eyewitnesses to the resurrection were still alive.

Therefore, the most likely opinion is that Mark sought to make the oral gospel more believable and to urge faith and obedience to its demands. He accomplished this by embellishing the text with the rhetorical device of Old Testament quotations. Similarly, by clustering the miracle anecdotes in one section of the text, he aimed at overwhelming his readers with the awesome deeds of Jesus on whom the oral gospel was premised. In so doing, he urged a faith response towards the oral gospel.

4.5 Summary

In summary, a delineation of the interlocutors in the Markan discourse shows that the Markan text comprises of a mimetic portrait of the audience's rhetorical situation on one hand and anecdotal rhetorical devices of Old Testament quotations, miracle stories, and passion narratives on the other hand. The mimetic portrait of the audience's rhetorical situation is employed to show the audience's unacceptable obduracy towards the oral gospel. Consequently, it evokes abhorrence of their obduracy and a desire to eliminate it by believing and obeying the gospel.

On the other hand, the rhetorical devices of Old Testament quotations, the miracle stories, and the passion narratives were meant to enhance the believability of the oral gospel by elevating the ethos of Jesus and by showing that the Jesus of faith was indeed the Christ of the Old Testament promises. These rhetorical devices are complimented by clustering the miracle stories, use of foils, and satire to catalyze reader-response to the oral gospel.

---

57. Gundry, *Survey of the New Testament*, 128.

CHAPTER 5

Markan Old Testament Quotations as a Rhetorical Device

5.1 Introduction

This section explores the nature and function of Old Testament quotations in the Markan text. Particularly, the survey is biased towards establishing the nature and function of Old Testament quotations in Mark 1:2–3 and 4:12. These two quotations have been selected because of their strategic importance in addressing the question of the identity of the Jesus of faith (1:2–3) as well as illuminating the rhetorical situation that occasioned the writing of the Markan text (4:12). Whereas Mark 1:2–3 is the narrator's quotation, Mark 4:12 is Jesus's use of excerpts from Isaiah 6:9–10. The purpose of the study is to ascertain whether these quotations are used as rhetorical devices to catalyze audience response to the oral gospel. The exposé also sheds light on the particular influencing thought and ideology of Mark and his audience. The major question that guides this section is: are these Old Testament quotations rhetorical devices and were they used to catalyze audience response to an oral gospel that was being simultaneously proclaimed? The study mainly uses rhetorical criticism method. It will however be complemented with grammatical historical analysis, speech acts theory, and discourse analysis.

5.2 Recent Trends in the Study of Old Testament Quotations in the Markan Text

In his book, *In Search of a Context: The Function of Scripture in Mark's Narrative*, Thomas R. Hatina has done a comprehensive review of the recent trends on the study of Mark's use of Old Testament Scripture. His review has covered the works of scholars from S. Schulz in 1961 to Rikk E. Watts in 1997. His main focus is on works that relied on the discipline of form-critical and redaction-critical approaches.

He notes that Schulz's method has limitations, which result from his stated position that Mark's reasons of using Old Testament quotations was "to give Phi.2:8 a historical framework in which it could function and that Mark used an entire narrative to meet this requirement."[1] On source-oriented approaches, Hatina has reviewed the works of J. Bowman and notes that he sought to establish parallels between Mark and the Old Testament Scriptures. His conclusion is that Bowman was not able to evaluate the evidence for his thesis that Mark was a new Haggadah. In his review of J. D. M. Derrett and W. Roth's work he notes that they sought to establish parallels between Mark and the Old Testament themes. On the work of Dale and Patricia Miller, he notes that they sought to show that "Mark is essentially midrashic and notes their uncritical use of Scripture that ignored explicit references to Scripture."[2] His final review in this section is the work of W. M. Swartley. He notes that Swartley suggested that the arrangement of the Markan material corresponds with the Old Testament tradition which includes the Exodus and the conquest traditions. He faults Swartley for overshadowing and omitting obvious scriptural quotations. Hatina's review on the work of Watts, which he says falls within the purview of his survey, argues that "the motif of the new Exodus in Isaiah provides the best integrative paradigm for reading Mark's gospel as a whole."[3]

In redaction-critical approaches, Hatina has reviewed various works which include U. Mauser, *Christ in the Wilderness*; A. Suhl, *Die Funktion der Alttestamentlichen Zitate und Anspielungen im Markusevangelium*.[4] His

---

1. Hatina, *In Search of a Context*, 11.
2. Hatina, 19.
3. Hatina, 21.
4. U. Mauser, *Christ in the Wilderness*; A. Suhl, *Die Funktion der Alttestamentlichen Zitate und Anspielungen im Markusevangelium*. Other works reviewed are H. Anderson, *The Old*

conclusions are that "despite the recent direction toward multiple methods, no study of Scripture has yet incorporated a narrative critical approach whereby the interpretive paradigm is based on Mark's own narrative program or the overarching aim of the plot."[5] These reviews were done to establish the then existing research gap in order to identify an entry point in the Markan research. In view of Hatina's comprehensive reviews, this chapter will review his work and that of Rikk E. Watts.

5.2.1 Review of Rikk E. Watts

In his book *Isaiah's New Exodus and Mark*, Watts has formulated a hermeneutical grid for interpreting the Markan text following Jacques Ellul's and Paul Ricoeur's view on how "ideology facilitates social cohesion."[6] He notes that "this is effected particularly through ideology's *revivification* of the group's founding moment such that it becomes A) the shared and almost unconscious basis of the group's self-definition and B) its interpretative framework for understanding the world."[7] He supposes that the foundational episode of a community provides a grid on which future episodes can be interpreted. As such, he bases his hermeneutical schema of Mark's Old Testament quotations on the supposition that they can be interpreted by understanding Israel's founding moment, which would be its "interpretative framework for understanding the world."[8] Another supposition is that Mark's community shares some commonality with Israel.

Watts's grid can be used aptly to explain the impact of how God dealt with Israel in the past as an interpretative grid of their present and how it shaped their prophetic future and eschatology. However, overstretching the grid to interpret biographical narratives of Jesus, as they are used as a rhetorical communication to address the rhetorical situation of a mixed gentile and Jewish Christian audience, is an over-interpretation. The challenge in Watts's supposition is that it seeks to use an interpretative grid that is based on God's

---

Testament in Mark's Gospel; H. C. Kee, *The Function of Scriptural Quotations and Allusions in Mark*; W. S. Vorster, *The Function of the Use of the Old Testament in Mark*; Douglas J. Moo, *The Old Testament in the Gospel Passion Narratives*; and Morna D. Hooker, "Mark."

    5. Hatina, *In Search of a Context*, 48.
    6. Watts, *Isaiah's New Exodus and Mark*, 33.
    7. Watts, 33.
    8. Watts, 33.

dealings with Israel as an ideological community, as a hermeneutical grid to interpret narratives on the life and times of a rational being (Jesus) and their impact in shaping the Jesus movement.

5.2.2 Review of Thomas R. Hatina

In his *In Search of a Context*, Hatina has argued that the hermeneutical key to understanding the Old Testament quotations and allusions "is found in the ideological point of view shared by Jesus and the narrator that the kingdom of God has come in and through Jesus . . . And it is within this framework that quotations and allusions participate."[9] Hatina's study is based on what he describes as "incorporation of an interpretive paradigm based on Mark's own narrative program within the context of his story world."[10] He further contends that

> the historical component cannot be overlooked in any investigation of the function of Scripture in Mark . . . Historical inquiry is indispensable for understanding Mark's genre, the language in which it is written, and the ideological viewpoint of Jesus and the narrator. Without regard for the historical, the conflicts in the story, to which the quotations and allusions make a contribution, lose their impact.[11]

Hatina's argument is that Old Testament Scripture quotations in the Markan text serve "not only to introduce the Baptist but more importantly they function as an introduction to and preparation for the coming of Jesus, Messiah, Son of God who comes to set up God's kingdom."[12] Second, he says that "they make important contributions to the characterization of Jesus and to the correctness of his ideological point of view."[13] Third, they were used to describe the Markan community by differentiating the insiders and outsiders and "on one hand to undermine the authority of the religious leaders and on the other to establish a hermeneutic that is rooted in the law of love, which

---

9. Hatina, *In Search of a Context*, 3.
10. Hatina, 375.
11. Hatina, 375.
12. Hatina, 377.
13. Hatina, 377.

Jesus establishes in 12.29-31."[14] While this work partly agrees with Hatina on this point, it notes that narrative study can be used to reconstruct the rhetorical situation that occasioned the writing of the text. Thus, it is possible to reconstruct the purpose of the text which includes the purpose of the Old Testament quotations in Mark.

The stories in Mark and indeed the use of Old Testament quotations are not used just to narrate a historical situation. They constitute a rhetorical communication. As such, a study of Mark's use of Old Testament Scripture would yield better results if it uses rhetorical criticism method. This study has argued that Mark used Old Testament quotations to eliminate his audience's obduracy towards the oral gospel. On the one hand, he sought to create a positive appeal towards Jesus, on whom the gospel was premised, by showing that he was indeed the Messiah who was promised in Scripture.

5.3 Ideological and Religious Point of View

This section analyzes the hermeneutical grid through which Mark and by extension his primary audience interpreted the Christ event in light of the Old Testament quotations that anticipated it. The aim is to shed light on how biographical episodes about Jesus were used in the Markan text and how they were understood by Mark's audience. While social theory indeed explains how social identity is fostered, it may not be adequate in explaining biographical and community events that are divinely controlled. Hagiography and prophecy fall within the ambit of literature that is concerned with events that are divinely ordered. Therefore, they cannot be interpreted using the same interpretive grid as issues that occur through rational choices, natural, and social forces.

The episodes and events narrated in the Markan text and the prophetic words that anticipated them are under divine province and providence. They are better authenticated by comparing them with their scriptural precedents, prophecies, and the consequent eschatological expectations. Against Watts's proposition, Mark is not explaining[15] the present but affirming the salvific episode in order to catalyze audience response to the salvific message. He

---

14. Hatina, 377.
15. Watts, *Isaiah's New Exodus and Mark*, 34.

aims to show that the salvific episode,[16] on which the message of salvation is premised, is supported by the community's scripture precedents, prophecies, and the consequent eschatological expectations.

Hatina proposes an interpretative perspective that downplays the one suggested by historical critics. That is, Jesus and Mark's shared ideology that the kingdom has come is supplied by both the historical and religious context of their time. However, Jesus and Mark's ideologies are not conceived in a vacuum. They are part of the community's hopes and aspirations that were supplied by the then Scripture and the religious context. To Jesus and Mark, the prevailing ideology was that the kingdom of God was overthrowing both the devil's kingdom and the hypocritical religious disposition of the Pharisees, scribes, and Sadducees. However, to the Jewish religious leaders, the eschatological kingdom was to "overthrow the Roman Empire and establish the rule of Jehovah."[17] It is therefore limiting to overlook the religious and historical contexts per se, as Hatina has suggested.

This study analyzes the use of Old Testament quotations in Mark 1:2–3 and 4:12. It is based on the supposition that the episodic narratives in the text are not just a mere record of the episodes within the Christ event but, rather, a rhetorical communication. As such, rhetorical criticism has been employed to analyze the function of Old Testament quotations in the overarching purpose of the text. Whereas the ideological schema illumines the scriptural precedent, prophetic, and eschatological matrix that inform the worldview through which the salvific episode was interpreted, the socio-religious context illumines the rhetorical situation that occasioned the writing of the text. As such, interpretation of the episodes within the Christ event rests on a clear understanding of the ideological schema through which the salvific episode was interpreted and the socio-religious context in which the text was written. In addition to interpreting the Christ event as a fulfilment of the Old Testament prophecy, the study also shows that the Christ event accords with the ideological schema supplied by Scripture, prophecy, and eschatological hope of the community.

---

16. The salvific episode includes God's fulfillment of the promise to establish his kingdom, the Christ event plus the eschatological hope that it portends.

17. Garland, *Mark*, 21.

Although the works of Jesus were divinely enabled, they were largely occasioned and shaped by the context in which they occurred. Jesus's life and ministry happened within a context in which different Jewish sects were competing for recognition as the bona fide custodians of the community's faith. His major antagonists in the Markan text were the Pharisees (Mark 3:6), the scribes (Mark 3:22), the Sadducees (Mark 12:18), and the teachers of the law (Mark 2:16). Their contentions with Jesus concerning religious matters suggest that, together, they viewed Jesus as an intruder and imposter to the messianic role. As such, major controversies with these groups were inevitable. Their obtuseness to the word of God and opposition to Jesus were the rhetorical situations that prompted Jesus to tell the parable of the sower (Mark 4:1–12) and the parable of the wicked tenants (Mark 12:1–11). As such, knowledge of the socio-religious context is an invaluable necessity to interpretation of the text. It helps the interpreter discriminate between the different hermeneutical positions that compete for consideration.

5.4 Analysis of Old Testament Quotations in Mark 1:2–3

Having lived in a Scripture-centered community, Scripture quotations and allusions were part of the speech convention of both Jesus's and Mark's milieu. This supposition is supported by the many Old Testament allusions in the New Testament. As such, in analyzing Scripture quotations in the Markan text, a word-for-word quotation will be considered to be suggesting a carryover of meaning from the Old Testament *vorlage* (original) from which the quotation is sourced while an allusion will be considered to be drawing thoughts from the rich Jewish religious heritage to communicate either Jesus's or Mark's point of view.

G. K. Beale says that:

> Some of the presuppositions that underlie the New Testament writers' interpretation of the Old Testament are that the age of eschatological fulfillment has come in Christ and as a consequence, the later parts of biblical history function as the broader context for interpreting earlier parts because they all

have the same, ultimate divine author who inspires the various human authors.[18]

He further posits, "The broad redemptive-historical perspective of these assumptions was the dominant framework within which Jesus and his followers thought, serving as an ever present heuristic guide to the OT."[19] This is a major supposition that should be kept in view in the study of use of Old Testament Scriptures in the New Testament.

The syntagmatic positioning of the composite citation in Mark 1:2–3 suggests that its rhetorical value was to support Mark's assertion in Mark 1:1 that Jesus is the Christ, the Son of God. It shows that the assertion conforms to the precedents and promises in the Torah and the Prophets. Stamps opines, "In general, the one distinction which many commentators note with regard to Christian rhetoric is its appeal to authority. This authority has been variously defined: God, Jesus, Holy Spirit, Hebrew Scripture, Christian tradition."[20] Particularly, the Torah and the Prophets are very reliable faith documents to the Jews and Christians. Consequently, they serve as a heuristic guide in validating occurrences that claimed place in shaping the community's faith and praxis. As such, highlighting the Christ event as the fulfillment of the Hebrew Scriptures had the effect of enhancing the belief value in the oral gospel that was premised on the person and work of Jesus Christ. Being a product of the community's Scripture, Old Testament quotations evoke belief, illocutionary act of calling the audience to respond in faith to the oral gospel, and perlocutionary effect of urging obedience to the gospel's demands.

5.4.1 Exegetical Analysis of Mark 1:1–3

Mark 1:1 introduces the subject of discussion in the Markan text with the phrase Ἀρχὴ τοῦ εὐαγγελίου Ἰησοῦ Χριστοῦ [υἱοῦ θεοῦ]. Being a phrase, the period that closes this verse is anomalous. The KJV has rightly replaced it with a semicolon. As such, it finds its meaning in the larger context of Mark 1:1–15 and its external context which includes the referent of the term τὸ εὐαγγέλιον in Mark's milieu. Since by the time of writing the text τὸ εὐαγγέλιον

---

18. Beale, *Handbook on the New Testament*, 96–97.
19. Beale, 98.
20. Stamps, "Rhetoric," 957.

referenced the oral gospel that Mark and his contemporaries were preaching,[21] then undoubtedly, the oral gospel that is referenced in Mark 1:1 was outside and independent of the Markan text. Arguably, this verse serves two purposes. First, it describes and sets the parameters of the subject under discussion in the Markan text as the episodes on which the gospel of Jesus Christ was premised. Second, it calls the audience to reminisce on the nature and significance of the salvific episode in order to spur a faith response to the salvific message.

Primarily, Ἀρχὴ suggests that Mark intends to locate and explain the episode or episodes on which the oral gospel was premised. The objective genitive Ἰησοῦ Χριστοῦ serves to identify the gospel as about Jesus and to identify Jesus as the Christ. The Old Testament quotation in Mark 1:2–3 and the subsequent narrative about the forerunning ministry of John the Baptist have been used to validate the assertion, in the genitive Ἰησοῦ Χριστοῦ, that Jesus is the Christ. In other words, the purpose was to demonstrate that the Jesus of history and Christian faith was the Christ of the Old Testament prophecy and promise. As such, the phrase is a prolegomenon setting the bounds and purpose for the entire Markan text.

Gundry intimates that "since Καθὼς in v. 2 defines 'beginning of the good news of Jesus Christ' as in accordance with the OT quotations in vv 2b–3, the phrase covers only those verses whose subject matter corresponds to OT quotations, i.e. vv 4–8, which tell how John the Baptizer's activities correspond to the quoted passages."[22] He sees the "beginning of the gospel" as the preaching ministry of John. However, though Gundry has rightly captured the fact that the word σου in verse 2b (ἰδοὺ ἀποστέλλω τὸν ἄγγελόν μου πρὸ προσώπου σου, ὃς κατασκευάσει τὴν ὁδόν σου) in the composite quotation refers to Jesus and not John, he has overlooked its implication that, whereas verse 2b describes the ministry of Jesus of emancipating and leading the captives in the similitude of the Exodus experience, verses 3–8 suggests that the ministry of Jesus is authenticated by an Old Testament Scripture which is fulfilled in yet another historical episode – John's ministry. Mark notes that "all held that

---

21. From the time of Jesus (Mark 1:14–15, 6:12) and as witnessed by the Acts of the apostles, the apostles were proclaiming the gospel orally. Later, administration of the Lord's Supper (1 Cor 11:26) was incorporated as a form of gospel proclamation.

22. Gundry, *Mark*, 31.

John really was a prophet" (Mark 11:32 ESV). Therefore identifying John as Jesus's forerunner identifies Jesus as the God whose highway John was making straight according to Isaiah 40:3. As such, whereas verses 4–8 shows the role of John as the messenger of verses 2b–3, verses 9–15 positions Jesus as the one whom prophecy had declared will be forerun by John according to verse 2b. Therefore, the subject of the composite quotation is not John but Jesus.

A plausible possibility that should also be brought to bear on the argument is that the narration about the gospel of Jesus begins in Mark 1:1 and not 1:15.[23] Reading 1:1–15 as a unified section shows that together with grounding the gospel on a scripturally supported historical episode, Mark 1:1–15 is also aimed at showing that indeed Jesus, who appeared in Galilee preaching τὸ εὐαγγέλιον τοῦ θεοῦ (1:14), is indeed the Christ who was promised and anticipated by the Torah and Prophets to which proof is offered in 1:2–13. Therefore, the narrative on John's ministry, whose climax is the baptism of Jesus, is used to identify Jesus as the Christ who, according to Scripture, was to be forerun by one with religious credentials similar to John's. Even the fulfilled prophecy concerning John in 1:3 was a further proof that, indeed, the prophecy in 1:2 had been fulfilled in the coming of Jesus.

Furthermore, the word "Καθὼς" (according as) in verse 2, which is a subordinate comparative clause[24] relates Ἀρχὴ τοῦ εὐαγγελίου Ἰησοῦ Χριστοῦ [υἱοῦ θεοῦ] to the Christ event which had been fulfilled according to Scripture and on which Mark was premising the oral gospel. Kilpatrick says, "Where καθὼς introduces a following quotation in the New Testament it invariably follows its main clause . . . Some editors break this rule in their punctuation of Mark 1:1ff., but there is no need to do this."[25] As such, Καθὼς calls attention to the comparison between the Jesus who was baptized by John with the Christ who was referenced as σου in the sentence, ἰδοὺ ἀποστέλλω τὸν ἄγγελόν μου πρὸ προσώπου σου, ὃς κατασκευάσει τὴν ὁδόν σου (1:2b) and on whom the gospel was premised (1:1). Gundry's assertion that,

---

23. The introduction of John's ministry vv. 2–9 was to identify the historical Jesus as the Christ of Scripture. The consequential benefit of affirming the coming of Jesus as in accordance to prophetic utterance (vv. 2–15) is in authenticating the episodes that constitute the beginning of the gospel of Jesus Christ (1:1). Therefore, vv. 2–15, serves to show that the coming of Jesus Christ was inaugural to the salvific episode which was the basis of the gospel proclamation.

24. Wallace, *Greek Grammar*, 663.

25. Kilpatrick, *Principles and Practice*, 355.

Since Καθὼς in v.2a defines "beginning of the good news of Jesus Christ" as in accordance with the OT quotations in vv 2b–3, the phrase covers only those verses whose subject matter corresponds to OT quotations, i.e. vv 4–8, which tell how John the Baptizer's activities correspond to the quoted passages,[26] overlooks the fact that the composite quotations describe the person and ministry of Jesus by use of the forerunning ministry of John. As such, the oral gospel is premised[27] on a scripturally supported Christ event which includes episodes recorded in the entire text, which were in the historical past of the Markan text, and not just the "Baptizer's activities."[28]

Other Scripture texts where Ἀρχὴ is similarly used are Genesis 1:1 and John 1:1. In these two references, the main concern of the authors is to ground both creation (Gen 1:1) and Jesus, the light of the world (John 1:1), on God. Use of Ἀρχὴ in the Markan text shows Mark's reliance on Genesis for his style. Moreover, this notion is supported by the fact that he is grounding the oral gospel about Jesus Christ on Old Testament Scripture and in God. Supporting John's ministry by Old Testament Scripture quotation is in essence founding Jesus's ministry on the same Scriptures. As such, Gundry's statement that "to extend the beginning by including further verses, and perhaps the whole of Mark, would violate the definition of the beginning by the Καθὼς clause,"[29] should take into account the consideration that Jesus and indeed the entire Christ event is the subject of the composite quotation. In other words, more than being an introduction to John's ministry, verses 4–13 serves to identify Jesus, on whose work the oral gospel was premised, as the Christ of Old Testament Scripture.

The gospel that is referred to in 1:1 is qualified as that of Jesus Christ by use of the genitive Ἰησοῦ Χριστοῦ [υἱοῦ θεοῦ]. Some manuscripts do not include the genitive of relationship υἱοῦ θεοῦ.[30] The geographical distribution

---

26. Gundry, *Mark*, 31.

27. The major event in the Christ event is the passion. It was a salvific and propitious episode. The gospel message is an announcement of the fulfilment of the Christ event and its salvific significance for those who put their faith in Jesus Christ. As such, the oral gospel is premised on the salvific episode.

28. Gundry, *Mark*, 31.

29. Gundry, 31.

30. Aland et al., *Greek New Testament*, 117.

of the manuscripts that include [υἱοῦ θεοῦ] is very vast and early.³¹ As such, it can be taken to be part of the phrase. Nonetheless, its inclusion or exclusion does not affect the general message and meaning of the phrase. It constitutes a theological interpretation of who Jesus Christ is. Rhetorically though, relating Jesus Christ with God also embeds the phrase with the illocutionary act of convincing and convicting the audience concerning the divinity of Jesus Christ as well as the perlocutionary effect of urging them to respond positively to the oral gospel.

The phrase Ἀρχὴ τοῦ εὐαγγελίου Ἰησοῦ Χριστοῦ [υἱοῦ θεοῦ] in Mark 1:1 has been used to introduce the subject of the Markan text – the beginning of the gospel. Richard Schneck, who holds an alternative view, avers that "the opening verse announces the central figure of the story; Jesus the Messiah, the Son of God."³² However, much as Jesus Christ plays a central role in the treatise, the Markan Jesus and all his works have been narrated to qualify and validate the oral gospel by founding it on the high pedestal of God, Jesus's exalted ethos, and scriptural promises. As such, though the inevitability of mentioning Jesus in any mention of the gospel should be noted, the purpose of the opening verse should be grammatically understood as a very apt introduction to the subject of the text: a discussion on the episode or episodes on which the oral gospel is premised.

According to France, "The genitive Ἰησοῦ Χριστοῦ may, in theory, be read either as subjective genitive ('the good news proclaimed by Jesus Christ') or objective ('the good news about Jesus Christ')."³³ He supports his argument by saying,

> There are no other uses in Mark of the genitive after εὐαγγέλιον; the noun used absolutely refers in three cases to a message to be believed (1:15) or proclaimed (13:10; 14:9) rather than to the act of proclamation, though in the remaining two uses (8:35; 10:29) either sense is probable. It is therefore probable and more natural to read the genitive after εὐαγγέλιον here as objective

---

31. Aland et al., 117.
32. Schneck, *Isaiah in the Gospel of Mark*, 28.
33. France, *Gospel of Mark*, 53. However, Mark did not intend any ambiguity. As has been argued, the gospel of God subsisted in the gospel of Jesus Christ which was the gospel by the church. As such, Ἰησοῦ Χριστοῦ was categorically an objective genitive.

(the gospel *about* Jesus Christ), and this is the more normal usage in the rest of the NT (though note to the contrary Rom. 2:26; 16:25, etc., and, denoting the *recipients* of the gospel, Gal. 2:7). But vv.14–15 will make it clear that the εὐαγγέλιον is in fact *preached* by Jesus as well. Whatever the dictates of syntactical pedantry, I think it likely, that Mark would have approved, and may well have intended, the *double entendre* which the genitive construction allows.[34]

Whereas France's argument may in theory be valid, textual evidence[35] shows that the gospel about Jesus (Mark 1:1) is a secondary development from the rudimentary gospel of God (1:14) which was the gospel that was being proclaimed by Jesus Christ. By the time of writing the text, the gospel by Jesus Christ (1:14) subsisted in the gospel about Jesus Christ (1:1). However, France's postulation that, "It is therefore probable and more natural to read the genitive after εὐαγγέλιον here as objective (the gospel *about* Jesus Christ), and this is the more normal usage in the rest of the NT"[36] cannot be faulted.

The connection of the noun Ἀρχὴ with the forerunning ministry of John the Baptist by use of a comparative clause, Καθὼς, shows that John's ministry was part of the eschatological events that were to usher in the messianic kingdom. Funk identifies the story about John's ministry as,

> The story of how the gospel concerning Jesus Christ took its rise and begins, so far as narrated events are involved, with the appearance of John the Baptist . . . Nevertheless, the prediction of Isaiah functions to introduce the first event of Mark's narrative, and it gives the narrative temporal depth by linking it to a memorable past.[37]

Funk's statement suggests that John's ministry is recorded as the first event in a text that is considered to be the content of the gospel. However, as has been argued in this study, the narrative on John's forerunning ministry was primarily used to identify Jesus as the Christ.

---

34. France, 53.
35. This point has been argued in chapter 4, section 4.3.3.
36. France, *Gospel of Mark*, 53.
37. Funk, *Poetics of Biblical Narrative*, 218.

Having qualified the gospel as being about Jesus Christ (1:1), indicating that Jesus is the one who inaugurated the proclamation of the gospel (1:14–15), and having used the echoes of Genesis 1:1, Mark showed that he, like Moses, who had grounded creation on God, was premising the preaching of the gospel on a scripturally supported and God-sanctioned Christ event (1:2–16:20). Whereas Mark 1:2–15 shows that the oral gospel was founded on a scripturally supported episode, Mark 1:16–16:8 shows that it was God sanctioned. In other words, by embellishing his text with rhetorical devices of Old Testament quotations (1:2–3), Mark is asserting that Jesus's was the Messiah and Son of God in accordance with prophecy in his community's scriptural heritage. Similarly, by narrating anecdotes of the mighty miracles that Jesus had performed and by affirming that God resurrected him from the dead (1:16–16:8), Mark is in effect establishing that Jesus's earthly ministry was sanctioned by God. One of the signs that a man was sent by God was performance of signs and wonders (John 3:2). Through narration of Jesus's miracle stories, Mark aptly demonstrated that Jesus was a man sent from God and as such, the gospel that was premised on his work on the cross was authentic and worthy of belief.

The subordinate comparative clause Καθὼς in the sentence Καθὼς γέγραπται ἐν τῷ Ἠσαΐα τῷ προφήτῃ· ἰδοὺ ἀποστέλλω τὸν ἄγγελόν μου πρὸ προσώπου σου, ὃς κατασκευάσει τὴν ὁδόν σου connects Mark 1:1 to predictive Scriptures that support its claims that Jesus, on whom the gospel is premised, is the Christ, the Son of God. Specifically, καθὼς serves to show that the salvific episode, on which the oral gospel was premised, happened in accordance to the community's predictive Scripture. καθὼς also shows that the narrative in the ensuing text is foundational to the gospel referenced in Mark 1:1.

Καθὼς is better interpreted as "according as."[38] Schneck interprets Καθὼς as "in conformity with"[39] which also carries an accurate description of the comparison between Mark 1:1 and Mark 1:2–3. Καθὼς makes more sense when it is connected to Ἀρχὴ in Mark 1:1 since Ἀρχὴ is the subject in the phrase Ἀρχὴ τοῦ εὐαγγελίου Ἰησοῦ Χριστοῦ [υἱοῦ θεοῦ]. Mark would have as well begun the verse by the words, "The gospel of Jesus Christ begun just as

---

38. Thayer, *Thayer's Greek-English Lexicon*, 314. This reading is also supported by Bagster, *Analytical Greek Lexicon*, 208.

39. Schneck, *Isaiah in the Gospel of Mark*, 31.

it is written . . ." Use of γέγραπται, a perfect passive, communicates the fact that the fulfilment of the salvific episode was anticipated in Scripture and that it had happened just as it was envisaged.

Observably, σου in προσώπου σου and σου in τὴν ὁδόν σου are connected by καθώς to refer to Ἰησοῦς χριστός. Mark sees God's intervention to lead his people in Exodus 23:20 as a precedent for future interventions. He therefore borrows words from Exodus 23:20 to describe John's forerunning work to Jesus's ministry of leading humanity in his redemptive Exodus from sin. The subject of the gospel referenced in 1:1 is therefore Ἰησοῦς χριστός. The Old Testament quotations concerning John and the supporting narrative about his ministry are meant to support the main subject of the oral gospel – Ἰησοῦς χριστός. Thus, both the Old Testament citations concerning John and the narrative about his work of preaching and baptizing Jesus are used to extol and validate the salvific ministry of Jesus. Extolling and validating the ministry of Jesus consequently grounds the oral gospel on a historical and scripturally supported episode thus mitigating the gospel's demand for a faith response.

ἰδοὺ ἀποστέλλω τὸν ἄγγελόν μου πρὸ προσώπου σου, ὃς κατασκευάσει τὴν ὁδόν σου· is an amalgam of Exodus 23:20 and Malachi 3:1. ἰδοὺ (הִנֵּה) in Exodus is covenantal in that it points the audience to the reason why they are obligated to obey the instructions in verses 21–33. Similarly, Mark is calling his audience to respond to the gospel referenced in Mark 1:1. It is similar, in purpose, to the word of God in Exodus 23:20. However, unlike in Exodus where the messenger is sent to go before the people of Israel, in Malachi, the messenger is sent to go before the sender. Malachi combines the subject of Exodus 23:20 and the indirect object to be one person. Observably, Mark has interpreted the "I" and "me" in Malachi as Jesus Christ. His interpretation shows his theological stance that Jesus Christ is indeed God. Graphically, he is showing that God, in Jesus, is leading the captivity in a New Exodus, while John is shown to have heralded his coming.

Καθὼς γέγραπται (as is written) in the New Testament texts is equivalent to כֹּה אָמַר אֲדֹנָי יְהֹוִה (thus says the Lord God) or even וְעַתָּה דִּבֶּר יְהוָה לֵאמֹר "But now the LORD has spoken saying . . .," (Isa 16:14) in reference to prophetic utterance in the Old Testament. In Exodus 4:22, God instructed Moses to use the phrase כֹּה אָמַר אֲדֹנָי יְהֹוִה as an identifying formula of his utterance so that the children of Israel may believe that it is God who had sent him to deliver them from the Egyptian bondage. During their stay in Canaan, the saying was adopted by the prophets as an identification formula for God's utterances through their various oracles. It absolved the prophets from the responsibility of the utterance and placed it solely on God. Its rhetorical significance was to load prophetic utterance with believability and conviction by imbuing it with illocutionary efficacy that is conferred by the audience's faith in God. This faith is prior, parallel and independent of the prophetic utterance. Speech acts in biblical speech have their efficacy rested in God who is believed to have inspired Scripture.

The Shift from כֹּה אָמַר אֲדֹנָי יְהוִה to καθὼς γέγραπται expresses the shift in mode of divine communication from oral speech to written text. Vanhoozer has rightly labelled this change as a shift from "Speech Acts to Scripture Acts."[40] The shift reflects different modes of divine communication. At other times, it suggests a shift of addressee from the primary to the secondary audience of the Torah, Prophets, and writings. However, there is no change in their rhetorical value which is to convince and convict both the primary and secondary audience concerning the truth value of the proposition in God's utterance.

Particularly, in its formative stages, the truth value and efficacy of the gospel of Jesus Christ lay in the gospel's conformity with the inherited faith of the Markan community. Quoting portions of the inherited canon of Scripture was meant to anchor the truth value of the oral gospel on an already established faith standard. As such, Old Testament quotations act as a rhetorical device to catalyze reader-response to the oral gospel. Stamps avers, "Generally, argumentation included citing respected authorities, authoritative writings and presentation of facts from life."[41] The other reason for using the citation formula is to endow the text with illocutionary acts that draw their efficacy from the audience's faith in God's sovereign stature and his divine ability to bestow new statuses to readers through the text's divine pronouncements. Vanhoozer aptly explains the power of divine pronouncements in stating that "the divine speech-acts, though humbly clothed *in human language forms* are nevertheless powerful enough to liberate the captive, empower the weak, fill the empty and sustain the suffering."[42]

---

40. Vanhoozer, *First Theology*, 159.
41. Stamps, "Rhetoric," 956.
42. Vanhoozer, *First Theology*, 157. Emphasis added.

Therefore, Mark's use of καθὼς γέγραπται is similar to the usage of כֹּה אָמַר אֲדֹנָי יְהֹוִה in the Torah and Prophets. The Qumran community who may have been contemporaries of Mark also used this identification formula in their varied communications. Manuscript 1QS 5:17, 8:13–14, CD 7:19[43] has used the formula כאשר כתוב which "corresponds to καθὼς γέγραπται (Mark 1:2a)."[44] Mark's use of this identification formula also serves in calling the audience to pay attention to the message being communicated. It was also a call, to the readers, to faith in the subject of his treatise – the gospel of Jesus Christ the Son of God. As such, the phrase καθὼς γέγραπται should not be understood in its general use in the Greek language but as carrying the force of its Hebrew cognate כֹּה אָמַר אֲדֹנָי יְהֹוִה. It also shows that the oral gospel was sanctioned by God and was in accord with the inherited canon of Scripture that alone had been accepted as the standard of faith and practice.

Old Testament quotations in the Markan text show Mark's familiarity with the Old Testament Scripture. For example, Mark 1:2b, ἰδοὺ ἀποστέλλω τὸν ἄγγελόν μου πρὸ προσώπου σου, ὃς κατασκευάσει τὴν ὁδόν σου is a quotation from Exodus 23:20 and Malachi 3:1. The Exodus LXX text reads καὶ ἰδοὺ ἐγὼ ἀποστέλλω τὸν ἄγγελόν μου πρὸ προσώπου σου. In the MT it reads הִנֵּה אָנֹכִי שֹׁלֵחַ מַלְאָךְ לְפָנֶיךָ. These two sentences agree word for word. It is more likely that though Mark was familiar with the Hebrew text, he used the translation in the LXX for his quotation.

Malachi 3:1 in the LXX on the other hand reads ἰδοὺ ἐγὼ ἐξαποστέλλω τὸν ἄγγελόν μου καὶ ἐπιβλέψεται ὁδὸν πρὸ προσώπου μου. The MT reads הִנְנִי שֹׁלֵחַ מַלְאָכִי וּפִנָּה־דֶרֶךְ לְפָנָי. Mark's rendition agrees more with the MT than the LXX. The translator of the Malachi quotation to Greek may also have borrowed the word ἐπιβλέψεται from the "qal reading of פָּנָה which denotes 'looking' or 'turning back.'"[45] However, it is better understood in its *pi'el* form in which case, it is a perfect third person masculine singular meaning to make clear. Mark may have compared the two and found the *pi'el* form in the MT as the one that better represents his position. This supports the notion that he was not interpreting the Old Testament Scripture in their contexts but the

---

43. Donahue and Harrington, *Gospel of Mark*, 60; this information is also available in Burrows, *Dead Sea Scrolls*, fascicle 2, plate viii.

44. Schneck, *Isaiah in the Gospel of Mark*, 33.

45. Hatina, *In Search of a Context*, 145. France, "Gospel of Mark," 64, adds that the choice depends on reading the verb as *qal* instead of *piel*.

Christ event in light of precedents and prophecy in Scripture. Donald English supports this view in his statement that, "Mark is not too tied to the literal text of the Old Testament as we know it . . . Even the received Scriptures, it seems, were being seen in a new light because of the coming of Jesus."[46]

Exodus 23:20 refers to a promise by God to send an angel to lead Israel on their way to the promised land. Malachi's use of the words of an already fulfilled episode to describe a future episode shows that his oracle envisioned a future Exodus in the similitude of the Egyptian Exodus – that is, a fuller and complete emancipation of God's people from the successive and oppressive colonizing Empires. He must have been privy to Isaiah's oracle which looked forward to a return of Israel from exile as recorded in Isaiah 40:1–3. It is arguable that Malachi did not consider the Isaianic second Exodus to have been fully realized by the return of the exiles from Babylon. Therefore, it was in order for him to await a fuller realization of the emancipation prophesied by Isaiah. Mark's use of the MT rendering of Malachi 3:1 to describe the beginning of the gospel suggests that he saw the redemption through the preaching of the gospel as the new exodus envisaged by Malachi, but this time around, it was an exodus of people being delivered from Satan's bondage in sin. As such, the exodus from Egypt was seen as a type of the messianic deliverance of his people from the bondage of sin. No wonder Matthew quotes the Angel telling Joseph, "She [Mary] will bear a son, and you shall call his name Jesus, for he will save his people from their sins" (Matt 1:21 ESV).

A comparative study of the citation of Exodus 23:20 and Malachi 3:1 in Mark 1:2–3 shows that unlike Matthew and Luke who were keen on highlighting John's ministry, Mark was not just concerned with narrating John's forerunning ministry. Rather, he was using an episode that was considered to be axiomatic to support his statement that Jesus is the Christ, the Son of God. That is, Mark used the story about the forerunning ministry of John the Baptist to show that Jesus, on whose work the oral gospel was premised, is indeed the Christ whom Scripture affirms would be forerun by one with credentials similar to John's. Consequently, the phrase καθὼς γέγραπται shows that the Old Testament quotations were used to validate the oral gospel about Jesus Christ. He was telling his audience that the salvific episode, whose salvific significance was being proclaimed as the gospel, conforms to its type in the

---

46. English, *Message of Mark*, 29.

Torah and to its prophetic portrait in both Isaiah and Malachi. Thus, all the episodes narrated in the Markan text were purposely used to validate Mark's thesis that the episodes on which the gospel of Jesus Christ was premised took place in conformity with the promises in the Torah and the Prophetic predictions and as such, the gospel was worthy to be believed and obeyed.

Mark 1:3, φωνὴ βοῶντος ἐν τῇ ἐρήμῳ· ἑτοιμάσατε τὴν ὁδὸν κυρίου, εὐθείας ποιεῖτε τὰς τρίβους αὐτοῦ, is a quotation from Isaiah 40:3. In its LXX rendering, it reads: φωνὴ βοῶντος ἐν τῇ ἐρήμῳ ἑτοιμάσατε τὴν ὁδὸν κυρίου εὐθείας ποιεῖτε τὰς τρίβους τοῦ θεοῦ ἡμῶν. In its MT rendering, it reads קוֹל קוֹרֵא בַּמִּדְבָּר פַּנּוּ דֶּרֶךְ יְהוָה יַשְּׁרוּ בָּעֲרָבָה מְסִלָּה לֵאלֹהֵינוּ. The LXX and the MT agree almost word for word. Mark's rendering agrees with both the LXX and the MT almost to a word. He interprets Jesus as the God referred to as θεοῦ ἡμῶν in the LXX and אלֹהֵינוּ in the MT. Use of Old Testament quotations to validate his claims suggests that Mark was addressing an audience to whom the Old Testament was authoritative Scripture.

Exodus 23:20 is programmatic to understanding the Old Testament faith corpus. Similarly, it is programmatic to studying the use of Old Testament quotations in Mark 1:2–3. God spoke the words in this text to the children of Israel during their sojourn after inaugurating the Mosaic covenant. Thereafter, as Isaiah 40:3, Malachi 3:1, and Mark 1:1–3 show, successive generations were deriving echoes from this Scripture when faced with situations that required similar interventions. It showed and convinced them that, the God who acted in history established a precedent and would intervene similarly in like situations in the future. Semantic descriptions of historical episodes with precedential value also contributed to the language nuances for describing similar expectations and predictions in the future. Episodes of how God acted and would therefore act in the future were vivified and perpetuated in the yearly feasts which celebrated and enacted God's grace acts in history.

Isaiah's prophetic oracle draws its language, hope, and usage from this faith matrix, that is, God will always deliver his people and will send an anointed messenger to prepare a way where there is no way and lead them to full emancipation. This conviction was premised on the echoes provided by the Exodus experience. As such, Isaiah's oracle of a future bondage and eventual emancipation of Israel derived its language of expression and interpretative framework from the Exodus motif. The Babylonian bondage and emancipation happened in conformity with Isaiah's prophecy. However, to Malachi, the results of the emancipation from the Babylonian exile did not conform to his interpretation of Isaiah's oracle. Therefore, he was in order to await a fuller emancipation from the empires that were still ruling Israel.

In light of Isaiah's oracle, Malachi anticipated a new exodus that was to happen someday in the future. He, like Isaiah, nuanced his prophetic utterance with the language of the Exodus motif that had become a precedent and reference point of God's future deliverance. Jesus was manifested within the context of a heightened hope of Israel's full emancipation from her colonizing Empire. R. Timothy McLay says, "The worldview of the first-century Jew generally consisted in the belief that the one God who had created the world and sealed the election of Israel by means of the covenant at Sinai (Exodus 19–23) would act to deliver and redeem the people of Israel from her enemies."[47]

Mark interpreted the Christ event as the fulfilment of the Torah, the Prophets, and the writings. As McLay says, "In the NT, the Jewish Scriptures were seen to be fulfilled in new ways and reapplied to a new context – the Early Church community – because of Jesus."[48] Mark therefore saw the Christ event as the salvific episode that Isaiah had prophesied and which Malachi had also reasserted in his oracle (Mal 3:1). He interpreted John's preaching and baptizing ministry as the voice of the one prophesied in Isaiah 40:3. Again he interpreted John as the messenger who was to come and prepare the way of the Lord – Jesus (Mal 3:1). Due to the heightened expectation of deliverance and its embedment in the religious psyche of Jews and the God fearers in other communities, identifying John's ministry as the forerunning ministry that was anticipated in the oracles of Isaiah and Malachi served as a rhetorical device to enhance the belief value of the oral gospel which proclaimed the fulfilment of the kingdom of God and its deliverer-king, Jesus.

McLay states, "The use of typology, midrash, or pesher does not exhaust the ways in which the NT writers employed Scripture because the Scriptures were also used to advance the particular message of the writers."[49] As such, Mark saw the entire Old Testament Scripture as having been fulfilled in the Christ event. In any case, Jesus had said, "Do not think that I have come to abolish the Law or the Prophets; I have not come to abolish them but to fulfill

---

47. McLay, *Use of the Septuagint*, 35.
48. McLay, 34.
49. McLay, 34.

them" (Matt 5:17 ESV). Mark's composite quotation can arguably be adjudged an interpretation of the Christ event in light of Isaiah's oracle.

Beale avers, "One of the mostly held positions is that Jesus and the NT writers used non-contextual hermeneutical methods that caused them to miss the original meaning of the OT texts that they were trying to interpret."[50] However, this position has not considered the effect of the presuppositions held by Jesus, and the New Testament authors. Jesus interpreted Scripture in light of the presupposition that he had come to fulfil the Law and the Prophets (Matt 5:17). He also sought to correct the wrong interpretation of Scripture by the Pharisees, the Sadducees, and the scribes (Matt 5:20). As such, Jesus used Scripture for the paraenetic purpose of exhorting his hearers to embrace Scripture-based faith.

Similarly, Mark's Old Testament Scripture interpretation was influenced by the supposition that Scripture had, in one way or another, been fulfilled in the Christ event. Therefore, every aspect of the Christ event had corresponding Old Testament Scripture texts that it fulfilled. The discernible difference with the hermeneutics of other epochs is that Mark and his contemporaries were interpreting the Christ event as a fulfilment of the Jewish Scriptures. In investigating the nature and function of Old Testament texts in the Markan text, it is necessary to consider the impact of this underlying presupposition.

Old Testament quotations in Mark 1:2–3 also illuminate the purpose of the Markan text. Whereas the Old Testament quotation that anticipated John's ministry stressed that he was a forerunner of Jesus, the nuancing of verses 7–8 shows that they were used as a foil to Jesus's more exalted persona and ministry. Moreover, the scarcity of details on John's forerunning ministry in Mark 1:4–8 compared to the detailed accounts in Matthew 3:1–14 and Luke 3:1–20 suggest that Mark's major reason for narrating the anecdote about John was not necessarily epistemological. The comparison between the person and ministry of John and the person and ministry of Jesus using such words as ὁ ἰσχυρότερος, a comparative, to express Jesus's more exalted persona in comparison to John's and in saying οὗ οὐκ εἰμὶ ἱκανὸς κύψας λῦσαι τὸν ἱμάντα τῶν ὑποδημάτων αὐτοῦ to diminutively express the persona of John in comparison to the exalted persona of Jesus shows that Mark narrated John's ministry as a foil to highlight the exalted persona and ministry of Jesus. This argument

---

50. Beale, *Handbook on the New Testament*, 1.

is further affirmed by John's description of the baptism that would later be performed by Jesus in saying, ἐγὼ ἐβάπτισα ὑμᾶς ὕδατι, in contrast to Jesus's more exalted baptism with the Holy Spirit using a contrasting clause αὐτὸς δὲ βαπτίσει ὑμᾶς ἐν πνεύματι ἁγίῳ (Mark 1:8).

The subject of verses 2–3 is Jesus not John. Mark's reason for using this composite quotation was also to subtly rebuke the audience for maintaining an obdurate and lukewarm response towards the oral gospel. Its exalted belief value was shown by magnifying the persona and ministry of Jesus on whom it was premised by use of a foil of a diminutively portrayed persona and ministry of none other than John, who was believed to be one of the most prominent persons ever to be sent by God (Matt 11:11). As such, Mark used this composite Scripture quotation and the narrative about its fulfilment as a rebuke that was aimed at calling his audience to reconsider their obduracy in view of God's demands in the oral gospel.

Summary of exegetical analysis of Mark 1:1–3.

An analysis of Mark 1:1–3 shows that Mark interpreted the Christ event as the fulfilment of the Torah and the Prophets. Interpreting John the Baptist as the one prophesied in Isaiah 40:3 and Malachi 3:1 was deliberately aimed at showing that the gospel message was in accord with predictive Scripture. Unlike Matthew and Luke who were keen to underscore John's forerunning ministry, Mark's quote in verse 2b on the scriptural support of Jesus's ministry shows that he intended to incorporate the Old Testament citation concerning the ministry of John in the main citation concerning Jesus's ministry. As such, the value of the Old Testament quotation in verses 2–3 was to support the assertion that Jesus was the Christ the Son of God (1:1). Mark's interest was to show that the oral gospel that was premised on the work of Jesus on the cross was worthy of belief. By anchoring the oral gospel on the inherited Scripture of the community, Mark embellished his text with a rhetorical device that enhanced the oral gospel's belief value.

By the time of writing the text, the pervading religious view in Mark's milieu was that the eschatological expectations concerning the coming of the Messiah had already been fulfilled in the Christ event and as such, the long-awaited kingdom of God was at hand (1:15). The nearness of the kingdom of God that is expressed in the saying ἤγγικεν ἡ βασιλεία τοῦ θεοῦ does not express chronological or geographical nearness. Rather, it expresses ease of availability to whosoever wills and responds to the gospel. Romans 10:7, ἐγγύς σου τὸ ῥῆμά ἐστιν ἐν τῷ στόματί σου καὶ ἐν τῇ καρδίᾳ σου, τοῦτ' ἔστιν τὸ ῥῆμα τῆς πίστεως ὃ κηρύσσομεν uses the preposition ἐγγύς to show nearness in terms of response. It is plausible to deduce that this was the nuance that was intended by Mark. As such, Mark communicated that the benefits of the kingdom are graciously available to whosoever wills.

5.4.2 Rhetorical Reading of Mark 1:1-3

The textual context of this portion is the wider pericope from Mark 1:1-15. A look at its structure reveals very important information concerning the purpose of the text.

    A. Introducing the beginning of the gospel about Jesus Christ 1:1-3

      B. John comes to the desert 1:4-8

        C. Baptized by John 1:9-11

      B^1 Jesus comes to the desert 1:12-13

    A^1 Introducing the proclamation of the gospel of God 1:14-15[51]

The chiastic structure of the text is a Hebrew rhetorical feature which emphasizes important aspects of the text. The parallelism of line A and A^1 emphasizes that the subject of the topic is the beginning of the gospel. It also shows that the gospel referenced in Mark 1:1 is similar to the referent of the gospel referenced in Mark 1:15. Since the gospel referenced in Mark 1:15 is obviously oral, outside and independent of the Markan text, then the gospel referenced in Mark 1:1 is also oral, outside, and independent of the Markan text. Whereas John's forerunning ministry as a precursor to the ministry of Jesus is emphasized by line B and B^1, the major emphasis is the introduction of Jesus and his preaching ministry in his baptism. The baptism episode in the narrative served to connect Jesus and his forerunner thereby affirming the assertion that Jesus is the Christ.

Gundry compares the oral gospel that is referenced in Mark 1:1 to the "word" referenced in Hosea 1:2 LXX, in which case "[the] beginning of the word of [the] Lord to Hosea consists in an oral word spoken long before the written report of it."[52] The oral word was later written as a text, in which

---

51. The gospel of God (Mark 1:14-15) subsists in the gospel about Jesus Christ (Mark 1:1).
52. Gundry, *Mark*, 33.

case, the oral word is synonymous to the written text. In the Markan text, Mark neither recorded the contents of the gospel that Jesus preached nor the gospel that the disciples preached after resurrection. Instead, he narrated episodes in the life and times of Jesus. These episodes include: Jesus's baptism, miracles, controversies with the Jewish religious leaders, passion, and resurrection. The few times a semblance of his teachings are recorded is in answer to questions by his disciples and those of his detractors (Mark 2:10, 21, 27; 3:28–29; 7:11–24; 10:1–12, 42–45; 12:25, 29–31; 13:5–37). Unlike Hosea who transcribed the word that had been spoken to him in the past, Mark is addressing a subject that had begun in the past and was a going concern in his day and that continued to thrive concurrently with his text. As such, the oral gospel was distinct from his text. In any case, if the witness of Papias is anything to go by, the oral gospel he is exhorting his readers to respond to was the one that had been orally preached by the apostle Peter.

Identifying and delineating the gospel under reference in Mark 1:1 as being outside and independent of the text reveals a direct tripartite discourse between the text, the audience, and the oral gospel. Indirectly, though, the text creates two interlocutors – the mimetic world of the text which is portrayed by the parable of the sower in Mark 4:1–9 and the rhetorical devices of Old Testament quotations, miracle stories and passion narratives that were used to identify and extol the person and persona of Jesus. This delineation reveals a dialogue between the text and the audience; an already existing but wanting dialogue between the audience and the oral gospel; a dialogue between the mimetic world of the text and the audience; and finally an enhancement of the belief value of the oral gospel using the rhetorical embellishments of Old Testament quotations, miracle stories, and the passion narratives. This study observes that the difficulties encountered in identifying the text's purpose and genre stem from lack of noting the important distinction between the Markan text and the oral gospel that is identified in this study as being outside and independent of the text. The Markan text's genre, structure and form are informed by Mark's intention to speak to and impact his audience's response to the oral gospel.

A hermeneutical enterprise that recognizes that the gospel referenced in Mark 1:1 is oral, outside, and independent of the text ought to establish the nexus between the oral gospel and the Markan text. Arguably, the text aims at creating an audience "appeal factor"[53] towards the oral gospel about Jesus Christ. It is not explicitly stated who was preaching the oral gospel to Mark's audience but from his concern, it can be inferred that he and his contemporaries who included the apostle Peter were the preachers. The other assumption is that the audience were aware of the oral gospel since they were interacting with the preachers on a day to day or week by week basis as the preaching exigency demanded (Acts 2:46). This explains why Mark did not belabor to explain the distinction between his text and the oral gospel. He had not anticipated that his treatise would one day be regarded as the bona fide gospel. However, it is apparent that his concern was his audience's dismal level of belief and obedience to the demands of the oral gospel.

Mark's opening phrase, Ἀρχὴ τοῦ εὐαγγελίου Ἰησοῦ Χριστοῦ [υἱοῦ θεοῦ], is rhetorically stated in an unequivocal way that introduces his topic as the beginning of the oral gospel. It also shows that Mark was conversant with the oral gospel, its foundation, and significance. Such equivocal presentation of the subject of the text, which is aimed at raising the reader's confidence in the author's grasp of his topic of discussion, is a rhetorical embellishment of the text with the author's ethos.[54] Highlighting the narrator's ethos arouses interest and engenders audience's trust in the authenticity of his message. This also shows that Mark was considered to be a trustworthy and knowledgeable custodian and narrator of the Christian traditions. As such, he inspired faith and confidence in what he taught. No wonder Matthew and Luke used his material without much change.[55]

Whereas a composite quotation from Exodus 23:20, Isaiah 40:3, and Malachi 3:1 is discernible in Mark 1:2–3, Mark envisaged that the verse be read as a single literary construction. It is more of an interpretation of the Christ event in light of Scripture than an interpretation of the individual texts that make up the composite quotation. Malachi looked forward to a fuller emancipation of Israel from its colonizing powers in the similitude of the

---

53. Cook, *Structure and Persuasive Power*, 288.
54. Moeser, *Anecdote in Mark*, 23.
55. A comparative analysis of the Synoptics shows a near direct transposition of Markan material into the other two synoptic writings. See Aland, *Synopsis Quattuor Evangeliorum*.

Exodus experience. Therefore, Malachi sees Exodus 23:20 as the precedent to the deliverance in his oracle in Malachi 3:1.

Mark interpreted Malachi 3:1 as an oracle that anticipated the emancipation of Israel as prophesied in Isaiah 40:3. Therefore, to Mark, both the Exodus 23:20 "type" and Malachi's anticipated emancipation in Malachi 3:1 were illuminated by Isaiah's oracle in Isaiah 40:3. As such, both the quotation on the "type" (Exod 23:20) and Malachi's oracle in Malachi 3:1 could be collapsed into the overarching oracle in Isaiah 40:3. No wonder, Mark interpreted the Christ event as a fulfilment of Isaiah's oracle in Isaiah 40:3.

An important question at this juncture is: What did Mark intend to accomplish by citing the composite quotation? As can be observed, the quotation was used to show that the historical Jesus, who had become the Christ of faith, was the Christ who was anticipated in Scripture. Consequently, the gospel about him was valid and worthy of his audience's belief. As such, the composite quotation was used as a rhetorical device to enhance believability of the oral gospel by validating the premise on which it was founded – Jesus and his work – through Scripture. Since the Hebrew Scripture was held as authoritative by the Christian community, anchoring the oral gospel on scriptural precedents and prophecy had the effect of convincing and convicting the audience about its truth value. The illocutionary benefit is the conferment of a new identity to the believers by identifying them with the Scripture-centered faith community, Israel.

Summary of rhetorical reading of Mark 1:1–3

Hatina notes, "The common eschatological hope of deliverance from exile shared by several groups in early Judaism is made to serve as the ideological background against which Mark's composite quotation is read."[56] Similarly, Richard B. Hays posits, "There is an ill-formed but widespread hope for God to send a 'Messiah' (*Christos*: 8:29; 14:61) who will restore the kingdom of David and put an end to Israel's suffering (10: 46; 11:9-10)."[57] In this respect, the Christ event was interpreted as the fulfilment of the Jewish Scripture albeit in new ways. As such, the salvific gospel that was premised on episodes within the Christ event could be aptly validated by quotations from Old Testament

---

56. Hatina, *In Search of a Context*, 156.
57. Hays, "Canonical Matrix of the Gospels," 55.

Scripture. Hatina further says, "The rhetorical force of an argument was certainly enhanced by an appeal to an authoritative source, such as Scripture, even if only a single line or phrase was quoted."[58] Because of the high value placed on Old Testament Scriptures, quoting them to validate the premise on which the oral gospel was founded generates illocutionary acts that invite reflection and evoke response to the oral gospel.

5.5 Analysis of Old Testament Quotation in Mark 4:12

Mark 4:12 reads ἵνα βλέποντες βλέπωσιν καὶ μὴ ἴδωσιν, καὶ ἀκούοντες ἀκούωσιν καὶ μὴ συνιῶσιν, μήποτε ἐπιστρέψωσιν καὶ ἀφεθῇ αὐτοῖς (so that they may indeed see but not perceive, and may indeed hear but not understand, lest they should turn and be forgiven). Jesus did not explicitly indicate from which Old Testament book he cited this quotation by use of the usual identification formula καθὼς γέγραπται. This means that, the saying βλέποντες βλέπωσιν καὶ μὴ ἴδωσιν, καὶ ἀκούοντες ἀκούωσιν καὶ μὴ συνιῶσιν, may have been a common saying in Hebrew/Aramaic as it is in many other languages. Clarke says, "To hear, and not understand; to see, and not perceive; is a common saying in many languages."[59] An expanded form of this saying is found in Isaiah 6:9–10.

Isaiah 6:9–10 in the LXX reads: ⁹καὶ εἶπεν πορεύθητι καὶ εἰπὸν τῷ λαῷ τούτῳ ἀκοῇ ἀκούσετε καὶ οὐ μὴ συνῆτε καὶ βλέποντες βλέψετε καὶ οὐ μὴ ἴδητε ¹⁰ἐπαχύνθη γὰρ ἡ καρδία τοῦ λαοῦ τούτου καὶ τοῖς ὠσὶν αὐτῶν βαρέως ἤκουσαν καὶ τοὺς ὀφθαλμοὺς αὐτῶν ἐκάμμυσαν μήποτε ἴδωσιν τοῖς ὀφθαλμοῖς καὶ τοῖς ὠσὶν ἀκούσωσιν καὶ τῇ καρδίᾳ συνῶσιν καὶ ἐπιστρέψωσιν καὶ ἰάσομαι αὐτούς. The NETS has translated this verse as, "And he said, 'Go, and say to this people: You will listen by listening, but you will not understand, and looking you will look, but you will not perceive. For this people's heart has grown fat, and with their ears they have heard heavily, and they have shut their eyes so that they might not see with their eyes and hear with their ears and understand with their heart and turn – and I would heal them.'"[60] Its rendering in the MT is:

---

58. Hatina, *In Search of a Context*, 158.
59. Clarke, *Clarke's Commentary*, 50.
60. Pietersma and Wright, *New English Translation*, 830.

⁹וַיֹּאמֶר לֵךְ וְאָמַרְתָּ לָעָם הַזֶּה שִׁמְעוּ שָׁמוֹעַ וְאַל־תָּבִינוּ וּרְאוּ רָאוֹ וְאַל־תֵּדָעוּ׃
¹⁰הַשְׁמֵן לֵב־הָעָם הַזֶּה וְאָזְנָיו הַכְבֵּד וְעֵינָיו הָשַׁע פֶּן־יִרְאֶה בְעֵינָיו וּבְאָזְנָיו יִשְׁמָע וּלְבָבוֹ יָבִין וָשָׁב וְרָפָא לוֹ׃

(And he said, "Go, and say to this people: 'Keep on hearing, but do not understand; keep on seeing, but do not perceive. Make the heart of this people dull and their ears heavy, and blind their eyes; lest they see with their eyes, and hear with their ears, and understand with their hearts, and turn and be healed'"). The similarity of the syntax between Mark 4:12 and Isaiah 6:9–10 suggests that most probably, Mark 4:12 is a paraphrase of Isaiah 6:9–10. As such, it can be adjudged an allusion of Isaiah 6:9–10. This section investigates the function of this Old Testament allusion in Mark 4:12.

5.5.1 Observations from Source Documents

A comparative reading of Isaiah 6:10 in the MT and LXX shows that, in the MT it is a continuation of God's commission to Isaiah that commences at verse 9. It is rendered in imperative form. However, in the LXX, it is a description of the obduracy of Isaiah's audience and is rendered in an indicative form. This suggests that verse 10 in the LXX is a translation of the interpretation of the idiomatic expression in the Hebrew *vorlage* into its meaning in Greek. As such, both the MT and the LXX have the same meaning. It also suggests that the interpreters of the Hebrew text into the LXX understood the irony in verse 10 of the Hebrew version to stand for the last condition of the audience after they hear the word of God and sleight it once more.

Observations from the outlines

Isaiah's prologue is an introduction to his visions and oracles concerning Judah and Jerusalem (Isa 1:1). Similarly, Mark has introduced the gospel that he and his contemporaries were preaching (Mark 1:1). Just as Isaiah is concerned about the rebellion of Judah against God and the impending judgment (Isa 1–5), Mark is also concerned about his audience's obduracy and lukewarm response to the oral gospel (Mark 2–4). Both texts are addressing their audience's response to a proclamation that is outside and independent of their written texts. Schneck has observed that "if the book of Isaiah is read in its sequential order, there is prophetic activity before Isaiah 6."[61] Isaiah's main purpose was to exhort his rebellious audience to obey the word of God that he and his predecessors had been proclaiming long before the written oracle. Similarly, Mark was exhorting his obdurate and lukewarm audience to respond in faith and praxis to the oral gospel that he and his contemporaries were proclaiming before and after the Markan text was written.

5.5.2 Comparative Outlines of Isaiah 1:1–6:10 and Mark 1:1–4:12

Outline of Isaiah 1:1–6:13	Outline of Mark 1:1–4:13
Introduction 1:1	Introduction 1:1–15
Isaiah's oracles before Uzziah's death 2:1–5:30	Jesus's preaching and audience's expression of obduracy 1:15–4:13
Prophecy on the glory of the last days 2:1–5	Calling of first four disciples 1:16–20
Judgment of God against the unbelieving 2:6–4:1	Jesus teaching and healing ministry 1:20–2:12
An oracle about the future glory of the redeemed 4:2–6	Introduction of controversy with religious elite 2:13–3:34
A portrait of Judah's obduracy in the song of the vineyard 5:1–7	A portrait of Jewish leaders' obduracy in the parable of the sower 4:1–9
Judgment of the obdurate 5:8–30	Judgment of obdurate 4:10–12
Explanation about the obdurate 6:1–13.	Explanation about the obdurate 4:13–20.

---

61. Hatina, *In Search of a Context*, 126.

The phrase "In the year that King Uzziah died" (Isa 6:1) locates the time that God sent Isaiah afresh to address Judah's continued rebellion. By telling the song of the vineyard in Isaiah 5:1–7, he painted a portrait of Judah's rhetorical situation which profiles his audience's attitude towards the word of God. The song depicts a well-tended vineyard that had, notwithstanding the best crop husbandry, failed to yield the expected fruit. This song is meant to awaken Isaiah's audience to God's view of their indifference to his word. It is used to call the readers to a reflection on their wanting response to the word of God and to provoke them to a positive response to its demands.

Similarly, Mark mirrored the rhetorical situation and profile of his audience by retelling the parable of the sower (Mark 4:1–9). The range of his audience, in terms of their response to the gospel message, is symbolized by different soils, the word of God by seeds, and the preacher by the sower. Audience obduracy is depicted through a disappointing scenario in which though the sower's intention and desire was to sow seeds on fertile soil, unfortunately, some fell on paths where they were eaten by the birds of the air. Others fell on rocky soils where they germinated but could not grow to fruitfulness because they were scorched by the sun for lack of deep soils to sustain growth. Some also fell on thorny ground and could not grow because they were choked by the thorns. Delightfully, some fell on fertile soils where they yielded thirty-fold, sixty-fold, and others a hundred-fold.

The reason for the negative audience response to the word of God in both Isaiah and Mark is described using a similar idiom (Isa 6:9–10 and Mark 4:12). The decision by Jesus to describe and decry his audience's undesirable response to the gospel using a similar idiom to Isaiah's has been a subject of various scholarly discussions. Some of these discussions will be surveyed to shed light on the use of Old Testament quotations as rhetorical devices in the Markan text.

Recent studies on the use of Isaiah 6:9-10 in Mark 4:12

The most recent and readily available studies that have been done on the relationship between these two enigmatic verses are that of Thomas R. Hatina, R. Schneck, and R. E. Watts. The major line of investigation by most scholars is the seeming "exclusivism determinism"[62] in the message of Mark 4:10–12.

---

62. Hatina, 184.

However, to some, this view is deemed to be contradicting the general teaching and theology of Jesus.

Hatina has pointed out that very few scholars have "attempted to understand the function of the quotation within the narrative context of Mark which is the only context available to us."[63] He has investigated the presumed exclusivism using a historical-critical and a narrative-critical reading of Mark 4:10–12. However, has neither identified the idiomatic and ironical aspect of the quotation nor its rhetorical and performative function. This study argues that God was urging Isaiah to continue proclaiming his word in the midst of opposition and rebellion of the people.

The idiomatic expression ἐπαχύνθη, הַשְׁמֵן "to be dull of hearing" or "to make fat" (Isa 6:10) describes the state of not hearkening to a message despite of it being incessantly spoken. George M. Landes has shown that the cognate of the term שָׁמֵן is "to become fat; (Hi.) to make fat, insensitive; put on fat."[64] As such, the idiomatic expression "to make fat" could be replaced by "become insensitive." This idiomatic expression is aimed at urging Isaiah to persist in proclaiming God's word in spite of his audience's stubbornness. The irony in which the Isaian text is rendered may have influenced Jesus's choice of the citation. It is imbued with rhetorical irony that is capable of awakening the audience to their stubbornness with the consequence of catalyzing their response to the oral gospel. Its performative function was to arouse the audience to respond to the gospel through the veiled threat that is communicated in the irony.

The oral message that Isaiah's audience were being exhorted to pay attention to is not explicitly identified in his oracle. However, it is presumed to have been a given among God's covenant people. Williamson has captured the implicit relationship between the text and oral message of Isaiah by saying that "there is clearly a gap between the oral proclamation of the prophet and the written form of his words which we have."[65] The oral message is the one that the people are being reproved through irony "to continue hearing and not comprehend, seeing and not perceive" (Isa 6:9–10). To understand

---

63. Hatina, 184.
64. Landes, *Building Your Biblical Hebrew*, 136.
65. Williamson, "Preaching from Isaiah," 141.

the nature and function of the passage we need to delineate the interlocutors in the discourse.

The interlocutors in Isaiah's discourse are Isaiah's oracle, his primary audience and the oral message that Judah is being accused of having heard but not understanding, and the portrait of their obduracy that is portrayed in the song of the vineyard (Isa 5:1–7). The discourse between Isaiah's oracle and his audience is meant to catalyze Judah's response to the proclamation of the word of God that was outside and independent of Isaiah's written oracle. The song of the vineyard is written using satire in dramatic rhetoric that portrays Judah's negative disposition towards the word of God in order to provoke them to respond favorably. Isaiah 6:9–10 is a paradoxical satire that communicates an indictment against Judah's unbelief. At the same time, it is an entreaty urging Judah to respond to the ongoing proclamation of the word of God. As such, Isaiah's oracle was meant to awaken the audience to the consequences of their blatant rejection of God's word.

Since Isaiah 6:9–10 is aimed at eliminating the exigence in his audience's rhetorical situation, it is a rhetorical communication. Bitzer says that "rhetoric alters reality by bringing into existence a discourse of such a character that the audience, in thought and action, is so engaged that it becomes mediator of change."[66] It is significant to note that this quotation has not been preceded by the identification formula "כֹּה אָמַר אֲדֹנָי יְהוִה" which in itself would be a rhetorical nuance to evoke belief. One would argue that the stature of prophet Isaiah was of a degree that conferred upon him ethos that evoked belief in his speech. Moreover, the satire in the text is embedded with sufficient rhetorical and illocutionary efficacy to both warn against slighting God's entreaty and evoke a positive response to God's word. However, in spite of Isaiah's exalted ethos, his audience were still obstinate to his proclamation.

Similarly, the interlocutors participating in the discourse that is generated by Mark 4:10–12 are: the Markan text, the audience, the mimetic world portrayed in the parable of the sower, and the oral gospel that Mark and his contemporaries had preached and continued to preach to their audiences. Again, Mark 4:10–12 is used to catalyze Mark's audience to respond to the gospel that he was proclaiming. Just as in Isaiah, Mark 4:12 is a paradoxical

---

66. Bitzer, "Rhetorical Situation," 4.

satire that communicates both an indictment and an entreaty to Mark's audience to respond to the oral gospel.

Schneck takes Mark 4:10–12 to be a quotation of Isaiah 6:9–10 saying that "it is used to describe the fate of those who do not accept Jesus' message."[67] He further avers,

> Jesus tells the parables not to divide the groups but as an act of judgment to conceal the mystery of the kingdom from those who are already outside. In other words, the divinely inflicted obduracy is the result of the crowd's already existing disposition, namely its failure to accept the word; it is not the result of a divine fiat.[68]

He has however not explained what to "make the hearts of the people fat, their ears dull and their eyes blind" (Isa 6:9–10) means. It would have shed more light and perhaps alter his conclusion. He interprets Isaiah 6:9–10 and Mark 4:10–12 as a form of judgment. He avers, "God will not intervene to protect the rebellious people from impending disaster. The process of punishment will be set in motion by Isaiah's preaching (6:9–10)."[69] Nonetheless, Schneck sees hope in God reserving a remnant in Judah who will rebuild the nation afresh (6:13). He sees the same judgment exercised in Mark 4:10–12 against the outsiders who have failed to believe in the gospel. According to Schneck, "the hardening spelt out in Mark 4:10–12 is a fulfilment of Isaiah's oracle in Isaiah 6:9–10."[70]

Watts places Mark 4:10–12 in a winder context that includes the controversy between the Jesus and the Jewish leaders from Jerusalem who labelled Jesus as a person who drives evil spirits by the power of Beelzebub. These are the people he considers to be outside the circle of insiders. He likens them to the obdurate in Isaiah 6:9–10. Whereas Watts's inclusion of Jesus's antagonists in the controversy narratives as part of those considered as being outsiders is irrefutable, nonetheless, he has not probed the rhetorical value of the retold parable by examining it in the context of the wider matrix of the Markan discourse.

---

67. Schneck, *Isaiah in the Gospel of Mark*, 235.
68. Schneck, 236.
69. Schneck, 123.
70. Schneck, 123.

Schneck, Hatina, and Watts have not delineated the interlocutors in the discourses generated by Isaiah 6:9–10 and Mark 4:10–12 in order to effectively analyze the nature and function of each interlocutor in the two discourses. As such, they have not identified the rhetorical function of these texts. Bereft of this information, the text is limitedly seen as a direct communication between the text and the audience. Such a limited view misses the important dialogue between the audience and the oral gospel as well as the catalytic effect of the rhetorical devices on audience response to the oral gospel.

5.5.3 Exegetical Analysis of Isaiah 6:9–10

LXX Isaiah 6:9 reads: καὶ εἶπεν πορεύθητι καὶ εἰπὸν τῷ λαῷ τούτῳ ἀκοῇ ἀκούσετε καὶ οὐ μὴ συνῆτε καὶ βλέποντες βλέψετε καὶ οὐ μὴ ἴδητε (And he said, "Go, and say to this people: 'Keep on hearing, but do not understand; keep on seeing, but do not perceive'").

LXX Isaiah 6:10 reads: ἐπαχύνθη γὰρ ἡ καρδία τοῦ λαοῦ τούτου καὶ τοῖς ὠσὶν αὐτῶν βαρέως ἤκουσαν καὶ τοὺς ὀφθαλμοὺς αὐτῶν ἐκάμμυσαν μήποτε ἴδωσιν τοῖς ὀφθαλμοῖς καὶ τοῖς ὠσὶν ἀκούσωσιν καὶ τῇ καρδίᾳ συνῶσιν καὶ ἐπιστρέψωσιν καὶ ἰάσομαι αὐτούς, (For this people's heart has grown fat, and with their ears they have heard heavily, and they have shut their eyes so that they might not see with their eyes and hear with their ears and understand with their heart and turn – and I would heal them) (NETS).

The MT rendering of Isaiah 6:9–10 is:

> וַיֹּאמֶר לֵךְ וְאָמַרְתָּ לָעָם הַזֶּה שִׁמְעוּ שָׁמוֹעַ וְאַל־תָּבִינוּ וּרְאוּ רָאוֹ וְאַל־תֵּדָעוּ: הַשְׁמֵן לֵב־הָעָם הַזֶּה וְאָזְנָיו הַכְבֵּד וְעֵינָיו הָשַׁע פֶּן־יִרְאֶה בְעֵינָיו וּבְאָזְנָיו יִשְׁמָע וּלְבָבוֹ יָבִין וָשָׁב וְרָפָא לוֹ:

> And he said, "Go, and say to this people: Keep on hearing, but do not understand; keep on seeing, but do not perceive. Make the heart of this people dull and their ears heavy and blind their eyes; lest they see with their eyes, and hear with their ears, and understand with their hearts and turn and be healed" (Isa 6:9–10 ESV).

In both the MT and LXX, these two verses spell out God's commission to Isaiah. There are two major observations from the LXX version: First, the use of ἀκούσετε and βλέψετε (indicative future second person plural), shows that the stress in Isaiah's message is its futuristic tense. As such, Isaiah's oracle was focused on his future proclamation and the people's response from the day of his commissioning. Second, the use of the word ἐπαχύνθη (indicative, aorist, passive, third person singular) in verse 10 suggests that the audience had been insensitive to God's word that had been proclaimed prior to this fresh commission and that this insensitivity was self-inflicted. The verbs, ἤκουσαν and ἐκάμμυσαν, are indicative, aorist, active, third person plural. The indicative mood and aorist tense show that the hearts of the audience became insensitive, their ears were made heavy, and their eyes were closed in the past of the time when the fresh message was to be delivered by Isaiah. As such, it is not Isaiah's new message that was to effect insensitivity of the heart, heaviness of ears and blindness of the eyes.

Isaiah 6:10 LXX describes the rhetorical situation of the people to whom Isaiah was sent. They are described as having an insensitive heart, heavy ears and blind eyes. On the other hand, verse 10 in the MT is rendered as a continuation of Isaiah's commission to Judah and Jerusalem in verse 9, that is, to make the hearts of his audience insensitive by a fresh and incessant proclamation of the word of God. Furthermore, הַשְׁמֵן֙ לֵב־הָעָ֣ם הַזֶּ֔ה וְאָזְנָ֥יו הַכְבֵּ֖ד וְעֵינָ֣יו הָשַׁ֑ע פֶּן־יִרְאֶ֨ה בְעֵינָ֜יו וּבְאָזְנָ֤יו יִשְׁמָע֙ וּלְבָב֣וֹ יָבִ֔ין וָשָׁ֖ב וְרָ֥פָא לֽוֹ׃ is an irony expressed in an idiomatic form whose intention is the opposite of its stated purpose. It impresses upon Isaiah God's intention to heal his people if they hearken to his entreaty and forsake their hardened position. As such, it is directed to the prophet encouraging him to be fervent and steadfast in the frustrating mission of proclaiming God's word to an obstinate people.

The LXX rendering suggests that the audience had been hearing the word of God preached in the past but had continued to harden their hearts. Nevertheless, Isaiah was being sent afresh to proclaim the word of God all the more. Similarly, the MT's expression recognizes that Isaiah's message is directed to an audience who have heard the word in the past and hardened their hearts. As such, telling him to go and harden his audience's hearts is in essence telling him to go and proclaim his oracle to an audience who, notwithstanding having been preached to before, had continued to harden their hearts. Robert B. Chisholm notes that "Rather than expressing God's desire, the oracle is a commentary on the people's attitude . . . this form of imperative is comparable to saying to a recalcitrant child who is bent on climbing a high tree, 'Go ahead, be stubborn! Break your neck!' The imperative expresses the speaker's frustration rather than his will or desire."[71] Just as in the LXX, the message is addressing the rhetorical situation of his audience. The aim of this rhetorical communication is to awaken the audience from the stupor of their stubbornness to consciousness and obedience to the word of God. As such the LXX does not contradict the MT; rather, it interprets and sheds more light into the meaning of the MT which is considered to be a derivative of the LXX's *vorlage*.

The saying לֵךְ וְאָמַרְתָּ לָעָם הַזֶּה שִׁמְעוּ שָׁמוֹעַ וְאַל־תָּבִינוּ וּרְאוּ רָאוֹ וְאַל־תֵּדָעוּ contains both a commission to Isaiah and an entreaty to his audience. The entreaty is couched in form of a warning. God's anger is revealed in the phrase לֵךְ וְאָמַרְתָּ לָעָם הַזֶּה. Notably, he does not address them using his usual loving titles, "My people," "sons of Israel," or "house of Israel" but uses "these people," an address that does not stress his covenant relationship with them. Rather, it expresses distance and estrangement between God and the addressees. However, paradoxically, God also reveals his enduring mercies when he says שִׁמְעוּ שָׁמוֹעַ. This can be interpreted as "keep on hearing." It means that they have been spoken to in the past and continue to be spoken in the present without taking heed to God's message. Notwithstanding, God is not relenting in sending his prophet to continue speaking to them. God is still willing to commission Isaiah afresh, to continue entreating them.

The clause שִׁמְעוּ שָׁמוֹעַ וְאַל־תָּבִינוּ וּרְאוּ רָאוֹ וְאַל־תֵּדָעוּ is a serious indictment on the people for not paying attention to God's message despite his incessant entreaty. God's entreaty is however delivered in a rhetorical irony that reveals both, the people's stance against his law and God's reaction towards their negative stance. This rhetorical irony seems to be a warning that the speaker's patience is running out and that he is about to take action because of being slighted despite his effort to be reconciled. Agreeably, John Goldingay posits that "the words in verse 9 and 10 may be ironic. They constitute a warning of where the people will find themselves unless they respond and turn."[72]

The warning is also couched with a message suggesting that this call is yet another chance that is being afforded. It reveals God's anger controlled by mercy. However, it is couched with a warning that mercy is slowly running out. Jeremiah 5:21–22 addresses an audience who are said to have eyes but

---

71. Chisholm, *From Exegesis to Exposition*, 105–106.
72. Goldingay, *Isaiah*, 61.

do not see, who have ears but do not hear. Yet he calls them to repentance. Describing people as having eyes to see but not seeing and having ears to hear but not hearing, idiomatically expresses their obstinacy towards the word of God as can be observed in Ezra 3:11 and 12:2. Psalm 119:70 describes people who are arrogant and who do not keep the law of God as callous and unfeeling.

Isaiah's commission to make the hearts of the people calloused; make their ears dull, and close their eyes is therefore a commission to proclaim the word of God persistently in the midst of audience opposition. Clarke posits, "The prophet speaks of the event, the fact as it would happen, not of God's purpose and act by his ministry. The prophets are in other places said to perform the thing which they only foretell: . . . Jer. 1:10."[73] He supports the supposition that the condition of obduracy is not resultant of prophetic proclamation but is self-inflicted. Goldingay summarizes his exposition of the two verses by saying that "it is designed to bring people to their senses, to repentance, and to forgiveness, even though it does not explicitly urge them to repentance and indicate that there is any way out. Isaiah will urge them to turn and will not merely repeat what 6:9–10 literary says, but he will meet a response that supports its truth."[74]

Isaiah's commissioning words reveal God's anger; however, history shows that it was contained by God's mercy for over a century until judgment was meted out through the Babylonian exile between 605 and 536 BCE. Such a paradoxical expression is described by Fowler as "two incongruous voices speaking at once."[75] In his study of the Amhara culture of Ethiopia, Levine found out that "ambiguity can provide an effective means of achieving affective response; it communicates 'expressive overtones and suggestive allusions.'"[76] Some scholars have posited that prophet Isaiah is pronouncing judgment which is in form of deafness and blindness.[77] However, verse 11

---

73. Clarke, *Clarke's Commentary*, 50.

74. Clarke, 61.

75. Fowler, *Let the Reader Understand*, 195. Fowler explains the language such as was used by Isaiah and Mark as one that is not referentially oriented.

76. Levine, *Flight From Ambiguity*, 29–36. Levine has argued that, pre-modern cultures generally were and are far more comfortable with ambiguity and other forms of indirection than we are, and therefore are better able to exploit its constructive uses.

77. Goldingay, *Isaiah*, 191.

suggests that the oracle was pointing to a time when total devastation would be visited upon the cities if they do not repent.

Interpreting Isaiah's oracle as a statement of judgment is an over-interpretation. The first of Goldingay's two positions that "Yahweh sends Isaiah to tell people that God is closing their minds (vv. 9–10).... They have reached the point when God's judgment must fall, and the closing of their minds is the form this judgment will take,"[78] may not have considered the value of the irony in the statement by the prophet to Judah. Mortyer has also taken a similar view in saying, "Isaiah's message (9) and his task (10) constitute, at first sight, the oddest commission ever given to a prophet: to tell people not to understand and to engender heart hardening and spiritual blindness."[79] Nobody has this far investigated how Isaiah's oracle was going to engender heart hardening and spiritual blinding besides a literal reading of the text. In the absence of such investigation, the most plausible proposition that can be proffered is that the saying is idiomatically nuanced with extant idioms that, with time, may have been obscured in the process of language development. For texts that outlive the life span of their language, the possibility that the idiomatic reference was lost in the course of language development is very high. As such, the possibility of interpreting idiomatic expressions in antiquity using methods influenced by later-day language conventions may not be overruled.

Williamson illumines the verse by saying that:

> Beyond this judgment, however, we find that this negative notion is reversed and turned positively. It is surprising, once one has this in mind, how often allusions in chapter 40–45 appear to show that eyes and ears that once were closed have now been opened or the like. And in even further development, the saying which was clearly originally given in a metaphorical or "spiritual" sense is turned in a more liberal direction so that physical blindness and deafness too will find healing (e.g. 35:5–6).[80]

---

78. Goldingay, 61.
79. Mortyer, *Prophecy of Isaiah*, 78.
80. Williamson, "Preaching from Isaiah," 146.

Williamson's supposition suggests that repentance and a faith shift are intended in the commissioning words to Isaiah. They do not envisage judgment per se without option of repentance and forgiveness to whosoever wills.

It is also apparent that the commission is idiomatically and ironically expressed and that making the hearts heavy, the ears dull and the eyes blind is an expression of a different referent than what the literal words signify. The challenge in locating the meaning is compounded when translating an idiomatic expression from Hebrew to the receptor language, in this case, Greek and English. Moreover, even referents of idiomatic expression in the same language may be lost in the course of changed language and religious contexts and concepts over time.

Klein, Blomberg and Hubbard Jr., have defined irony as a "device in which a writer says the very opposite of what he means."[81] Such idiomatic expressions are difficult to interpret by analyzing the semantics and syntax of the text. They are more understandable through analysis of the rhetorical situation and exigence that occasioned the text. The semantics and syntactical formations have been translated into English without taking into account their idiomatic referents. A scan of the religious context in which Isaiah's commission was spelt out shows that obstinacy to the word of God was the occasion that prompted God's commission. As such, the verse was used to both indict and entreat Isaiah's audience concerning their response to an oral preaching that was outside and independent of the text.

5.5.4 Exegetical Analysis of Mark 4:12

Mark 4:11 supplies an illuminating background and context to Mark 4:12. It says; 11καὶ ἔλεγεν αὐτοῖς· ὑμῖν τὸ μυστήριον δέδοται τῆς βασιλείας τοῦ θεοῦ· ἐκείνοις δὲ τοῖς ἔξω ἐν παραβολαῖς τὰ πάντα γίνεται, 12ἵνα βλέποντες βλέπωσιν καὶ μὴ ἴδωσιν, καὶ ἀκούοντες ἀκούωσιν καὶ μὴ συνιῶσιν. (And he said to them "to you is given the mystery of the kingdom of God. But to those outside everything becomes parables, such that, seeing they may see and not understand and hearing they may hear and not understand.")[82] Describing the disciples and those who had followed him as the ones given τὸ μυστήριον τῆς βασιλείας τοῦ θεοῦ in essence addresses the fact that because of the divine nature of the

---

81. Klein, Blomberg, and Hubbard, *Introduction to Biblical Interpretation*, 314.
82. Researcher's interpretation of Mark 4:11–12a.

kingdom of God, it requires divine illumination to be understood by mere mortals (Matt 16:17). As such, in ordinary parlance the divine nature of the kingdom makes it a mystery. Therefore, whereas to those inside Jesus's circle of followers, parables are readily understood through divine illumination, to those who are outside everything (τὰ πάντα) that is spoken by Jesus becomes (γίνεται) parables whose meanings are not easily grasped. The difference is not therefore in Jesus's different mode of communication to the outsiders and insiders, it is in pragmatics – that is, the divine enablement to understand the gospel about the kingdom of God.

Mark's parable of the sower (Mark 4:1–12) is a portrait of Jesus's audience's response to the gospel. As originally told, Jesus used it to provoke his audience to respond positively to the word of God. Whereas Mark was also provoking his audience to respond positively to the oral gospel through retelling the parable, his reminisce and narration of Jesus's use of Old Testament quotation in Mark 4:12 was to embellish his text with a rhetorical device to warn his audience against slighting God's entreaty through the oral Gospel message in view of God's negative perception of obduracy that was aptly shown in Jesus's allusion to Isaiah 6:9–10.

The parable of the sower is a rhetorical masterpiece that is aimed at eliminating the exigence of obduracy towards the oral gospel. At the end of the parable, Jesus invoked another rhetorical idiom, "whoever has ears to hear, let them hear" (Mark 4:9). Again, this is not an act of demarcating between the ones who have ears and those who do not have ears, as has been postulated in some quarters. Rather, its use to address a similar situation in Isaiah 6:9–10 suggests that it is either a Hebrew or Aramaic rhetorical saying that was in normal use, and whose use was to embed the text with efficacious illocutionary acts that would evoke a desire to positively respond to the oral gospel. Mostly, when this saying is used, it serves to both urge belief in what has been said and at the same time it serves as a dire warning against stubbornness to the word of God (Rev 2:7, 11, 17, 29; 3:6, 13, 22).

ἵνα βλέποντες βλέπωσιν καὶ μὴ ἴδωσιν, καὶ ἀκούοντες ἀκούωσιν καὶ μὴ συνιῶσιν, μήποτε ἐπιστρέψωσιν καὶ ἀφεθῇ αὐτοῖς in Mark 4:12, appears to be communicating the same message as "he who has an ear let him hear." However, part of scholarship has said that it differentiates between the stubborn audience who are destined for damnation and the believing who are destined to be saved, or alternatively those who are outside and those who are inside. In this view, the disciples are identified as part of the insiders. However, this argument wanes when it is viewed in the backdrop of Jesus's rebuke to the disciples for not understanding the parable in Mark 4:13 which would identify them with the outsiders. Moreover, Mark has used the same saying in Mark 8:17–18 in reference to his disciples' lack of perception. If Jesus's disciples can be referred to as hard-hearted and as people having eyes but not seeing and having ears but not hearing, then Mark 4:12 is not using the saying to differentiate between insiders and outsiders. Rather, by virtue of enjoying the illuminating power of the Holy Spirit, Jesus's teachings do not become parables to the disciples but to the unbelieving who do not have the illuminating power of the Holy Spirit everything becomes parables. This explanation introduces a new definition of the term "parable." In Jesus's view, therefore, a teaching becomes a parable to an audience who by virtue of their obduracy, it is not comprehended.

Mark 4:12 is a description of the audience's opposition of Jesus, a rebuke for their obduracy, as well as an entreaty to the audience to respond to the oral gospel. As such, the paraphrased Old Testament citation of Isaiah 6:9–10 in 4:12 is a rhetorical embellishment that underscores God's grave view of obduracy and the value of diligently hearkening to the oral gospel. At the same time, it sermons the audience to positively respond to the oral gospel. The parable of the sower shows the centrality of the oral gospel proclamation in the Markan text. Its salvific value demands that it be preached against all kinds of opposition. The fact that, most times than not, even the fruitful ones produce a paltry thirty-fold and sixty-fold demands that the gospel be preached until people become dull of hearing.

5.5.5 Comparative Analysis of Isaiah 6:9–10 and Mark 4:12

A comparison between Isaiah 6:9–10 and Mark 4:12 shows that Jesus's saying in Mark 4:12 is not a direct citation of any of the Old Testament versions. Mark did not quote Jesus as having preceded his citation with Καθὼς γέγραπται ἐν τῷ Ἡσαΐᾳ τῷ προφήτῃ as is used in Mark 1:2. This suggests that Jesus was the source of this particular saying. Despite the differences between Isaiah 6:9–10 and Mark 4:12, the rhetorical situations being addressed by Isaiah, Jesus, and Mark are similar. Isaiah's audience is composed of people who hear the word and see the works of God but are obstinate. Isaiah was sent to warn these people that unless they respond to God's varied ways of rapprochement, judgment was sure to be visited upon them. The language of God's message to Isaiah is laden with rhetorical irony as a persuasive tool. However, to Isaiah's audience the message would be received as a satire. According to Ryken,

> Satire is the exposing, through ridicule or rebuke, of human vice or folly. It becomes literary when the controlling purpose of attack is combined with a literary method such as story, description or metaphor. Satire can appear in any literary genre (such as lyric, narrative or drama) and can be either a minor part of a work or the main point of an entire work. Although satire usually has one main object of attack, satire often make a number of jabs in various directions, a feature that that can be called "satiric ripples." . . . Satire is a subversive form. It assaults the deep structures of our thinking and aims to make us uncomfortable. It questions the status quo and unsettles people's tendency to think that their behavior is basically good.[83]

The message of Isaiah exposes his audience's self-inflicted obduracy which is in dire need of correction otherwise God's judgment would be meted against them.

As portrayed in the preceding parable (Mark 4:1–9), Jesus's audience was composed of people who lacked commitment to the word of God; those who are detracted from responding to the word of God by temptations, persecution, and worldly cares. To some relief, there were some who were keen on hearing and acting on the word of God. This study has argued that Mark retold the parable of the sower to mirror the rhetorical situation of his audience. Comparatively, the rhetorical situations of Isaiah, Jesus, and Mark can be described using similar idiomatic expressions. As such, their exigencies can be eliminated using the same rhetorical communication.

Isaiah 6:9–10 and Mark 4:12 are better described as satirical entreaties. They are in the form of portraits of the audience's rhetorical situations that mimetically depict the prevailing exigence. These portraits evoke abhorrence for the audience's rhetorical situation and a desire to eliminate the exigence therein by responding to an ongoing proclamation of God's word. Isaiah, Jesus, and Mark used the same sayings, arguably sourced from their rich

---

83. Ryken, *Words of Delight*, 329.

Scripture-centered language convention. They were employed to embellish their message with rhetorical devices to enhance believability and to call their respective audiences to respond to the word of God that was outside and independent of the respective texts. By virtue of God's ability to act on his word and peoples' ingrained faith in him and Scripture, rhetorical devices that are God and Scripture centered are laden with speech acts that are efficacious enough to convince and convict the audience concerning the belief value of the gospel that is premised on a God-sanctioned episode, like the Christ event.

Mark 4:12 is arguably a summary of the assessment of the rhetorical situation of the audience of Jesus that he has portrayed in the parable of the sower (4:1–9). This notion is further fortified by the fact that the saying is not a direct quotation from Isaiah 6:9–10. As such, Mark 4:12 should be interpreted in view of its immediate context of Jesus's parable of the sower as well as the larger controversy narratives. Matthew, who has been adjudged to have used the Markan text as his source understood the quotation to have been from Isaiah 6:9–10 which he quotes in its LXX version (Matt 13:14–15). The difference between Mark and Matthew in rendering this quotation fortifies the argument that Mark was not keen to have the text read in light of Isaiah 6:9–10 but as Jesus's own composition that employed lexemes from his rich Scripture-centered language convention.

5.6 Summary

The study shows that the salient reasons for using Old Testament citations in Mark are one, to connect the oral gospel with the faith heritage of the Markan community which was premised on their Scripture – the Old Testament. The belief in the Old Testament as the Christian Scripture confers convincing and convicting efficacy to Scripture acts that are quoted in the text. As such, citations of the Old Testament were used to enhance the belief value of the oral gospel by showing that its subject, Jesus, was the Christ who was promised and anticipated in Old Testament Scripture.

The parable of the sower is indeed programmatic to interpreting the Markan text. The rhetorical situation that Mark was addressing with his treatise is aptly captured in this parable. It identifies the audience by profiling them as people who ranged from those who showed complete lack of interest in the gospel, those who were unwilling to surrender fully to demands of the gospel, those who had half-heartedly embraced the gospel message, to those who were optimally fruitful. To each of these groups, Mark was writing to urge a faith shift to optimal response in faith and praxis to the oral gospel that was outside and independent of the text.

CHAPTER 6

Markan Miracle Stories as a Rhetorical Device

6.1 Introduction

This section analyzes the nature and significance of miracle stories in the Markan text. The aim is to affirm the plausibility of the supposition that the Markan miracle stories were used as rhetorical devices to enhance the belief value of the oral gospel. The study is premised on the supposition that the Markan text is a rhetorical communication that is aimed at eliminating the exigence of obduracy and lukewarm response to the oral gospel in Mark's audience. The study will utilize rhetorical criticism method. It will however incorporate speech theory in explicating the impact of the miracle stories on the readers.

A distinction has been made between the study of the Markan miracle stories and the study of Jesus's miracle episodes. This distinction is helpful in focusing the study on the main thesis of this study. The bulk of extant research on miracles is biased towards studying the nature of Jesus's miracle episodes.[1] So far, there is limited study that has been done on the nature and significance of the Markan miracle stories within the matrix of the Markan discourse. Research on miracle stories is old enough to warrant fresh research.

---

1. Craig S. Keener has authored a two-volume book on the credibility of New Testament miracles. See Keener, *Miracles*, vols. 1 and 2.

Notable researchers on this topic have been Alan Richardson in 1941, H. Van Der Loos in 1965, Gerd Theissen in 1983, and Werner Kahl in 1994.

The question that guides this analysis is: have individual or groups of miracle stories been used as rhetorical devices? Answering this question sheds light on whether miracle stories are written as a repository of tradition thereby suggesting that the textual genre of the Markan text is either history or biography. On the other hand, if they are rhetorical units then it would suggest that they are written for either theological or paraenetical purposes. Either way, the results have important hermeneutical implications. The study identifies the most plausible designation of the Markan genre. Narrowing the study further, the salient question is: are miracle stories in any way catalytic to faith and praxis demanded of in the oral gospel? An answer to this question sheds light on the purpose of miracle stories in the Markan text.

Whereas most of Jesus's miracles were performed to meet certain needs, the Markan miracle stories are explicitly and essentially communicative tools. To answer the question whether an individual or a group of miracle stories is a rhetorical device, the section has analyzed their structure, syntax, and their language nuances. This is in line with Gorman's suggestion that "elements of design – structure, patterns, and so on – manifest both the artistic beauty of a text and its function or intended impact."[2] The communicative purpose of miracle stories can be discerned in the narrative's speech acts, the author's commentaries, and their syntactic and semantic formations.

6.2 Definition of a Miracle

Richardson defines a miracle in biblical sense as "an event which happens in a manner contrary to the regularly observed process of nature."[3] Verbrugge intimates that "*semeion* denotes a miracle worked by a deity or a miracle worker that contradicts the natural course of things."[4] Both definitions have captured the supernatural aspect of miracles. This "supernaturalness" is the aspect that confers the performance of a miracle and the hearing of a miracle story the efficacy to evoke awe and hence creating an exalted view of the miracle

---

2. Gorman, *Elements of Biblical Exegesis*, 84.
3. Richardson, "Miracle, Wonder, Sign, Powers," 152.
4. Verbrugge, *New International Dictionary*, 523.

worker. Consequently, it enhances believability in the miracle worker (John 3:1–3), his word, and the gospel about him. Van Der Loos avers, "The virtue of divinity or of the 'divine man' was impressively illustrated by a display of miraculous power."[5] A miracle or miracle story also affirms the plausibility of other stories, promises or faith that are premised on the work and sayings of the miracle worker. As such, miracle stories in the Bible serve to convince and convict the audience about the connectedness of the miracle worker and his message to God (John 3:2). Consequently, the connectedness of miracles to God confers miracle stories with rhetorical efficacy, illocutionary acts, and perlocutionary effects that evoke a response, in faith and praxis, to the gospel that is premised on the teachings and work of the miracle worker.

6.3 Miracles in the Old Testament

The word miracle as used in the Bible has its roots in antiquity. It first surfaces in the Old Testament in Exodus 4:1–9. The miracles performed by Moses – turning his rod into a serpent, his hands becoming leprous, and turning the Nile water into blood – are called אוֹת in the clause וְלֹא יִשְׁמְעוּ לְקֹל הָאֹת הָרִאשׁוֹן which is translated into σημείου, genitive, neuter, singular of σημεῖον, in the clause "μηδὲ εἰσακούσωσιν τῆς φωνῆς τοῦ σημείου τοῦ πρώτου . . ." in the LXX.[6] These miraculous deeds are meant to be signs נִפְלְאֹתַי from פָּלָא (Exod 3:20). This term has the meaning of supernatural deeds or miracles. In some contexts, it can simply mean "wonders," "extraordinary things," or "marvelous things."

Miracles were primarily performed to meet the needs of the community. For example, Miracles that were performed before Pharaoh and the Israelites in Egypt were meant to convince Pharaoh and the Israelites that God had indeed sent Moses to urge Pharaoh to let Israel free from the Egyptian bondage. God was seen as the only source of numinous power that enabled performance of supernatural acts (John 3:1–2). Even in cases where non-deities performed miracles, God was believed to have superintended them and as such they were subordinate to his power (Exod 7:10–12).

---

5. Loos, *Miracles of Jesus*, 118.
6. Rahlfs, *Septuaginta*, 91.

God's provision of manna (Exod 16:4–35) supplied the need for food to the Israelites. Moreover, the aspect of affirming God's presence among the people was very much alive in performance of miracles. This is affirmed by the saying by Moses and Aaron that "in the evening, you shall know that it was the Lord who brought you out of Egypt" (Exod 16:6). Therefore, much as Mosaic miracles were performed to meet the needs of the children of Israel, they also served to affirm that God was in their midst and that he had indeed sent Moses to deliver them. To Pharaoh, miracles were used to as a judgment and to compel him to set Israel free.

Some miracles were requested by God's people to prove that he was actually the one who was communing with them. In Judges 6:17–22 and 6:36–40, Gideon asked for signs from God to prove that he was really the one talking to him. Later, miracles were seen as signs to authenticate God's approval of prophets and their ministries. Both Elijah and Elisha performed miracles which showed that God had indeed called them to be prophets (1 Kgs 17:16; 19–24; 2 Kgs 2:13–14; 4:5–7, 32–35; 42–44; 5:1–15). Daniel, Shadrach, Meshach, and Abednego also witnessed God's miraculous deliverances in captivity (Daniel 3:1–27; 6:21). These miracles caused the foreign kings to acknowledge that YHWH was the only true God. As such, miracles in the Old Testament served a redemptive and revelatory purpose. They also acted as signs that God was with his people and that his word was authentic and worthy of belief. Verbrugge says, "Miracles are equally regarded as divine confirmatory signs for the proclamation of a rabbi."[7]

Later, in the life of the community, stories of these miracles were narrated for their rhetorical efficacy in urging belief in the teachings that are premised on the person and work of the miracle worker. For example, the Exodus miracles were narrated in various ways and times to stir love, admiration, and faith in YHWH and to engender fidelity to his covenant. During the Passover celebrations, celebrants were reminded of God's deliverance (Exod 12:26). Though these miracle stories were independent of the Scripture, they nevertheless catalyzed fidelity and obedience to the covenant stipulations.

In investigating the nature and significance of miracle stories, it is worth noting that, the messianic age, a time when miracles were believed to be authenticators of the divine commission of the Messiah (Isa 42–61), was the

---

7. Verbrugge, *New International Dictionary*, 523.

context in which Jesus began his ministry. As such, Jesus viewed his miracles as proof that the eschatological kingdom of God had been ushered into the world. He told the Jews who were contending with him that if indeed he cast out demons by the finger of God, "then the kingdom of God has come" (Luke 11:20). As such, since Jesus's miracles connected Jesus with the Christ of the eschatological promises, then miracles and stories about them could catalyze response to the gospel that was premised on his person and work on the cross.

6.4 Miracles Stories in the New Testament

Stories about Jesus's miracles were circulating in his lifetime. The woman who had an issue of blood (5:27), the Syro-Phoenician woman (7:25), and Bartimaeus (10:47) had heard about Jesus prior to their first meeting with him. This means that, though, at times, Jesus had prohibited the beneficiaries of his miracles not to announce their healing, they had actually talked about it.

Miracles in the New Testament can be grouped into two categories, the miracles that Jesus performed in his ministry and the miracles that the apostles performed after Pentecost. The absence of diaries of Jesus's miracles suggests that the miracles were not diarized as they were taking place. If there were such diaries, they would have been treasured and preserved as repositories of the deeds of Jesus. External evidence shows that miracle and other New Testament stories were "reminisces of the apostles."[8] This means that the actions and sayings of Jesus were embedded in the eyewitnesses' memory. Some eyewitnesses are believed to have been alive by the time of writing some of the books of the New Testament (1 Cor 15:6). Writers and preachers of the gospel drew from this noetic repository for their communicative needs.

6.5 Extra-Biblical Miracle Stories

Other than miracles that are recorded in the Old and New Testaments, there were also extra-biblical accounts of miracles. Keener avers, "Deities like Asclepius and Serapis were believed able to provide benefits like healing."[9] In addition to ascription of healing miracles to deities, individual pagans were

---

8. Allert, *Revelation, Truth, Canon*, 100.
9. Keener, *Miracles*, 37.

also reported to have performed miracles. Keener says, "Ancient writers report the healings attributed to Vespasian before the inauguration of his flavian dynasty, undoubtedly a form of propaganda meant to authenticate his claim to rule."[10] However, Keener further posits that "the most significant pagan parallels to Christian miracle-worker stories such as the only extant literary account of Apollonius of Tyana, first appear in third century literature after Christian miracle stories had become widely known, and Christian and pagan expectations influenced each other more generally."[11] Christian or pagan, miracle stories were narrated to embed certain beliefs or notions about the miracle worker or his teachings in the audience.

6.6 Miracles as a Function of the Eschatological Kingdom

Scripture regards miracles, and especially healings, as aspects of the eschatological kingdom of God (Isa 53:5). Therefore, their occurrences in an era when there was a heightened expectation of the establishment of the kingdom of God were signs that the eschatological kingdom had finally been ushered into the world stage. As such, stories of miracles performed during the life and times of Jesus Christ bore rhetorical and illocutionary efficacy to convince the audience that indeed the eschatological kingdom had dawned and as a result, all the accruing benefits could now be procured upon faith in the gospel about the kingdom and its king, Jesus Christ. Richardson says that "there cannot be any doubt that they are intended to assert that the Messianic Age of the Isaianic prediction had already arrived. The significance of the miracles of Jesus lies in the fact that they are the miracles of the New Age."[12] As such, stories about the miracles of Jesus were used to show that indeed he was the Christ.

---

10. Keener, 62.

11. Keener, *Miracles*, 46; Philostratus, *Apollonius of Tyana*, Book I–IV, V–VIII edited and translated by Christopher P. Jones (Cambridge, Massachusetts: Harvard University Press, 2005), 419, V–VIII, 115;301–303.

12. Richardson, *Miracle Stories of the Gospels*, 43.

6.7 Miracle Stories in the Markan Text

According to Gerd Theissen, "miracle stories can replace miracles."[13] He argues that Acts shows that "conversions resulted not directly from miracles, but from the spread of news of them in the narratives: 'it became known throughout all Joppa, and many believed in the Lord (9:42; cf. 19:17f.).'"[14] However, though miracles and miracle stories sometimes serve the same purpose, they are not synonymous. In the Markan text, miracles are a function of Jesus and his disciples while miracle stories are a function of the author. Miraculous acts elicit awe leading to faith in the miracle worker or the one in whose name the miracle is performed. Vanhoozer refers to such acts as strategic action to which he says, they "bring about an intended result, some change in the world, other than understanding."[15]

On the other hand, miracle stories are mainly communicative speech acts. Vanhoozer describes communicative acts as acts that produce effect on other people through "proper communicative action."[16] He further posits, "The success of communicative action wholly depends on bringing about this one effect; understanding."[17] However, as will be argued,[18] miracle stories in Mark are functionally more of strategic actions than communicative acts. The way they are clustered together, their promptness as shown by highlighting immediacy, and their stupendous nature that could not be kept secret elicit awe in the person of Jesus thereby catalyzing a response to the gospel about him.

6.7.1 Current Trends in Research on Markan Miracle Stories

Over the years, the nature and significance of miracle stories have been understood in diverse ways. In 1941, Alan Richardson said that:

> they are told against the background of the theology of the early Church by preachers and teachers who saw in them not merely the supernatural ratification of that theology but rather the means of the instruction of converts in the truth of it. The

---

13. Theissen, *Miracle Stories*, 260.
14. Theissen, 260.
15. Vanhoozer, *First Theology*, 185.
16. Vanhoozer, 184.
17. Vanhoozer, 184–185.
18. This proposition has been argued in chapter 6, sections 6.7.2 and 6.7.4.

miracle-stories formed a characteristic part of the pedagogic technique of the earliest Christian missionaries.[19]

He further says that "St. Mark uses stories of miracles as vehicles by means of which instruction and exhortation may be conveyed... Their interest centers in their theological rather than in their historical character."[20] Whereas Richardson's argument is largely plausible, it is however directed by the presupposition that the contents of the Markan text constitute the gospel message. As such, narrating the episodes in the Christ event constitutes proclamation of the gospel.

However, it is arguable that, in a context where exegesis of biblical texts forms the only pedagogic technique of instructing both converts and believers, the contents of the text can be viewed as instructional material. That is why Richardson downplays the rhetorical value of miracle stories in ratifying the oral proclamation that he refers to as the theology of the early church. He is however right in positing that the stories are more centered on "ratifying a theological than a historical purpose."[21] Of special note, however, is that before, within, and after the writing of the Markan text, the main mode of preaching and teaching was ritual in celebrating the Lord's ordinances (1 Cor 11:23–26) and oral in proclamation of the salvific value of the Christ event[22] (Mark 16:15).

Theissen says, "Primitive Christian miracle stories are symbolic interactions on the part of groups within ancient society."[23] His position is that miracle stories are an expression of belief in miracles. He also regards them as social expressions that defined the group and that sharing the stories helped to bond the members and give them their unique identity. In support of his supposition that the primitive Christian miracle stories had a social function, he argues that "the men and women to whom they are addressed are intended to be moved to join the community which has escaped perdition... They have a missionary intention."[24] He concludes his argument by saying,

---

19. Richardson, *Miracle Stories of the Gospels*, 1.

20. Richardson, 1.

21. Richardson, 1.

22. Whitacre, *Patristic Greek Reader*, 232. This excerpt is quoted from Eusebius and Ecclesiastical History and Life of Constantine, Ecclesiastical History 3.24.3.

23. Theissen, *Miracle Stories*, 231.

24. Theissen, 259.

"the intention of primitive Christian miracle stories is to bear witness to a revelation of God which is directed to the whole world and seeks to bring all human beings to recognize that revelation."[25] As such, Theissen ascribes a missionary function to miracle stories.

Blackburn posits that "almost all scholars believe that Jesus saw a direct connection between the miracles he performed and his proclamation of the coming of God's kingdom."[26] His comment suggests that the aim of miracles was to authenticate the fulfilment and proclamation of the eschatological kingdom. An alternative view that has been advanced by Wright is that "miracles performed to the infirmed outcasts, Samaritans and Gentiles bore witness to their inclusion within the people of YHWH of those who had been outside."[27] He further avers that "it was to reconstitute those healed as members of Israel's God. In other words, these healings at the deepest level of understanding on the part of Jesus and his contemporaries would be seen as part of his total ministry."[28] Wright's comments suggest that he considers receipt of miracles as a confirmation that the recipients of miracles had been converted.

Bruce sees New Testament miracles as "signs of the messianic age."[29] Craig Keener's recent book on miracle surveys the credibility of the New Testament Miracle accounts,[30] while Theissen has surveyed miracle stories of the early Christian tradition. According to Riches, "Theissen's concern was their form and how they functioned in regard to existing social conditions, to the development of religious movements and traditions, and to individual self-consciousness."[31] Overall, there is a dearth in research on miracle stories and more so an investigation into Markan miracle stories as rhetorical devices that is not limited and bridled by the presupposition imposed by the second-century labelling of the Markan text as the gospel in written form. Notwithstanding evidence from Luke 1:1–4 and John 20:31 that these texts are written to ascertain and enhance belief in a proclamation that is outside

---

25. Theissen, 264.
26. Blackburn, "Miracles and Miracle Stories," 558.
27. Wright, *Jesus and the Victory of God*, 192.
28. Wright, 192.
29. Bruce, *New Testament Documents*, 84–89.
30. Keener, *Miracles*, 2011.
31. Riches, "Editor's Foreword," viii.

and independent of these texts, because of the blind resulting from the said presupposition, the value of miracle stories in authenticating this independent proclamation has not been identified and appreciated.

6.7.2 Mark's Commentaries in the Narration of Miracle Stories

This section investigates Mark's commentaries within the miracle stories. Lanes aptly refers to Mark's commentaries as "the literary device of a parenthetical statement to underscore the significance of a particular action or pronouncement."[32] As such, Mark's parenthetical comments do illuminate the nature and function of both the miracle episodes and the miracle stories. However, since this study is probing the rhetorical function of the miracle stories, its focus is more biased towards Mark's commentaries that illuminate the nature and function of the miracle stories. This has been done through a semantic and syntactic analysis of words or clauses that comment on the miracles using the historical present, comparative and superlative nuances, use of hyperbole, show of amazement, and appreciation. The cognitive and affective effects of the commentaries, as speech acts, on the audience have also been underscored so as to illuminate the purpose of the miracle stories in the Markan text.

Mark's commentaries on the context of miracles

Mark's use of hyperbolic language as in καὶ ἦν ὅλη ἡ πόλις ἐπισυνηγμένη πρὸς τὴν θύραν ("and the whole city was gathered together at the door" [1:33 ESV]) highlights the large reach of Jesus's teaching and healing ministry. It shows that, at the outset of his treatise, Mark intended to highlight the exalted portrait of Jesus and his teaching-cum-healing ministry by eliciting awe in his audience so as to draw them to greater response towards the oral gospel that was premised on Jesus's person and work on the cross.

Mark's commentaries on the reactions of the recipients of miracles

In the story of Jesus's miracle of calming the sea storm (4:30–41), Mark comments that the disciples feared to the point of asking "who can this be, that even the wind and the sea obey Him!" (4:41). By showing the disciples'

---

32. Lane, *Gospel According to Mark*, 26–27.

emotion of fear, Mark was in essence arousing his audience's empathy towards the disciples' emotional situation thereby enjoining them in their awe concerning the exalted persona of Jesus. Lane says, "The use of such literary devices as the parenthetical statement or the rhetorical question was designed to keep men from a spectator-relationship to what Jesus said or did."[33] Whereas the question "who can this be, that the wind and the sea obey him?" showed the profound wonder of Jesus's audience, as to who Jesus was, a narrated version to Mark's audience, who were simultaneously hearing the oral gospel about Jesus, works towards drawing them to greater response to the oral gospel.

In narrating the miracle of the healing of the demon-possessed man in Gerasenes[34] (5:1–20), Mark observes that the demoniac worshiped Jesus even before his deliverance took place (5:6). The word used to describe the demoniac's action is προσεκύνησεν – literally to do obeisance. In essence, Mark was highlighting the exalted persona of Jesus through the foil of the narrative about the subordination of demons under the authority of Jesus. Finally, after the healed demoniac was commissioned to go and proclaim what had happened to him, his proclamation caused his audience to marvel (5:20). By noting the level of amazement using the adjective πάντες and an imperfect ἐθαύμαζον, Mark showed the extensive reach of the news about Jesus. It also shows that Mark would like his audience to also marvel at the stories about the miracles that Jesus performed. Once more, in reporting that Jesus declined the healed demoniac's request to follow him but instead commissioning him to go and proclaim his healing, Mark is communicating to his readers, who are also hearing the oral gospel, that Jesus's priority was the proclamation of the gospel thereby drawing them to value, believe, and obey the oral gospel that he and his contemporaries were proclaiming.

Similarly, after the healing of the woman who had a flow of blood for twelve years, Mark comments that she feared and trembled and fell before Jesus (5:33). Fear and trembling are reported using a participle aorist phrase, φοβηθεῖσα καὶ τρέμουσα (fearing and trembling), a parallelism, to dramatize the action. Dramatization of the story has the effect of drawing the audience

---

33. Lane, 27.
34. Following manuscripts (ℵ*) B C ᵗˣᵗ (Δ) Θ syrˢ,ᵖ,ʰ, UBS 4th rev. ed. 1993, Matthew 8:28 identifies this location as Gadarenes.

to emotionally participate in her desperation so as to equally be overwhelmed by Jesus's gracious act of healing her. In effect, the audience is drawn to believe in the oral gospel about him.

Mark's commentaries on the reaction of the crowds

In the first miracle in Capernaum, Mark communicates the effect of Jesus's miracles by using words that describe the feelings of those who witnessed Jesus's preaching and miracles (1:22, 27; 2:12). With such words as ἐξεπλήσσοντο (1:22), an indicative imperfect of ἐκπλήσσομαι, he is able to communicate not just the fact of the episode but to dramatically transport and draw the audience into the imaginative arena of the action. Wallace notes that the imperfect tense "portrays the action as it unfolds."[35] The impact of the text in catalyzing a response towards the gospel about Jesus is thereby enhanced.

After the healing of the demoniac in Gerasenes (5:1–20), those who saw him healed and heard about the nature of the exorcism are reported to having been afraid (5:15) to the point of begging Jesus to depart from their region. This reaction is strange. The reason for their asking Jesus to depart from their region can only be speculated. However, whatever the case, to a reader of the miracle story, Jesus's persona is magnified thereby drawing the reader to respond to teachings that are premised on Jesus's work.

On the raising of Jairus's daughter (5:1–43), Mark narrates that after she was restored to life, the people were greatly amazed ἐξέστησαν [εὐθὺς] ἐκστάσει μεγάλη. Both ἐξέστησαν and ἐκστάσει form a parallelism to amplify the amazement that came upon the crowd. It is followed by an adjective μεγάλη which serves to magnify the "amazement" all the more. These same people had ridiculed Jesus when he had described the state of the girl as being asleep. This juxtaposing of ridicule and amazement acted as a foil to the exalted persona of Jesus thereby enhancing the gospel's belief value.

Similarly, in the healing of the deaf and mute (7:31–37), Mark observes that the people were astonished beyond measure, saying, "He has done all things well" (7:37). This great endorsement of the works of Jesus by the crowds coming almost at the close of his ministry in Galilee, in a way, summarizes the success of Jesus's ministry in Galilee. Though he had faced serious opposition, his ministry of healing and preaching had achieved remarkable

---

35. Wallace, *Greek Grammar*, 541.

success. At least, even in the midst of the obdurate, that is, the Scribes and Pharisees (2:6, 16; 3:22), there were times when he achieved optimum fruitfulness as the endorsement in 7:37 shows. Arguably, Mark would have wished his audience to give the same endorsement to the oral gospel that he and his contemporaries were preaching (1:1).

Mark's comments on the nature of miracle

Mark is very keen on noting the immediacy of the healing miracles. In narrating the healing of the leper (1:40–42), Mark notes that he was healed immediately upon being touched by Jesus. The paralytic, in Mark 2:11–12, was also healed immediately upon being told by Jesus to take up his bed and go home. Jairus's daughter was also restored to life immediately upon Jesus taking her up by her hand (5:42). Describing immediacy in the Markan text using the adverb εὐθέως is more of a rhetorical nuancing of his narrative to describe promptness and effectiveness rather than an expression of hurriedness to go over his "long introduction"[36] to the passion narrative as has been supposed by a section of scholarship. Noting the immediacy with which miracles happened demonstrates Jesus's power over the infirmities and calamities that he was solving.

Mark's use of miracle stories as a rhetorical device is aptly shown in the summary of the effect of Jesus's miracles in Mark 6:56, "καὶ ὅπου ἂν εἰσεπορεύετο εἰς κώμας ἢ εἰς πόλεις ἢ εἰς ἀγρούς, ἐν ταῖς ἀγοραῖς ἐτίθεσαν τοὺς ἀσθενοῦντας καὶ παρεκάλουν αὐτὸν ἵνα κἂν τοῦ κρασπέδου τοῦ ἱματίου αὐτοῦ ἅψωνται· καὶ ὅσοι ἂν ἥψαντο αὐτοῦ ἐσῴζοντο." Use of ὅπου and εἰς κώμας, ἢ εἰς πόλεις, ἢ εἰς ἀγρούς, is developmental parallelism of the adverb ὅπου that is used to emphasize the indiscriminate and extensive reach of the power of Jesus. "ἵνα κἂν τοῦ κρασπέδου τοῦ ἱματίου αὐτοῦ ἅψωνται."and "καὶ ὅσοι ἂν ἥψαντο αὐτοῦ ἐσῴζοντο" are also used for their rhetorical power to demonstrate the diminutive power of illnesses when confronted with the exalted power of Jesus Christ. This nuancing is a rhetorical embellishment that has rhetorical efficacy to evoke awe and enhance believability in Jesus. Consequently, it catalyzes audience response in faith to the oral gospel about Jesus Christ the Son of God (1:1).

---

36. Sections of Markan research have taken it as axiomatic that the Markan text is largely a long introduction of the passion narratives.

In summary, Mark's commentaries in the narration of miracle stories shows that he used miracle stories as both strategic and communicative acts. As strategic acts, they create awe in the person of Jesus thereby drawing his audience to respond to the oral gospel. They are also communicative acts in that they also engender understanding of who Jesus is. All in all, Mark's commentaries are rhetorical devices and speech acts that were used to catalyze reader-response towards the oral gospel that Mark and his contemporaries were proclaiming.

6.7.3 Genre of Miracle Stories

The literary genre that narrates virtues and deeds to exalt a person's stature is referred to as aretalogy. The Markan miracle stories are narrated in a form that suggests that their genre is similar to Greek aretalogy. Etymologically, "aretalogy" is derived from the Greek word ἀρετῆς, meaning "virtue, uprightness, and goodness."[37] According to Van Der Loos, in aretalogy, "the virtues and deeds of the 'divine man' had to be proclaimed and celebrated for the purpose of edifying the readers and pleasantly occupying their minds, but at the same time in order to spread the fame of the one concerned."[38] The virtues and deeds of Jesus Christ are narrated in the Markan text not only for the purpose of edifying the readers and pleasantly occupying their minds but more so to enhance the belief value in the gospel about him.

Miracles were also seen in Jewry as a sign that the performer was sent by God (John 3:2). As such, narrating miracles that had been performed by Jesus had the effect of showing that he was a man who had come from God. According to Van Der Loos, narrating the miracles done by a "divine man" was meant "to uplift, to build up the ranks of the believers, their highest aspiration is psychagogy, guidance of the soul."[39] Thus, he suggests that miracle stories had an affective effect on the audience. He concludes by saying that some scholars also see "the stories of miracles in the New Testament in this genre as well: the virtues and miracles of the 'divine man' Jesus are described for the purpose of glorifying Him and making Him known to wide circles."[40]

---

37. Kubo, *Reader's Greek-English Lexicon*, 244.
38. Loos, *Miracles of Jesus*, 118.
39. Loos, 119.
40. Loos, 119.

Whereas the purpose for which Jesus performed miracles were not, purposively, either to draw crowds or even to increase his fame, as demonstrated by his injunction to the people healed not to broadcast the miracle, the narrator's purpose of telling the story, at a later day, would be to make his views and proclamations about Jesus more believable.

Mark's use of immediacy in explaining Jesus's promptness in attending to his daily preaching and miracle-performing ministry and also in the promptness in which the miracles took place shows that the genre of the Markan miracle stories is aretalogy. In aretalogy, the results of the narrated miracles are shown to have happened "immediately."[41] According to Van Der Loos, aretalogy narrates "not only the admiration, surprise, dismay, acclamation, but also skepticism and derision" that the "divine man's ministry evoked in his audience."[42] This explains Mark's narration of the controversies between Jesus and the Jewish religious leaders some of who said, "'He is possessed by Beelzebub . . . by the prince of demons he casts out the demons'" (3:22 ESV).

Though aretalogy was a genre that is identified as a handbook Greco-Roman genre, it is however not unique to Greco-Roman literary convention. The portrayal of Moses as a miracle worker and confidant of God, in the Pentateuch, suggests that its genre has aspects of aretalogy. However, in Hebrew literary convention, different genres had not been identified and an apt nomenclature for each type developed. A comparison of the description of Moses and his miracles in the Pentateuch with the description of Jesus and his miracles in the Markan text suggests that the genre of the Markan miracle stories can be described as Hebrew aretalogy.

6.7.4 Rhetorical Structuring of the Miracle Stories

This section reviews the structure and syntactical formation of the Markan miracle stories in order to ascertain their rhetorical purpose within the matrix of the Markan discourse.

Structure of Mark's miracle stories

Whereas the first miracle recorded in Mark 1:23–28 is set within Jesus's preaching ministry, the corresponding miracle story is set within the church's

---

41. Loos, 120.
42. Loos, 120.

preaching ministry. The same applies to other miracles recorded in the Markan text. This shows that the church's preaching ministry is the context in which all miracle stories should be interpreted. This miracle story affirms Mark's assertion that Jesus taught people as one having authority. It is apparent that Mark narrated the miracle story to support his comment on Jesus's teaching that καὶ ἐξεπλήσσοντο ἐπὶ τῇ διδαχῇ αὐτοῦ· ἦν γὰρ διδάσκων αὐτοὺς ὡς ἐξουσίαν ἔχων καὶ οὐχ ὡς οἱ γραμματεῖς (1:22). His use of the conjunction "γαρ" highlights, at the outset of the narrative, that "Jesus's teachings," which constituted aspects of the oral gospel, were the major albeit latent theme of his text.

Mark used the first miracle story to set the direction, tempo and purpose of miracle stories in the text. It demonstrates that it was narrated to succinctly highlight the virtue and persona of Jesus for the purpose of enhancing the belief value of the gospel that Mark and his contemporaries were preaching. Basically, the choice of syntax, genre, and structure were purposely made in view of Mark's purpose of highlighting the ethos and persona of Jesus.

The seriousness and impact of the problem needing a miracle

Mark's miracle stories show a similar script. The problem that calls for the miracle is normally intensified. Examples are: how intense the affliction calling for the miracle was, (5:1–5, 25–26, 35); how boisterous the waves of the sea were (4:37); or how great the multitude that required to be fed was (6:35–38; 8:1–5). In the first miracle story (1:21–28), Mark intensified the problem by highlighting the fact that the miracle was performed on a Sabbath day when, according to Sabbath Laws, work was not allowed. It was also a time when Jesus would have faced serious opposition by the religious leaders for performing a miracle. Thus, the miracle story was used as a foil to Jesus's exalted persona and grace by first showing the odds that were against his performance of the particular miracle. This method of highlighting the seriousness of the odds that Jesus needed to surmount to perform his miracles shows that Mark used miracle stories not as a mere biographical or historical repository of the life and times of Jesus but as a rhetorical device to enhance the belief value of the oral gospel.

Similarly, the miracle story about the exorcism of the demoniac who was living in the tombs (5:3–17) was told for its rhetorical function of highlighting the exalted persona of Jesus and by extension enhancing the belief value of the oral gospel. In Mark 5:3–5, Mark magnifies the problem by narrating how the demoniac lived in ritually unclean places, that chains could not restrain him, and that nobody was strong enough to subdue him. The demoniac's agony was captured by his cries and self-inflicted injuries. However, Mark narrates that, at the sight of Jesus, he fell on his knees in fear and when Jesus rebuked the unclean spirits, they left him and he was immediately healed.

Stating the long duration that the recipient of the miracle had lived with the problem (5:25–34) also shows that the problem had defied all extant methods of resolution. Subsequently, the immediacy of Jesus's miracle went a long way in highlighting the great numinous power inherent in Jesus compared to all other persons and methods used in the past. Again, such nuancing of the story using rhetorical embellishments that magnify the person of Jesus evokes a positive response towards a gospel that is premised on his person and work.

Failure of conventional healing methods

Another aspect that is noticeable in how miracle stories are narrated is highlighting the failure of the extant conventional methods in tackling the infirmities that are finally solved by Jesus's numinous power. Narration about the failure of the extant healing methods that the sick person had tried to no avail is meant to expose the supernatural aspect of the power in the healer. The woman who had been bleeding for twelve years is said to have visited all doctors to no avail, notwithstanding the fact that she had spent all her living (5:26). Contrariwise, at a mere touch of the hem of Jesus's garment, at no cost at all, she is completely healed.

Mark used the portrayal of the failure of Jesus's disciples (9:14–29) as a foil to Jesus's elevated persona. Mark could not spare any rhetorical arsenal in his disposal to magnify Jesus in order to enhance the belief value in the oral gospel that was premised on his person and work. Narrating the failings of the disciples suggests that the Markan text was written at a time when the apostles had not been accorded a larger than life persona by the church. It is arguable that it could have been written in the mid-fifties when most of the apostles were still alive. Treatises written during the time when the disciples were accorded a reverenced status would in a way concentrate more on their positive exploits.

Injunction not to reveal the miracle worker

A rather interesting phenomenon in Mark's miracle stories is highlighting that Jesus restrained some of the healed persons not to broadcast both the miracle and the miracle worker (1:44; 5:43; 7:36; 8:26; 9:9). Interestingly, Mark also narrates that the recipients of the miracles would not remain quiet but would broadcast their healing. Some scholars have argued that this injunction was meant to conceal Jesus's identity. As such, this phenomenon has been labelled "the messianic secret."[43]

The question that arises is not why Jesus would issue such injunction for any answer would be speculative. A more useful question would rather be why Mark narrated the story emphasizing the failure of the beneficiaries of the miracle to keep quiet despite being told by their benefactor not to broadcast the miracles? Though it could be construed as evidence from silence, Kahl has noted that "the healed subjects are not punished by Jesus for their disobedience."[44] The answer has to do with the expected perlocutionary effect of Mark's story on his audience. Thiselton aptly distinguishes such communication as having perlocutionary speech acts. He says, "I distinguish between 'illocutionary' speech acts, which depend for their effectiveness on a combination of situation and recognition, and 'perlocutionary' speech acts which depend for their effectiveness on sheer causal (psychological or rhetorical) persuasive power."[45] Jesus's injunction, which could not have been fully complied with, was meant as a strategic communication to elicit the opposite of its stated intention. Vanhoozer defines strategic communication as "an action that aims to produce perlocutionary effects on readers other than by means of understanding."[46] He is, however, not comfortable with dissemination of truth through use of rhetoric. He avers, "If all truth is a species of rhetoric, as some postmoderns and apparently some first-century Corinthians believed, then all illocutions become perlocutions."[47]

To Mark's audience, both the story of the miracle and the disobeyed injunction worked in a complementary way to magnify the intended impact of narrating the story, that is, exalting the person of Jesus by magnifying the effect of the spectacle that Mark dramatizes in the story. Mark therefore highlights Jesus's injunction and the beneficiary's inability to obey as a foil

---

43. Wrede, *Messianic Secret*, 141.
44. Kahl, *New Testament Miracle Stories*, 223.
45. Thiselton, *First Epistle to the Corinthians*, 51.
46. Vanhoozer, *First Theology*, 185.
47. Vanhoozer, 187.

to show the excellence of the miracle through its impact on the audience. The inability to keep silent shows that the impact of the miracle was too overwhelming to be swept under the carpet of silence. Gundry argues that "Mark is interested in the stupendousness of the miracle, which causes the crowd, 'however much he was ordering them,' to 'proclaim' the miracle 'all the more' (μᾶλλον περισσότερον)."[48] As such, Mark's highlight of the injunction functions as a dramatic rhetorical embellishment in the Markan text.

It is also arguable that Jesus's injunction was loosely given to be disobeyed. It is noticeable that most of these miracles except the healing of Peter's mother in law were performed either in the temple or other public places. The question that arises is: why would Jesus issue such injunction when he was not keen to conceal the miracles by performing them in secret? Even the healing of the woman with an issue of blood that had happened in secret was broadcast by Jesus himself (5:25–35). The answer to this question lies in the beneficiaries' inherent inability to obey the injunction due to the inevitability of the disclosure, a fact that Jesus knew and rhetorically exploited for its efficacy in impacting the hearers of his deeds. It ended up magnifying the real-time witness of those who observed the episode and those who heard the story of the miracle. This can be identified as one of Jesus's methods of increasing the reach and impact of his ministry.

Jesus used the same device when he requested the disciples to give food to over five-thousand people knowing very well that they could not afford to buy it (6:30; 8:1–9). These feeding miracles were performed in a way that first magnifies the problem in order to bring out greater effect on his disciples and the rest of the multitude that was listening to his teachings, once the miracle is performed. Later, when Mark tells the story, he adopts the same rhetorical device to magnify Jesus's person to his readers.

It would be strange for Jesus Christ to be performing a miracle that prompts the audience to ask in awe "Who can this be, that even the wind and the sea obey Him!" (4:41) and at the same time seem to be hiding his identity? To Mark's readers, who had heard about Jesus in the oral gospel proclamation, the question must have been read as a rhetorical question which was used to affirm the notion about Jesus's divinity. It is arguable that Mark chose and used these rhetorical narratives about Jesus's ministry to both

---

48. Gundry, *Mark*, 385.

pose and answer the same question that the audience of Jesus had asked, "who can this be?" The miracle stories answer the question by affirming the thesis of his treatise that Jesus was indeed the Christ, the Son of God (1:1). As such, what has been touted as maintenance of secrecy is actually a trumpeting of Jesus's identity and an enhancing of the belief value of the oral gospel about him. Whereas, by performing miracles, Jesus was elevating his status as the object of faith while also showing that the kingdom of heaven was at hand, Mark's miracle stories are a rhetorical device to urge belief and obedience to the oral gospel about Jesus Christ.

Clustering the miracle stories as a rhetorical device

Over and above embellishment of a text or speech, rhetoric is also concerned in how texts are structured so as to attract, interest, and direct its readership. In this connection, this section has analyzed the function of clustering most of the Markan miracle stories in one location of the book and whether such restructuring constitutes a rhetorical device.

It is evident that Mark clustered most of the miracle stories in the first section of his text (1:1–8:26). Out of the eighteen miracle episodes recorded in the Markan text, fifteen are reported in the first half of the book in Galilee and its environs. Witherington notes that "Almost all of Mark's miracles are clustered in the first half of his Gospel, the stories about them making up 47 percent of the half."[49] Placement of stories of one kind of episode that constitute a common theme in one section of the book must have been deliberately done. Watts noticed this unusual formation and posited, "One of the arresting features of Mark's gospel is the disproportionate distribution of Jesus' miracles."[50] He has given the following statistics:

> Although the inherent uncertainties in verse counting make it a rather blunt instrument, nevertheless, the importance of Jesus' miracles for Mark can be seen in that approximately 177 out of 666 verses, or 27% of Marks gospel deals with miracles, taking (the shorter ending). If the passion narrative (ch. 11ff) is excluded, this rises to 40% (some 168 out of 425 verses) . . . If we concentrate on the first section alone (to 8:26) Jesus' miracles

---

49. Witherington, *Gospel of Mark*, 92–93.
50. Watts, *Isaiah's New Exodus and Mark*, 139.

comprise an even higher 47% (approximately 145 out of 311 verses), while in the remaining two sections (8:27–16:8) miracles (an exorcism, a healing, a "cursing", and the resurrection) represent only 11% (about 47 out of 355 verses). Furthermore, Mark's summaries, confined as they are to the first section, also reflect a similar interest in Jesus' healings and casting out of demons (1:32–32, 39; 3:10–12; 6:5, 53–56). Even allowing for some variation due to disagreement over what constitutes miracle material, this represents a rather lop-sided distribution.[51]

Watts suggests that this concentration of the miracle stories in one section is "consistent with an Isaianic New Exodus hermeneutic,"[52] which "presents Jesus in terms of the Yahweh-Warrior who delivers the captives from demonic bondage, as Israel's healer, and as the one who forgives their sins."[53] It is doubtful that this is the reading and understanding that Mark intended for his readers, some of whom, considering the low rate of literacy, may not have been conversant with the motif of Isaianic new exodus let alone Watts's interpretation. A theological purpose to prove the divinity of Christ may not also be the reason since reporting fewer miracles and in a proportionate manner would have achieved the same purpose. Arguably, this formation is meant to be a rhetorical device that was chosen and employed to awe the audience in view of the many and varied miracles that Jesus performed.

Just as parallelism is used to emphasize an aspect of the text, even so clustering anecdotes of miracle episodes in one location of the book of Mark serves to magnify the person of Jesus and as such increases the belief value of the oral gospel. According to Ryken, Wilhoit, and Longman, this "cataloguing of deeds"[54] constitutes a rhetorical device. As such, clustering miracle stories in Mark can be considered as a rhetorical device since it is employed to solely convince and convict the audience of the belief value of the oral gospel message through its affective power to amaze the audience and therefore elevate their view of the person of Jesus and consequently draw them to respond to the gospel that is premised on his person and work.

---

51. Watts, 139.
52. Watts, 139.
53. Watts, 140.
54. Ryken, Wilhoit, and Longman, *Dictionary of Biblical Imagery*, 724.

The effect of juxtaposing miracles stories with Jesus's conflict with Jewish leaders

Mark juxtaposed miracle stories about Jesus with stories of Jesus's controversy with Jewish religious leaders. A Juxtaposition of positive and negative deeds is a foil that succeeds in highlighting the positive deeds and their subject when they are viewed against the background of the negative deeds and their subject. It also succeeds in distancing the readers from the negative deeds whose distaste is pronounced when viewed together with the positive deeds.

Jesus's reason for performing miracles of various kinds was not the same reason why Mark told the stories of the same miracles. Performing miracles such as healing and casting out demons from people was part of the overall mission of Jesus Christ (Luke 4:18). Some of the miracles were performed to initiate particular teachings while others were mere benevolent acts. For example, in Mark 3:1–6, Jesus initiated the healing on a Sabbath in order to teach and correct the wrong notions that the religious leaders held about the Sabbath laws. In some occasions he performed miracles to teach on the necessity of faith (2:1–12). However, Mark's reason for narrating the miracle stories is different. The rhetorical efficacy to raise the miracle worker's profile that is inherent in narrating miracle stories shows that they were narrated to paint an exalted persona of Jesus.

A review of Jesus's missionary itinerary suggests that he went to different locations purposely to preach the gospel and not to perform miracles (1:38–40; 2:2, 13; 6:2, 6, 12, 30). However, in all these instances, the content of the preaching and teaching is not specified. Instead, Mark has enumerated the miracles that Jesus performed. Highlighting that Jesus went to different places to preach suggests that preaching the gospel was the main function and context within which the miracles and controversies with the Jewish religious leaders happened. Similarly, the church's preaching was the main function and context within which the miracle stories were narrated. This suggests that the miracle stories were narrated to enhance the belief value of the gospel which was premised on the salvific deeds of the miracle worker.

6.7.5 Function of Miracle Stories in the Markan Text

Theissen notes that

> the development which can be seen here from Jesus to primitive Christianity consists of two contrary tendencies. On the one

hand there is a tendency to smooth out characteristic features, a "popular adaptation," which can be observed in other traditions. On the other hand, there is a tendency to intensify, to make the miraculous even more striking, which goes well beyond the historical and factual.[55]

Theissen's observation and especially his suggestion that the miraculous "goes well beyond the historical and factual,"[56] tends to push the text towards being considered a myth. Notwithstanding this contentious assertion, his observation suggests that the Markan miracle stories are used as rhetorical devices to enhance the persona of Jesus and thus the gospel concerning him.

The difference in form and emphasis of miracle stories in the books by the four evangelists suggests that they were employed to eliminate different exigencies in different rhetorical situations. A removal of the miracle stories from Matthew, Luke, and to some extent John, would not irreparably alter the plot of their storyline. Matthew is biased towards narrating the teachings of Jesus. Arguably, the aim is to guide the church in its catechetical work. Luke is biased more towards writing a historical treatise about Jesus. Arguably, his aim was to meet his stated purpose of affirming to Theophilus the things that he had been taught (Luke 1:1–4). John has written a christological treatise with the purpose of showing that Jesus is the Christ, the Son of God in order to spur faith in his name (John 20:30–31). However, minus the miracle stories, Mark would be irreparably destroyed. Its miracle stories are core to its purpose of catalyzing audience response to the oral gospel that was majorly premised on Jesus's work on the cross. Jesus's persona could not have been better enhanced by narrating any other of his ministry functions than the miracles that he had performed including the miracle of his resurrection.

Miracle stories as a rhetorical device

Barrett states, "The Markan miracles stories themselves are commonplace enough, but it is their Christological and eschatological context and interpretation which set them apart from either Jewish or Greco-Roman miracle tales about figures such as Honi the Circle Drawer or Apollonius of Tyana."[57]

---

55. Theissen, *Miracle Stories*, 281.
56. Theissen, 281.
57. Barrett, *Holy Spirit and the Gospel*, 57.

Particularly, the scriptural prediction that miracles would be aspects of the eschatological kingdom is important in illuminating the significance of miracle stories in the Markan text. Keener posits that "among the signs of the Messianic era, Isaiah predicted that the sick would be healed and the mute tongues would speak (Is. 35:5–6), and that God's people would be witnesses for him (Is. 40:10)."[58] As such, the Markan miracle stories also served to position the preaching of the gospel about Jesus Christ as an aspect of the messianic age.

As such, Mark narrated Jesus's miracles as rhetorical device to convince his audience that the historical Jesus, who was the subject of the oral gospel, was approved by God through the miracles that he performed and therefore he was the eschatological Christ. Through the Markan miracle stories, Mark demonstrated that the Christ-centered gospel that was being orally proclaimed was authentic and as such, it was worthy of the audience's faith.

A rhetorical reading of Mark 4:35–5:43

This portion is a cluster of four miracles, the first is a nature miracle, the second an exorcism of evil spirits, the third a healing, and the fourth a restoration of a dead girl to life. The cluster is a good representative of the spectrum of the miracles that Jesus was performing in the course of his preaching ministry. In his study of the miracles in this section, Blomberg notes, "They are enacted 'objects lessons' about the nature and arrival of the kingdom of God."[59] Blomberg has analyzed miracles from an episodic point of view. However, this study has analyzed the Markan miracle stories in the context of the church preaching and then evaluated their rhetorical value in drawing Mark's audience to respond to the oral gospel.

This cluster of miracle stories epitomizes the rhetorical aspect of miracle stories in the entire book. The supernatural aspect of the miracles that show Jesus's control over nature, demons, incurable diseases, and even death can cause the audience to question Jesus's humanity and see him as either sent of God or having a form of God (John 3:2). This in turn enhances Jesus's ethos. According to Phillips, ethos is an "appeal to character."[60] Mark is appealing to Jesus's exalted character to enhance belief in the oral gospel that is premised on his propitious work on the cross.

---

58. Keener, *IVP Bible Background Commentary*, 184.
59. Blomberg, *Jesus and the Gospels*, 268.
60. Phillips, "Rhetoric," 229.

In the story of the first miracle in this section (4:37–41), Mark first introduces the problem that called for the performance of the miracle. Unperturbed by a sea storm, Jesus was sleeping on a cushion in a boat. The scene of a boisterous sea that is contrasted by Jesus sleeping comfortably in the boat is intended to magnify the person of Jesus who is not worried by the storm. Arguably, Mark is showing that Jesus was not worried of the natural phenomenon since he had power over nature. Rhetorically, this narration portrays Jesus as one who is Lord over nature. Gundry captures the rhetorical aspect so well in his statement that,

> The use of the historical present tense, γίνεται dramatizes the power of the threat about to be described . . . Several other data likewise magnify the threat: (1) the choice of λαῖλαψ, "gale"; (2) the addition of μεγάλη, "great," and ἀνέμου, "wind," which apart from emphasis on the power of the threat are superfluous . . . to sharpen the point of emphasis.[61]

The awe evoked by this miracle was so great that the disciples feared to the point of asking, "Who can this be, that even the wind and the sea obey Him!" (4:35–41). However, to Mark's audience, who are not strangers to Jesus, having heard the oral gospel, the story would doubtlessly engender greater response to the gospel that was premised on Jesus's work on the cross.

The second miracle in the pericope is the healing of a demon-possessed person in the region of Gerasenes (5:1–20). Mark narrates that no man could bind him even with chains by use of the phrase καὶ οὐδὲ ἁλύσει οὐκέτι οὐδεὶς. This phrase further magnifies the problem that was to be solved by Jesus's miracle. This is a rhetorical structuring that is aimed at, correspondingly, magnifying both the miracle and the miracle worker. Specifically, it was structured to show that Jesus had supernatural power.

Though the demons in the man recognized Jesus as the Son of the Most High God, Jesus needed no approval and witness of Satan. Mark wanted his audience to understand that Jesus had no league with the devil. Jesus's opposition of the devil must have evoked a positive perception of his person and mission. The reason for highlighting that the demons possessing the man were many was to once more amplify the problem so as to correspondingly

---

61. Gundry, *Mark*, 238–239.

magnify the numinous power of the miracle worker. In other words, the narration is used as a foil to Jesus's power.

After healing the demoniac, Jesus told him, "Go home to your own people and tell them how much the Lord has done for you" (4:19). After broadcasting what Jesus had done to him, all the people were amazed. This story flies against the notion of the so-called "messianic secret." This point shows that the supposition that Jesus was hiding his identity is not founded on an exhaustive analysis of biblical data. The reason for Jesus issuing injunctions to some people not to broadcast their healing as in Mark 5:43 should be traced to other reasons other than hiding his identity[62] from his audience.

The next miracle in this cluster is the miracle of healing the woman who had an issue of blood for twelve years. Immediately upon touching the hem of Jesus' garment she was healed (5:29). Interestingly, Jesus began to enquire loudly who had touched him. Upon the woman identifying herself he spoke to her and acknowledged her healing before the crowd that was following him. Again this action, and others like, it negate the argument that Jesus wanted to keep his identity secret. If Jesus wanted to keep his identity secret, then he could not have enquired about the one who had touched him. The fact that Jesus wanted her to identify herself openly as the one who had been healed, is enough proof that the so-called messianic secret is not a notion that finds general consistency and traction in the text.

The final miracle in the pericope is the raising of Jairus's daughter. Mark narrated the death and the miracle of raising Jairus's daughter in a very dramatic fashion. After she is raised, Jesus gives the parents the command not to "let anyone know about this" (5:43 NIV). Interestingly, all the people who had come to mourn the dead girl were outside of the house where the healed girl was, how is it that Jesus would tell the parents of the girl not to let anyone "know about this"? Is it conceivable that they could have kept quiet? Or was it rhetorically said to be a reference point to the witnesses that the miracle was too great not to be broadcast even though Jesus had told the parents not to broadcast it? Quoting Reimarus, Schweitzer posits, "He forbid these miracles to be made known, even in cases where they could not be possibly kept hidden, 'with the sole purpose of making people more eager to talk of

---

62. This study has argued that the injunction is a rhetorical device that was used to intensify the impact of the miracle and the miracle story on the audience.

them.'"[63] Schweitzer's assertion is plausible. Mark's method of narrating these injunctions to magnify the effect of the miracle story on the audience is a unique Markan innovation.

Mark was so keen to highlight Jesus's injunction to the beneficiaries of miracles not to broadcast the miracles. He was equally keen to highlight that the injunctions were not obeyed. Arguably, such narratives act as rhetorical devices to magnify his audience's view of both the miracle and the miracle worker. This method of narrating a story functions as a foil at two levels. At the episodic level, the injunction served to amplify both Jesus's miracle and the witness thereof in consideration of the inevitability of broadcasting the miracles. It is a strategic action. At the narrative level, the inevitability of broadcasting the miracles despite Jesus's injunction not to broadcast them, itself being a strategic communication, served a rhetorical purpose of magnifying the miracle, the miracle worker, and consequently the gospel that was premised on Jesus's person and work on the cross.

6.8 Summary

The Markan miracle stories have one thing in common: the need that calls for the miracle is dramatically highlighted. For example, the demon-possessed person is said to be so violent that no one could bind him (5:3). Similarly, the woman who had an issue of blood is reported to have visited all the physicians but instead of getting better she was growing worse (5:26). Again, by the time Jesus arrives at Jairus's home, the girl who was sick is said to have died (5:35). Highlighting the magnitude of the need that required a miracle seems to have been used as a rhetorical foil to correspondingly magnify the miracle and the miracle worker.

Arguably, Mark's miracle stories are not narrated as mere repositories of tradition. Instead, they are a rhetorical communication that is aimed at eliminating an exigence in an identified rhetorical situation. The genre of the Markan miracle stories is Hebrew aretalogy. However, the aim is to accomplish a paraenetic purpose. Specifically, they were aimed at highlighting the ethos of Jesus with the consequential effect of enhancing audience belief in the oral gospel that is premised on his person and work on the cross.

---

63. Schweitzer, *Quest of the Historical Jesus*, 19.

CHAPTER 7

Markan Passion Narratives as a Rhetorical Device

7.1 Introduction

This section surveys the Markan version of Jesus's passion story. The main focus of the enquiry is to establish whether the passion story was used as a rhetorical device to catalyze audience response to the gospel about Jesus Christ, the Son of God. As such, it probes the nature and function of the passion story in the matrix of the Markan discourse. A distinction has been made between the passion episode and the passion story. Though there is some congruence between the study of the passion episode and the study of the passion story, their concerns are however dissimilar. The questions being answered in the study of the passion episode are mainly what, how, and why, the passion episode? However, the important questions being answered in the study of the passion story are how and why Mark narrated the passion story?

Specifically, the questions that guide the analysis are, first, how does the form of the passion story suggest that the story serves a rhetorical purpose? Answers to this question will shed some light on whether the passion story was intended to be a written repository of the tradition of the life and times of Jesus or it was a rhetorical communication serving a paraenetical purpose. Second, how is the passion related to predictive Scripture? This question is important in establishing whether the passion aligns with the faith heritage of the Markan community. In this regard, in addition to rhetorical criticism, a historical analysis will be done to establish the nexus between the passion and the Old Testament prophecy and promises. The "why" question is: why did Mark narrate the passion story? This question probes the narrator's interpretation of the passion episode. It is skewed towards probing the significance of the Markan passion story in the Markan text.

7.2 Form of the Passion Story

Contextually, the episodes narrated in the Markan text are set within the overriding context of the oral proclamation of the gospel. As evidenced by the inaugural sayings of the Last Supper, and as has been argued elsewhere in this book,[1] the proclamation of the passion and its implications on soteriology was an important addendum to the preaching of the oral gospel (1 Cor 11:26). Marshall notes, "The stress in the apostolic message did fall more upon the death and resurrection of Jesus than upon His earthly ministry."[2] Matera concurs with this annotation in opining, "The proclamation of Jesus' death and resurrection is the heart of the Christian faith. In the Creed, the Church confesses: 'For our sake he was crucified under Pontius Pilate; he suffered, died, and was buried. On the third day he rose again in fulfilment of the Scriptures.'"[3] However, the primitive proclamation of the death and resurrection was neither a creedal confession of the death and resurrection of Jesus, nor was it a narration of the passion episode. Rather, it was a witness of his death and resurrection and their salvific implications.

Indeed, the theme of Jesus's passion was introduced quite early in the controversy narratives. Guthrie notes, "It is near the outset of Jesus' public ministry, as Mark narrates it, that the Pharisees turn against him and begin to conspire with the Herodians how to destroy him (3:6)."[4] As early as Mark 2:1–3:5, "Jesus mission and message brings him into conflict with the religious authorities."[5] Notably, the passion is a major theme in the Markan text. The story is set within the context of the theme of gospel proclamation and the resultant controversy narratives.

---

1. This argument has been fronted in chapter 2 section 2.3.4, under "Gospel in the Pauline Epistles."
2. Marshall, *Luke*, 50.
3. Matera, *Passion Narratives*, 1.
4. Matera, 23.
5. Green, *Death of Jesus*, 141.

7.3 Passion Was God Willed

The matter-of-fact style in which the passion story is told suggests that Mark's primary audience were already in the know of the facts about Jesus's death and resurrection. Peter's sermons in Acts show that the passion of Christ was part of the early apostolic proclamation (Acts 2:22–24; 3:12–18). Mark's concern was not to narrate the passion episode for mere epistemological purpose; rather, it was to show that the death of Jesus was God willed. Therefore, it was not a common human death but a sacrificial, propitiatory and vicarious death. As such, the passion story was narrated to urge the audience to respond to the oral gospel that was primarily premised on the person and work of Jesus on the cross.

7.3.1 Passion Was Anticipated in Scripture

The Markan passion narratives contain many Old Testament allusions. Notably, Mark 14:27 cites LXX Zacharias 13:7, Mark 14:18 alludes to LXX Psalm 40:10, Mark 14:61 alludes to MT Isaiah 53:7, Mark 15:24 alludes to LXX Psalm 21:19, Mark 15:34 alludes to LXX Psalm 21:2, and Mark 14:24 alludes to MT Isaiah 53:12. These citations and allusions show that they were carefully chosen to show that the passion episode was anticipated by the Jewish Scripture which had also become the Christian Scripture. Bryan says, "Our choice of style and language is not primarily an indication of the truth or falsehood of what we say, but of the significance with which we wish to endow our words."[6] Mark's choice of words and his Old Testament quotations was not just a matter of providing a firm historical record to the gospel, he was very conscious of the rhetorical and illocutionary efficacy of supporting a statement or topic under discussion with Scripture.

The Markan text's feature of premising the passion on the promises of the Hebrew Scriptures highlights the agreement between the passion and the community's faith heritage thereby positioning the passion as a divine prerogative. Moo says that "Scripture was appropriated for the task of proclaiming the significance of Jesus' passion and justifying it as a divinely willed circumstance."[7] If the death of Jesus had not been anticipated by Scripture, then it would have been interpreted as any other death with no salvific value

---

6. Bryan, "Passion Narratives," 563.
7. Moo, *Old Testament in the Gospel*, 4.

to humanity. In grounding the passion on Scripture, Mark was embellishing his story with a rhetorical device with speech acts that would draw his audience to respond to the oral gospel which was majorly premised on Jesus's salvific accomplishment in the passion.

Although Jesus did not explicitly cite any other scriptural text to support his imminent passion except Zechariah 13:7 (Mark 14:27), he explicitly stated that his suffering and death must happen according to Scripture (Mark 9:12; 14:49). Moo rightly sees the purpose of quoting Old Testament Scriptures in the passion narratives as essentially "apologetic."[8] Arguably, it is the rhetorical nature and the illocutionary acts in the Old Testament quotation that engenders the apologetic function. An apology is essentially a rhetorical function aimed at convincing and convicting the audience and to draw them to faith in the gospel.

7.3.2 Jesus's Predictions of the Passion

The importance of the passion story to the Markan text is underscored by the number of times Mark recorded Jesus's prediction of his death. Within a relatively small portion in the text's structure, Mark narrates three occasions that Jesus predicted his passion; the first in 8:31–33 and an allusion in 9:30–32, and 10:32–34. In the first two predictions, Mark stresses the disciples' and particularly Peter's misunderstanding of the foretold death while in the third, though it seems that John and James had already accepted Jesus's fate, they completely misunderstood its salvific significance. They sought place of honor in the time of resurrection. This triad recall of Jesus's prediction of his death within a very short span of his text shows the importance of place Mark attached to the passion.

In quoting Jesus's saying, "From now on I am telling you before *it* comes to pass, so that when it does occur, you may believe that I am *He*" (John 13:19 NASB), John is suggesting that Jesus's purpose of predicting aspects about his passion was to make his disciples believe that he was indeed the Christ. As such, his predictions were meant to reveal his identity as the Christ.

---

8. Moo, 2.

7.4 Passion in the Parable of the Tenants

The controversy that was started by the Scribes in Galilee (3:6, 20–30) was rekindled when Jesus went to their turf in Jerusalem. In Mark 11:2–33, they questioned Jesus's audacity to enter Jerusalem on a colt with the crowds singing "Hosanna," driving out those who sold and bought in the temple, and the validity of his teachings (11:7–33). In return he rebuked and confronted their obstinacy and murderous attitude towards him and the gospel, by painting a satirical portrait of their opposition to God's messengers and his word using the parable of the unfaithful tenants (12:1–11).

A comparison between the parable of the sower (4:1–12) and the parable of the unfaithful tenants (12:1–11) underscores the difference in attitudes towards Jesus by the people in Galilee and Jerusalem. Though Jesus encountered an obdurate audience in Galilee, some of them were at least receptive with some measure of fruitfulness described as thirty-fold, sixty-fold and a hundred-fold (4:8). However, in Jerusalem, he was facing deadly hostility. By telling the parable of the wicked tenants, Jesus is in effect calling the Jerusalem religious leaders ungrateful murderers of the past prophets who had been sent to speak to them the word of God (12:1–11). Cole says that "this only showed their identification with their ancestors: one generation that killed the prophets, while another generation buried them."[9] This suggestion is supported by Mark's comment that after Jesus told the parable, they "looked for a way to arrest him because they knew he had spoken the parable against them" (12:12 NIV). The irony in the parable is that the Jerusalemites had been entrusted by God to be the custodians of the Torah, its covenants, and promises but they had turned into the worst breakers of the same and were incognizant of its eschatological promises that had been fulfilled in their time through Jesus.

By retelling this parable as a prelude to the passion narratives, Mark is implicitly warning his audience against such obstinacy as was exhibited by the religious leaders in the times of Jesus. As such Mark was retelling this parable to lay blame of Jesus's death on the Jewish religious leaders. In effect, he was wittingly portraying the religion of the Jews in bad light and, by this indirect foil, he was "manipulating the readers to respond"[10] to the oral gospel

---

9. Cole, *Mark*, 259.
10. Tolbert, *Sowing the Gospel*, 224.

about Jesus Christ. To the believing audience, the negative portrayal of the Jerusalem religious leaders served to warn them against handling the gospel deposit, which had been entrusted to them, in a similar way as the religious leaders in Jerusalem had done. As such, from the onset, the passion narrative is identified as a rhetorical device to provoke Mark's audience to respond to the oral gospel, to honorably and faithfully hold the gospel in trust, and to urge a faith shift from the religion of the Jews to faith in the oral gospel. Since proclamation of the salvific significance of the passion had become part and parcel of the gospel message, Mark was not just interested in narrating the passion story for the sake of preserving information, but also to affirm and endear the oral gospel message that was majorly premised on the sacrificial, propitiatory, and vicarious aspect of the passion episode.

7.5 Passion Was Sacrificial, Propitiatory, and Vicarious

Green posits, "Jesus' public humiliation and execution on a cross ran counter to practically every strand of first century messianic expectation. The cross of Christ constituted a scandal of no mean proportion that needed to be explained."[11] This section has explored the supposition that, by narrating the passion story, Mark intended to show that Jesus's death was not the scandal that it was thought to be but that it was sacrificial, propitiatory, and vicarious. A scan of Scripture and, more so, the words of the institution of the Lord's Supper have been done to explain the nature and significance of the passion of Jesus Christ.[12]

7.5.1 Interpreting the Passion in Light of Scripture

The Old Testament has variously described the nature and significance of the eschatological servant king through whom God was to establish his kingdom. It was to this description that the synoptic evangelists, and indeed all Christians, turned to for supporting material to verify the claims of Jesus and to show the salvific significance of the passion of Christ. In narrating Jesus's death by crucifixion, Mark employed the Old Testament to show that it was

---

11. Green, "Passion," 603.
12. See chapter 7, section 7.5.2.

both sacrificial and vicarious. The portrait of the Messiah and his suffering in Psalms 22:1 and 31:5 predicted his agony during his suffering; Psalm 22:18 foretold the sharing of his garments; Psalm 42:10 predicted his mocking; and Isaiah 52:13–54:12 foretold his suffering. The synoptic writers frequently referred to these texts to compare the historical Jesus with his eschatological portrait in the Old Testament. This can be discerned in the Markan text in 15:24, 28, 29–32, 34, and 36. As such, the Markan passion narratives served to enhance the belief value of the oral gospel which had, by that time, incorporated the passion as part of its proclamation.

7.5.2 Passion Foreboded in the Lord's Supper Narratives.

This work has argued that participation in the Lord's Supper serves the same purpose as the oral proclamation of the gospel. Whereas the oral gospel was an explicit proclamation (1:1), participating in the Lord's Supper was a festal proclamation (1 Cor 11:26). Matera posits,

> A Targum (an interpretative, Aramaic paraphrase of the Old Testament), on Exodus 12:42, for example, speaks of four nights when Yahweh delivers his people. The first was when he overcame the night of chaos and created the world. The second was when he appeared to Abraham who was one hundred years old and Sarah who was ninety years to bring about the marvelous birth of Isaac. The third was when he appeared in Egypt and delivered Israel from bondage. But the fourth night is yet to come. It will occur at the end of time, when Yahweh accomplishes his final salvation. That night will come at Passover . . . For the first Christians, the majority of whom were Jewish; Jesus' death was the fourth night, God's final and definitive act of redemption.[13]

As such, just as the preaching of the gospel witnessed the fulfilment of the time and promises that the Torah, the Prophets, and the Hebrew writings had anticipated, so also the inauguration and continued participation in the ordinance of the Lord's Supper (1 Cor 11:26).

The inauguration of the Lord's Supper achieved four objectives. First, Jesus's prediction that Judas would betray him and its eventual fulfilment

---

13. Matera, *Passion Narratives*, 18.

entrenched the passion as scripturally sanctioned (Psalm 41:9–10) and, in effect, God willed. Second, it affirmed that the impending death would be sacrificial, propitiatory, and vicarious (Mark 14:22–24). Gundry aptly notes, "'Of the covenant' and 'being poured out for many' (cf. Isa. 53:12 MT) indicate the sacrificial character of Jesus' approaching death, its violence and atoning value for others – an indication of divine approval and salvific benefit . . . in opposition to human condemnation and shameful crucifixion."[14] In saying, "This is the blood of the covenant," Jesus is in effect confirming that the time of ratification of the new covenant anticipated in Jeremiah 31:31 would be fulfilled by his passion. Third, the Last Supper encapsulates the entire gospel message in festal form.[15] The broken bread, cup and wine expressed the humbling act of incarnation of God into humanity, his suffering, and eventual death (Phil 2:6–8) which were prompted by God's grace and love for humanity (John 3:16). Lastly, it served to explain the meaning and purpose of the passion of Christ. It is no wonder that the narration about the inauguration of the Last Supper is contextually positioned at the beginning of the explicit passion narratives (14:32–15:41). By using allusions from Exodus 24:8 and Jeremiah 31:31–34 about the blood and institution of the covenant in the narratives about the Lord's Supper, Mark rooted the gospel message on a scriptural precedent and a prophetic promise. Because of the Markan community's prior belief in God and sanctity of Scripture, the Passion story was embedded with illocutionary efficacy to convince and convict his audience concerning the truth and believability of the oral gospel.

The passion narrative affirmed the oral gospel that was also expressed in the festal celebration of the Lord's Supper. The apostle Paul describes participation in the Lord's Supper as a proclamation of Jesus's death until he comes (1 Cor 11:26). Whereas the gospel message was about the salvific significance of Jesus's coming, his work, his death, and his resurrection, the broken bread signifies his body that was given in incarnation while the cup of wine signifies his life that was given up in his death on the cross (14:22–24). Notably, both the Lord's Supper and the oral gospel witness the nature and significance of the salvific episode. As such, celebrating the Lord's Supper

---

14. Gundry, *Mark*, 832.

15. This point has been argued in chapter 2, section 2.3.4, under "Gospel in performance of ordinances."

is a gospel proclamation albeit in festal form. It perpetuates and inculcates the oral gospel and its praxis in the community's culture. It also serves to convince, convict and urge the Markan community to believe and perform the gospel's demands.

7.6 Rhetorical Function of the Passion Narratives in Identifying Jesus

The Markan passion story was, in a major way, revelatory. Mark used the trial and crucifixion narratives to show that, indeed, Jesus was the Christ the Son of God.

7.6.1 Disclosure of the Person of Jesus in the Trial Narrative

During the trial by the Jewish leaders, Jesus was asked whether he was "the Christ, the Son of the Blessed?" (14:61 ESV). He gave them a very categorical answer "I am, and you shall see the Son of Man seated at the right hand of Power, and coming with the clouds of heaven" (14:62 ESV). Jesus's answer is an allusion to Daniel 7:13. In effect, Jesus was affirming that he was indeed the son of man who is described in Daniel 7:13. Mark's narration of these disclosures serves the overall aim of disclosing the messiahship of Jesus thereby catalyzing audience response to the oral gospel about him.

7.6.2 Disclosure of the Person of Jesus in the Crucifixion Narrative

The narrative of Jesus's crucifixion achieved two objectives, which subsequently accomplished a paraenetic function within the matrix of the Markan discourse. Jesus's crucifixion is commenced by Pilate's handing over Jesus to the soldiers after he had him flogged (15:15). In a way, the story of this handover highlights a continuation of the fulfilment of Jesus's prediction that he would be handed over to the Gentiles (10:33–34). To a reader who is following the sequence of the narrative, the crucifixion story serves to affirm the truth value of Jesus's claims that were reiterated in the oral gospel.

The historical presents ἐνδιδύσκουσιν and περιτιθέασιν in the statement καὶ ἐνδιδύσκουσιν αὐτὸν πορφύραν καὶ περιτιθέασιν αὐτῷ πλέξαντες ἀκάνθινον στέφανον ("And they clothed him in a purple cloak, and twisting together a crown of thorns, they put it on him" [15:17 ESV]), highlight the dramatic irony with which the episode is narrated. Instead of just saying that the soldiers mocked and led Jesus for crucifixion, Mark details every aspect of the mockery from how he was led to the Praetorium, the calling of the entire garrison, how he was mockingly clothed in kingly purple robes, the preparation and placing of a crown of thorns on his head, how they mockingly hailing him as the King of the Jews, and finally, the soldier's mock worship. Once more, Mark achieved the purpose of highlighting the fulfilment of Jesus's prediction (15:33–34) to his readers, who all along have been following the story, by this time, they have formed an opinion of who Jesus is. As such, the irony in the mocking and taunting of Jesus as the king of the Jews served to reinforce the conviction in the salvific aspect of Jesus's person and work. The narrative style seems to have been aimed at drawing the audience to empathize and identify with the suffering of Christ. As such, the passion story is structured and told with a rhetorical bent that is strategic and communicative. It is aimed at evoking conviction in the oral gospel that was primarily premised on the salvific benefits accruing from the vicarious death of Christ.

The second purpose of the crucifixion narrative in the Markan text is to affirm the identity of Jesus as the Christ (1:1). The irony of the mockery of Jesus by the Roman soldiers and the placing of a plaque showing the reason for his execution as his claim to being the king of the Jews served as a preparation to their confession that "Truly this Man was the Son of God" (15:39). The narration about the unusual darkness that engulfed the land (15:33), the tearing into two the curtain in the Temple after Jesus had died (15:38), and the confession by the centurion that "Truly this Man was the Son of God" (15:39) shows Mark's theological point of view that Jesus was the Christ, the Son of God.

Again, in his characteristic style, Mark is leading his readers into a predetermined interpretation of the significance of Jesus and his death. The entire passion narrative, both in form and literary outlay, shows a rhetorical formation whose main purpose is to convince and convict the readers concerning the truth value of the oral gospel in which the historicity and significance of passion episode formed part of its proclamation. It was also aimed at evoking and urging faith and practice of the teachings in the oral gospel.

7.7 Rhetorical Function of the Narrative about Jesus's Prayers in Gethsemane

The story about Jesus's prayers in Gethsemane (Mark 14:32–42) was narrated to show the setting of Jesus's arrest. Whenever Jesus intended to do an extraordinary miracle or some other important assignment, he solicited the company of Peter, James, and John (5:37; 9:2; 14:33). Mark's narration that Jesus took these disciples along and that he enlisted their prayers underscores the importance of the passion story to Mark's overall purpose. It also suggests that Mark wanted to show that Jesus's capture was not occasioned by any wrongdoing on his part; thus elevating his death to a sacrificial status. Also, he wanted to show the fulfilment of Old Testament and Jesus's predictions that the disciples would forsake him.

In addition, the story of Jesus's capture while in prayer arouses a favorable view towards him and the gospel that was premised on his work. His guiltless nature is so glaringly portrayed by the Gethsemane prayers. Highlighting that Jesus prayed three times was a rhetorical method of superlatively showing the intensity of Jesus's prayers and hence the import of the suffering, which he refers to as τὸ ποτήριον (14:36), in this case a dose of God's judgment that he was to vicariously undergo for the salvation of humanity as shown in the Last Supper narratives. Mark was also interested in portraying the disciples' inability to watch (γρηγορῆσαι) with him (14:37) as an aspect of forsaking him. Here "γρηγορῆσαι" references praying together with him. An alternative view that has been offered by Gundry is that γρηγορῆσαι referenced watching for the coming of Judas.[16] This is not likely since Mark is not in any way demonstrating that Jesus looked forward to being delivered from arrest. After all, the salvific significance of the passion was the high point of the gospel proclamation.

The rhetorical value of the narration about Jesus's prayers and impending arrest is so vital to Mark's purpose. He employed language nuances that arouse empathy and audience engagement. Words like περίλυπός ἕως θανάτου (sorrowful unto death – 14:34), ἔπιπτεν (he fell – 14:35), and τὸ ποτήριον (the cup – 14:36), that describe Jesus's inner turmoil and fears were employed to

---

16. Gundry, *Mark*, 854.

emotionally draw the audience to empathize with the agony that Jesus had experienced. Gundry agreeably says that "Mark uses his authorial omniscience of Jesus' inner feelings to excite sympathy for him."[17] His remark supports the supposition that the story is told with a bent of drawing the audience to respond favorably to the preaching about the salvific significance of the death of Jesus.

7.8 Rhetorical Function of the Narrative about Jesus's Arrest

The setting of Jesus's arrest was the Mount of Olives at a place called Gethsemane (Mark 14:26–32). Normally, Jesus used this place as a prayer haven (13:3; 14: 26). Mark's portrayal of Jesus as being in prayer during his arrest served both an apologetic and rhetorical purpose. It was apologetic in that it shows that Jesus did not die because he was a sinner but that he was, in all ways, a godly person. It was rhetorical in that it served to endear Jesus to Mark's audience and to paint him in a positive light for the purpose of drawing them to faith in the gospel about him.

The narrative about Judas's participation in Jesus's arrest shows that the passion fulfilled scriptural predictions (Psalm 41:9). France avers, "Mark has been happy to develop the theme of scriptural fulfilment and the fulfilment of Jesus' own prediction through Judas' own actions."[18] The connection of Jesus's betrayal by Judas as fulfilment of his predictions served Mark's purpose of amplifying Jesus's stature which consequently enhanced faith in the oral gospel about him. The narration about how the disciples forsook Jesus after his arrest and how Peter denied him achieved the purpose of enhancing Jesus's ethos by showing that his prior prediction concerning how the disciples would forsake him came to pass. It also affirmed that the passion was in line with predictive Scripture and that Jesus was the promised shepherd (Zech 13:7). Overall, the narrative on Jesus's arrest shows that Mark's intention was to magnify Jesus's persona with the consequential aim of drawing his audience to believe the oral gospel. It also served to sanitize the death of Jesus by showing that it was a divinely willed salvific death.

---

17. Gundry, 854.
18. France, *Gospel of Mark*, 526.

7.9 Rhetorical Function of the Narrative about Jesus's Trial

Mark narrated a two-tier trial. The first was before the chief priests, the elders and the scribes (Mark 14:53–72). The second tier was before Pilate (15:1–14). Narrating this two-tier trial achieved the purpose of enjoining both the Jews and Gentiles in the culpability for the death of Jesus. It also achieved the purpose of connecting the episode with Jesus's earlier prediction that he would be handed over to the chief priests, teachers of the law and the Gentiles (10:33). Noting the fulfilment of Jesus's prediction served to enhance the belief value in Jesus and the oral gospel message.

7.9.1 Jesus's Trial before the Sanhedrin

In narrating Jesus's trial before the Sanhedrin (14:53–65), Mark shows that Jesus's accusers are seeking false evidence against him to no avail. This is supported by his use of a progressive imperfect[19] ἐζήτουν (14:55). Use of this progressive imperfect also suggests that the narrative's rhetorical purpose was to reveal that Jesus had been arrested and accused without cause. This exposé reinforces the notion that his death was not occasioned by any wrongdoing on his part and as such it qualified to be a sacrificial ransom for sinners. Mark does not also leave his audience to make independent interpretation of the trial narratives but uses leading comments to show Jesus's innocence. For example, after his comment, "For many bore false witness against Him," Mark further comments that, "but their testimonies did not agree" (14:56). Thus, he leads his readers into his purpose for the narration by these comments. For example, after his narrative that some witnesses were saying, "We heard Him say, 'I will destroy this temple made with hands, and within three days I will build another made without hands'" (14:58), Mark leads the reader in how to understand this assertion by refuting it with a comment, "But not even then did their testimony agree" (14:59). These and other comments show that the narrator is taking charge of directing his audience on how Jesus's trial should be interpreted.

In the narrative of Jesus's trial before the Sanhedrin, Mark implicitly but vividly portrayed the religion of the Jews in a negative light. This is a foil to laud faith in Jesus Christ and the oral gospel. Mark also highlighted the

---

19. Wallace, *Greek Grammar*, 543.

exalted ethos of Jesus by showing that, though they had judged him fit to die, he was indeed a righteous man. As such, the claims in the oral gospel about him were shown to be trustworthy.

7.9.2 Jesus's Trial before Pilate

The narration about Jesus's trial before Pilate shows that the Jewish leaders accused Jesus of claiming to be the king of the Jews (Mark 15:2). They supposed that such a charge would be viewed as sedition by a leadership that eschewed claimants of kingship, for they were likely to lead an insurrection against Rome. According to Josephus, Herod killed John the Baptist because he feared that because of his popularity he might "be inclined to lead a rebellion."[20] However, it is plausible to say that Mark highlighted the charge that Jesus claimed to be the king of the Jews so as to reap rhetorical capital from the sarcasm of labelling Jesus "the king of the Jews" that turns out to be Jesus's real identity. Moreover, in the narrative about Jesus's trial before Pilate, Mark put the Jewish religion on trial in the court of his audience by showing that, in practice, the Jewish religion (as practiced by the Jewish leaders) was more callous than the colonizing empire whose laws and ethics were represented by Pilate's positive appraisal of Jesus as one who had done no evil to deserve death (15:14). Once more, the narrator leads his audience in noting the innocence of Jesus by his interpretative comment that ἐγίνωσκεν γὰρ ὅτι διὰ φθόνον παραδεδώκεισαν αὐτὸν οἱ ἀρχιερεῖς (15:10). Apparently, the rhetorical effect of the narrative of the trial before Pilate was to catalyze a faith shift in some of Mark's readers, who may have had allegiance to Judaism, into faith in the gospel of Jesus Christ the Son of God.

Barabbas was a freedom fighter[21] – who had committed murder in an insurrection (15:7). Gundry rightly avers, "The chief priests successfully used the popularity of a freedom-fighter with the crowd to combat the popularity that Jesus had with them."[22] Mark has used the crowd's preference for a

---

20. Josephus, *Works of Flavius Josephus*, 581.

21. Rees, "Barabbas," 172, says that Barabbas could have been a freedom fighter. However, though some doubt whether the priests (the pro-Roman party) would urge the release of a political prisoner, and that Pilate would grant it, Rees notes that "to say that the Jews would not have been interested in the release of such a prisoner is to forget the history of the mobs."

22. Gundry, *Mark*, 927.

freedom fighter for a political cause as a foil to the preference of Jesus who was proclaimed in the oral gospel as a giver of a better kind of freedom and who ushers in not a temporal but an eternal kingdom (1:15). Mark's narration highlighted the irony that a more superior freedom than that which the Jews sought to attain through insurrection had paradoxically been offered through the sentence of crucifixion that they had successfully lobbied for. Mark's readers who had the double advantage of having heard the oral gospel and reading the text this far could however note the irony and be drawn to believe the oral gospel that Mark and his contemporaries were preaching.

In summary, Mark used the narrative on the trial and sentence of Jesus to death by crucifixion as a foil of Jesus's persona when viewed against the hypocrisy of the Jewish leaders. Consequently, the story enhanced the belief value of the oral gospel about Jesus Christ. As such, the narrative was fashioned as a rhetorical piece and device to catalyze audience response to the oral gospel that was by this time principally premised on the passion episode.

7.10 Summary

The rhetorical focus of the passion narratives in the Markan text is manifest in two fundamental ways. The form and structure serve to show that it was used as a rhetorical device to ground the oral gospel on both the historical fact of the Christ event and the Markan community's faith heritage. At the locutionary/literary level, the story aims to convince, convict and urge the readers to believe and obey the demands of the oral gospel.

The passion story served to establish the passion episode as a historical fact. The story is narrated in a way that shows the nature of the passion. It exposes the chronological order of the entire episode in a dramatic way that obviously serves to imprint the happenings in the reader's mind. As has been pointed out, the positioning of the Last Supper narratives before the passion narratives served to show that the death of Jesus was not a normal death but a sacrificial, propitiatory and vicarious death.

The redemptive significance of the passion episode to both the Christian community and Mark's unbelieving audience elevated the proclamation of its certainty and significance to be part of the oral gospel proclamation. It forms part of the phenomenon on which the oral gospel about Jesus Christ is premised. It is part of the episodes that Mark regards as the beginning of the gospel of Jesus Christ the Son of God (1:1). The passion narrative is a good repository from which past and present preachers draw information to affirm the gospel about Jesus Christ the Son of God.

CHAPTER 8

Conclusion

8.1 Introduction

Mark 16:9–20 has been adjudged a secondary[1] addendum to the Markan text. However, an analysis of this part of the text has value in showing how its writer understood the purpose of the Markan text. Being a kind of obiter dictum to the undisputed portion of the text, an analysis of the contribution of the longer ending to the understanding of the rhetorical value of the Markan text has been appended as an excursus. However, its usefulness in generating insights concerning the purpose of the text cannot be underrated.

8.2 Excursus

This excursus will delve into a short probe of the contribution of the author of Mark's longer ending to the understanding of the purpose of the Markan text. Authenticity of this section has been an area of dispute. However, the importance of any disputed portion is highlighted by Taylor's supposition that, "Readings that are not original are often of much importance; because they show how the gospels were understood by copyists in later times, and because existing oral tradition is sometimes revealed by the additions, as for example, when Codex Bezae adds after Lk. 6:4 the story of the man working on the Sabbath."[2] As such, a probe of this portion will go a long way in

---

1. Metzger, *Textual Commentary*, 125.
2. Taylor, *Formation of the Gospel Tradition*, 4.

shedding more light on the function and significance of the Markan text as understood by the author of the longer ending.

8.2.1 Importance of the Longer Ending (Mark 16:14–20)

If the current argument that Mark 16:8 is the ending of the Markan text[3] is sustained, then the Markan text's conclusion is an anticlimax. Mark's themes and rhetorical purpose seem lost. As has been noted in the analysis of Mark's passion narratives, Mark is fond of leading his readers with interpretative comments within the narration of the various episodes.[4] As such, it is out of tune with Mark's narrative style to end his text at 16:8 without leading his readers into the consequences of Jesus's resurrection in connection with his major theme of proclamation of the oral gospel.

If the presupposition that Mark wrote his text haphazardly and without any discernible order, as has been argued by some analysts as early as Papias,[5] is sustained, then, Mark 16:8 can be adjudged an authentic ending of the Markan text. However, as has been argued in this study, the Markan stories are not haphazardly but deliberately structured to generate maximum rhetorical efficacy to catalyze audience response to the oral gospel that was outside and independent of the text.

Arguably, Mark comes out as an astute rhetor with the same persuasion as was with Moses when he wrote the Genesis account.[6] In this understanding, ending the Markan text at Mark 16:8 is out of tune with his intents and purpose. The text could be adjudged a treatise with an introduction, a body but lacking a conclusion that resonates well with its introduction and body, that is, an argument without cause and conclusion. As such, a suggestion that the original ending of Mark might have been torn off from some manuscripts in the process of transmission is plausible. Metzger suggests that, "Three possibilities are open: (a) the evangelist intended to close his Gospel at this place; or (b) the Gospel was never finished; or, as seems most probable, (c) the Gospel accidentally lost its last leaf before it was multiplied

---

3. Metzger, *Textual Commentary*, 126.
4. See chapter 7, section 7.10.1.
5. Eusebius, *Ecclesiastical History*, 113.
6. See section 1.9.3.

by transcription."[7] As such, some later copyists who noticed this anomaly tried to address the problem by writing summary addendums. However, it is also possible that some manuscripts retained the original endings which however, could become collateral damage in the process of verifying which manuscript is the original. A keen and cautious approach in textual criticism ought to guide this analysis.

Contribution of the longer ending to exegesis

It is apparent that whoever wrote Mark 16:14-20 understood Mark 1:1 as referring to the gospel that Jesus inaugurated in Mark 1:15, that which he sent his disciples to preach (6:7-13), and finally that which Mark and his contemporaries were preaching. He also understood that this gospel was outside and independent of the text. This is suggested by his use of Jesus's commissioning words as the concluding remarks to the Markan text (16:15-20). Some scholars have suggested that the author of this portion may have sourced his material from the rest of the Synoptic writings and Acts.[8] However, the opposite scenario is more plausible. It is more probable that the contents of the endings of the other Synoptics were sourced from the longer ending of the Markan text. Moreover, Jesus's commissioning words in Mark 16:17-18 cannot be traced to any of the Synoptics. Therefore, it is more likely that the other Synoptics redacted the Markan version other than whoever authored the larger ending of the Markan text to have sourced material from other Synoptics and then added more extraneous information that is contained in Mark 16:17-18 and lacking in the other Synoptic texts.

Moreover, if the longer ending is a later appendage to the text, then, the writer must have appended this addendum sometimes in the first century before Papias's commentary on the Markan text.[9] The information in Mark 16:18b in which Jesus is promising those who believe that "if they drink any deadly poison, it will not hurt them" (16:18 ESV) is collaborated by Papias's account that the daughters of Philip of Caesarea who were contemporaries of the apostles witnessed that, "Barnabas, who was also called Justus, drank poison of a snake in the name of Christ when put to the test by the unbelievers

---

7. Metzger, *Textual Commentary*, 126.
8. Cole, *Mark*, 335.
9. Holmes, *Apostolic Fathers*, 739-741.

and was protected from all harm."[10] If Papias's testimony is true as many of his testimonies are taken to be, then it was a polemical piece on the reliability of these accounts which, plausibly, were in the Markan text that was in his possession. As such, Papias and his audience must have been in possession of the Markan text that contained the longer ending of the Markan text.

Furthermore, the longer ending seems to provide not only an apt ending but one that resonates very well with the entire structure and theme of the Markan text. The author seems to recognize that the subject of the text is the beginning of the gospel and he correspondingly appended a conclusion with the same theme and especially one that seeks to identify the gospel that Mark and his contemporaries were preaching (1:1) as the gospel that Jesus commissioned his disciples to preach to the whole world (16:15).

Notwithstanding arguments that this portion of the text is spurious,[11] the rhetorical structuring of the text supports it. Metzger sees a difference in its rhetorical tone which he says "differs totally from the simple style of Mark's gospel."[12] Though Metzger sees a lexical difference, the writer's structure and message are perfectly in agreement with the rest of the structure and message. The *exordium*, *narratio* (1:1–15), and *confirmatio* (Old Testament quotations, controversy narratives, miracle stories, and the passion narrative) are aptly complemented and in agreement with the conclusion (16:9–20). The external evidence supplied by the earliest apostolic fathers – Papias, Justin Martyr, and Irenaeus mitigates its inclusion. Metzger posits that "it is present in the vast number of witnesses, including A C D K X W Δ Θ Π Ψ 099 0112 f^{13} 28 33 *al*. The earliest patristic witnesses to part or all of the long ending are Irenaeus and the diatessaron."[13] If it was added by a different person other than Mark, then he may have been privy to the contents of the lost ending of Mark which he reconstructed in his own language. Alternatively, his source could have been the oral tradition of the deeds and sayings of Jesus. To have appended such an apt conclusion, he must have been a person who understood the form, structure, and purpose of the Markan text.

---

10. Holmes, 743.
11. Metzger, *Textual Commentary*, 122–126.
12. Metzger, 126.
13. Metzger, 124.

Having gone through the arguments that the longer ending of the Markan text may have been a secondary appendage, the doubts that emerge suggest that the conclusions on the question of who authored the ending of the Markan text be held in abeyance. This study is of the view that it forms a very apt conclusion to the Markan text. It supports the hypothesis that the overriding theme of the text was proclamation of the oral gospel that was outside and independent of the text and that it was aimed at catalyzing audience response in faith and obedience to its demands.

8.3 Summary

This summary brings together the results of the study of the topics forming its conceptual framework. It is aimed at establishing the synergy of the Markan text's rhetorical devices in the grand function of catalyzing audience response to the one and only gospel that was outside and independent of the Markan text. Further, it determines the role played by the Scripture acts within the rhetorical embellishments of Old Testament quotations, miracle stories, controversy narratives, and the Passion narratives.

Pursuant to an analysis of the interlocutors within the matrix of the Markan discourse and the rhetorical devices that embellish the text that is unencumbered by the presupposition imposed by the second-century labelling of the Markan text as the "Gospel according to Mark," it has been argued that the gospel referenced in Mark 1:1 was an oral gospel that was outside and independent of the Markan text. It has also been established that, primarily, the Markan text served a paraenetic purpose of catalyzing audience response to the oral gospel.

This work has also shown that, in minor ways, Mark's genre reveals aspects of Greco-Roman aretalogy, but in a major way, it is similar to the genre of the book of Genesis. Just as the Genesis narratives urged the Exodus pilgrims to keep the covenant that they had entered with God at Sinai, the Markan text also reminisces and narrates the episodes in the immediate history of Mark's community to catalyze audience response to the gospel that undoubtedly proclaims the new covenant.

The parable of the sower (4:1–12) has been identified as both programmatic and paradigmatic to the interpretation of the Markan text. It paints not only the portrait of the rhetorical situation of Jesus's audience to mirror the rhetorical situation of Mark's audience with its exigency of obduracy and lukewarm response to the oral gospel, but also spells out the preferred norm of optimal fruitfulness. Through this mirror portrait, Mark not only rebukes the obdurate audience, who were not responding positively to the oral gospel, but also commends the faithful as he exhorts and enjoins the entire spectrum of his audience to aspire for optimal fruitfulness.

The Markan anecdotes that were hitherto seen as without order[14] by Papias and others throughout the interpretation history, have been shown to be rhetorical devices[15] that Mark used not only to ground the oral and ritual gospel on the belief matrix of the Markan community but also to convince, convict and urge faith and obedience to the oral gospel.

The major author supposition that directs the course of the text and choice of rhetorical devices is the understanding that the promises of the Torah, the Prophets, and the writings had been fulfilled in the Christ event (1:2-3). This identification is in line with Bitzer's postulation that, "A rhetorical discourse does obtain its character-as-rhetorical from the situation which generates it."[16] Thus, the Markan text, as a rhetorical communication, addresses the rhetorical situation that produced it. It has been argued that the occasion that prompted the writing of the Markan text was the exigency of obduracy and lukewarm response towards the gospel by Mark's audience, whose portrait he painted in retelling the parable of the sower.[17] This portrait acts as a mirror image of his audience's rhetorical situation that provokes them to dramatically visualize and therefore abhor obduracy and lukewarm response to the oral gospel when contrasted with the equally dramatically portrayed norm of optimal response. As such, Mark's retold parable of the sower (4:1-12) and the parable of the unfaithful servants (12:1-11) are programmatic in that they supply an apt hermeneutical grid and context for interpreting the Markan text.

In Gundry's review and critique of the studies that have been done so far on the purpose of the book of Mark, he concludes by stating, "In the final

---

14. Eusebius, *Ecclesiastical History*, 113.

15. This study has argued that the Old Testament quotations in the Markan text, the miracle stories and the passion narratives are rhetorical devices that were used to catalyze audience response to the oral gospel that was outside and independent of the Markan text.

16. Bitzer, "Rhetorical Situation," 3.

17. This point has been argued in chapter 3, section 3.5.

analysis, we are left once again with the competing views that Mark wrote to put forward a theology of suffering, a theology of glory, or a theology of both suffering and glory."[18] He then roots for the theology of glory as the overriding theme. His argument is that Mark colored the miracle stories, and predictions with "statements of admiration, crowd attraction, narratives of fulfilment, etc. . . . Mark dresses up the passion in colors of fulfilment, decency, dignity, and the supernatural."[19] As such, he concludes, "The little paraenetic tradition that appears in this gospel he puts to the service of an apology for the cross."[20]

However, after identifying and accounting for the blind and bridle that the editorial label of the text as "the Gospel according to Mark" introduces and having also identified the oral and ritual gospel as an independent interlocutor with the audience, this study has shown[21] that Mark's Old Testament quotations, the miracle stories, and the passion narratives were used as rhetorical devices. The aim was to ground the oral gospel, which he and his contemporaries were preaching, on his community's faith heritage. Of note is that the Markan text and indeed all the texts by the four evangelists were written by the church for the church. Consequently, he demonstrated that the oral gospel was divinely sanctioned and that it was not a myth but a message that was premised on a historical and divinely ordered episode. Looked at from this perspective, the Markan text assumes a paraenetic purpose. As a result of this premise, its genre harmonizes with its purpose. Consequently, its form and structure become more understandable.

The pearls suggested by Schmidt can now be identified as the rhetorical devices that are not just hanging on a string but supporting the all-important theme of the salvific oral and ritual gospel that is outside and independent of the text. Thus, there is a functional relationship between the Markan text and the audience response to the oral gospel that was being proclaimed by Mark and his contemporaries. The genre of the Markan text can be accurately ascertained as a paraenesis. The text aims to exhort both believers and unbelievers to uphold, believe, and act upon the gospel that was being orally and festally proclaimed through administration of the ordinance of the

---

18. Gundry, *Mark*, 1024.
19. Gundry, 1024.
20. Gundry, 1024.
21. This aspect has been argued in chapters 5, 6 and 7.

Lord's Supper. In other words, the Markan text catalyzes audience response towards the gospel. Specifically, the rhetorical devices embellishing the text function affectively to urge the audience to respond to the gospel about Jesus Christ the son of God.

Glossary

aretalogy: A genre by which virtues, uprightness, and good deeds of a person are narrated.

biography in biblical literature: A literary genre by which the life and times of an individual, in this case Jesus Christ, is narrated.

epexegetical: Describes a word in a genetive case which is used to shed more light on a word previously used with some ambiguity.

gospel: In the first century, gospel refered to the good news that the Christ event that was once promised in the Old Testament had been fulfilled and that consequently, salvation was availed through the work of Jesus Christ on the cross.

Gospel as a genre: Describes a unique literary genre (*sui generis*) in which the four books by Mark, Matthew, Luke and John are written. It is a new development in biblical studies.

historiography in biblical literature: A literary genre through which an orderly and actual account of a people or an individual person, in this case Jesus Christ, is written.

illocutionary act: The action intended by a speaker. For example, the becoming of husband and wife after pronouncememt of "I now pronounce you as husband and wife."

memoir: The name was used to refer to written accounts of the eyewitnesses' remembrances of the life and times of Jesus. It could also refer to a journal record of the acts of Jesus that may have been written down as they happened. It was the initial reference of the books currently labelled "Gospels."

mimesis: Describes the depiction of a narrative world in fiction or text wherein the readers can mirror their own life for the purpose of provoking them to form and transform their character and behavior. The parable of the sower in the text of Mark is described as mimetic because it mirrors the state of Mark's audience.

noematic: Describes something that is of the mind or intellect. It is used in the book to denote the content and meaning that is intended in the mind of the author

noetic remembrances: It is used to show remembrance of the acts and sayings of Jesus that were aided by the information that was stored in the eyewitnesses' minds.

numinous power: Refers to power to perform signs and wonders. Biblical faith holds that God is the source of all numinous power.

paraenesis: Is a technical word used to describe a literary genre whose main purpose is to exhort readers to certain ethical and faith responses

paraklectic: The word is used to describe the edificatory function of ordained feasts and ordinances.

perlocutionary act: An action that is engendered by a speech act in lives of the audience.

pleonastic: An adjective used to describe the book of Mark as overly wordy in narrating episodes in Jesus's life.

programmatic: A concept that sets forth a procedure or method for dealing with a certain subject.

reader-response: Refers to Mark's reader's response to the extant oral gospel that was independent and outside the Markan text.

rhetorical efficacy: Refers to the effectiveness of a rhetorical communication to convict and convince the reader to act to change perceived problems in the historical situation of the reader.

rhetorical situation: It refers to the situation in the life of the author's audience that prompted the writing of a text.

semiotic: Adjective describing the noun semiosis. Semiosis is the study of the information that is conveyed through signs and symbols.

strategic acts: Acts that are done to elicit a reaction or response. Strategic acts perform similar functions as speech acts.

thaumaturgic: Adjective derived from the noun thautamagy. It describes a spiritually aided response to the world.

wisdom as genre: Generally, wisdom as a literary genre refers to the genre in which the sapiential books of the Old Testament are written.

Bibliography

Primary Sources

Aaron, David H. *Biblical Ambiguities: Metaphor, Semantics, and Divine Imagery.* Leiden: Brill, 2001.

Aeschines. "The Defence: Aeschines." In *Demosthenes and Aeschines*, translated by A. N. W. Saunders, edited by Robert Baldick, Betty Radice, and C. A. Jones, 143–188. Aylesbury, Bucks: Hazel Watson & Viney, 1975.

Aland, Barbara, Kurt Aland, Johannes Karavidopoulos, Carlo M. Martini, and Bruce M. Metzger, eds. *The Greek New Testament.* 4th ed. Stuttgart: Deutsche Bibelgesellschaft, 1993.

Aland, Barbara, Kurt Aland, Johannes Karavidopoulos, Carlo M. Martini, Eberhard Nestle, Erwin Nestle, and Bruce M. Metzger, eds. *Novum Testamentum Graece.* 28th ed. Stuggart: Deutsche Bibelgesellschaft, 2012.

Aland, Kurt, ed. *Synopsis Quattuor Evangeliorum: Locis Parallelis Evangeliorum Apocryphorum, et Patrum Adhibitis.* Stuttgart: Deutsche Bibelgesellschaft, 1995.

Demosthenes. "Demosthenes: For Megapolis." In *Greek Political Oratory*, translated by A. N. W. Saunders, edited by Betty Radice, 169–249. Harmondsworth: Penguin Books, 1970.

———. "The Prosecution: Demosthenes." In *Demosthenes and Aeschines*, translated by A. N. W. Saunders, edited by Robert Baldick, Betty Radice, and C. A. Jones, 57–139. Aylesbury, Bucks: Hazel Watson & Viney, 1975.

Eusebius, Pamphilus. *The Ecclesiastical History of Eusebius Pamphilus.* Translated by C. F. Crusé. London: Bell & Sons, 1892.

Fragments of Papias 1:1. Accessed via BibleWorks.

Holmes, Michael W. *The Apostolic Fathers: Greek Texts and English Translations.* 3rd ed. Grand Rapids, MI: Baker Academic, 2007.

Homer. *The Iliad.* Translated by Martin Hammond. London: Penguin Books, 1987.

———. *The Odyssey.* Translated by E. V. Rieu. London: Penguin Books, 1946.

Josephus, Flavius. *The Works of Flavius Josephus*. Translated by William Whiston. Nashville, TN: Thomas Nelson, 1998.

Philo. *The Works of Philo: Complete and Unabridged*. Translated by C. D. Yonge. Peabody, MA: Hendrickson, 1993.

Philostratus. *Apollonius of Tyana, Volume I: Life of Apollonius of Tyana, Books 1-4*. Edited and translated by Christopher P. Jones. Loeb Classical Library 16. Cambridge, MA: Harvard University Press, 2005.

———. *Apollonius of Tyana, Volume II: Life of Apollonius of Tyana, Books 5-8*. Edited and translated by Christopher P. Jones. Loeb Classical Library 17. Cambridge, MA: Harvard University Press, 2005.

Saunders, A. N. W. *Greek Political Oratory*. Edited by Betty Radice. Harmondsworth: Penguin Books, 1970.

Thucydides. "Pericles' Funeral Speech." In *Greek Political Oratory*, translated by A. N. W. Saunders, edited by Betty Radice, 33-38. Harmondsworth: Penguin Books, 1970.

Secondary Sources

Aland, Kurt. *Quattuor Evangeliorum: Locis Parallelis Evangeliorum Apocryphorum, et Patrum Adhibitis*. Stuttgart: Deutsche Bibelgesellschaft, 1995.

Allert, Graig D. *Revelation, Truth, Canon and Interpretation: Studies in Justin Martyr's Dialogue with Trypho*. Leiden: Brill, 2002.

Arnold, Carroll C. "Introduction." In *The Realm of Rhetoric*, translated by William Kluback, vii-xx. Notre Dame, IN: University of Notre Dame Press, 1982.

Aune, David E. *The New Testament in Its Literary Environment*. Philadelphia: Westminster, 1987

Bagster, Samuel. *The Analytical Greek Lexicon*. London: Samuel Bagster & Sons, 1977.

Barr, James. *The Semantics of Biblical Language*. Oxford: Oxford University Press, 1969.

Barrett, C. K. *The Holy Spirit and the Gospel Tradition*. London: SPCK, 1947.

Barton, John. "Marcion Revisited." In *The Canon Debate*, edited by Lee Martin McDonald and James A. Sanders, 341-354. Peabody, MA: Hendrickson, 2002.

Bauckham, Richard. *Jesus and the Eyewitnesses: The Gospels as Eye Witnesses Testimony*. Grand Rapids, MI: Eerdmans, 2006.

Beale, G. K. *Handbook on the New Testament Use of the Old Testament: Exegesis and Interpretation*. Grand Rapids, MI: Baker Academic, 2012.

Beavis, Mary Ann. *Marks' Audience: The Literary and Social Setting of Mark 4:11-12*. Sheffield: Sheffield Academic Press, 1989.

Bellinzoni, A. J. *The Sayings of Jesus in the Writings of Justin Martyr*. Leiden: Brill, 1967.

Bitzer, Lloyd F. "The Rhetorical Situation." *Philosophy and Rhetoric* 1, no. 1 (1968): 1–14.
Black, C. Clifton. *The Rhetoric of the Gospel: Theological Artistry in the Gospels and Acts*. St. Louis, MO: Chalice, 2001.
Blackburn, Barry. "Miracles and Miracle Stories." In *Dictionary of Jesus and the Gospels: A Compendium of Contemporary Biblical Scholarship*, edited by Joel B. Green, Scot McKnight and I. Howard Marshall, 549–560. Downers Grove, IL: InterVarsity Press, 1992.
Blomberg, Craig L. *The Historical Reliability of the Gospels*. Downers Grove, IL: InterVarsity Press, 1987.
———. *Interpreting the Parables*. Downers Grove, IL: IVP Academic, 1990.
———. *Jesus and the Gospels: An Introduction and Survey*. Nottingham: Apollos, 1997.
Blomberg, Craig L., and Jennifer Foutz Markley. *A Handbook of New Testament Exegesis*. Grand Rapids, MI: Baker Academic, 2010.
Bolt, Peter G. *Jesus' Defeat of Death: Persuading Mark's Early Readers*. Cambridge: Cambridge University Press, 2003.
———. "Mark's Gospel." In *The Face of the New Testament: A Survey of Recent Research*, edited by Scot McKnight and Grant Osborne, 391–413. Grand Rapids, MI: Baker Academic, 2004.
Boucher, Madeleine. *The Mysterious Parable: A Literary Study*. Washington, DC: Catholic Biblical Association of America, 1977.
Bovon, Francois. "The Canonical Structure of Gospel and Apostle." In *The Canon Debate*, edited by Lee Martin McDonald and James A. Sanders, 516–527. Peabody, MA: Hendrickson, 2002.
———. "The Reception and Use of the Gospel of Luke in the Second Century." In *Reading Luke: Interpretation, Reflection, Formation*, edited by Craig G. Bartholomew, Joel B. Green, Anthony C. Thiselton, 379–397. Grand Rapids, MI: Zondervan, 2005.
Brandon, S. G. F. *The Fall of Jerusalem and the Christian Church*. 3rd ed. London: SPCK, 1974.
Bryan, Christopher. "Passion Narratives." In *Dictionary for Theological Interpretation of the Bible*, edited by Kevin J. Vanhoozer, 562–564. Grand Rapids, MI: Baker Academic, 2005.
Breytenbach, Cilliers. "The Gospel of Mark as Episodical Narrative: Reflections on the 'Composition' of the Second Gospel." *Scriptura*, special issue 2 (1989): 1–26. German original, 1985.
Briggs, Richard S. "Speech-Act Theory." In *Words and the Word: Explorations in Biblical Interpretation and Literary Theory*, edited by David G. Firth and Jamie A. Grant, 75–110. Downers Grove, IL: InterVarsity Press, 2008.

Brown, Gillian, and George Yule. *Discourse Analysis*. Cambridge: Cambridge University Press, 1983.

Broyles, C. C. "Gospel (Good News)." In *Dictionary of Jesus and the Gospels*, edited by Joel B. Green, Scot McKnight and I. Howard Marshall, 282–286. Downers Grove, IL: InterVarsity Press, 1992.

Bruce, F. F. *The New Testament Documents: Are They Reliable?* 6th ed. England: InterVarsity Press, 2000.

Bryan, Christopher. *A Preface to Mark*. Oxford: Oxford University Press, 1993.

Burridge, Richard A. "Biography." In *Handbook of Classical Rhetoric in the Hellenistic Period 330 B.C.–A.D. 400*, edited by Stanley E. Porter, 371–391. Leiden: Brill, 2001.

———. "The Gospels and Acts." In *Handbook of Classical Rhetoric in the Hellenistic Period 330 B.C.–A.D. 400*, edited by Stanley E. Porter, 507–532. Leiden: Brill, 2001.

———. *What Are the Gospels?: A Comparison with Graeco-Roman Biography*. 2nd ed. Grand Rapids, MI: Eerdmans; Dearborn, MI: Dove Booksellers, 2004.

———. "Who Writes, Why, and For Whom?" In *The Written Gospel*, edited by Markus Bockmuehl and Donald A. Hagner, 99–116. Cambridge: Cambridge University Press, 2005.

Burrows, Millar, ed. *The Dead Sea Scrolls of St. Mark's Monastery*. New Haven, CT: ASOR, 1951.

Camery-Hoggart, Jerry. *Irony in Mark's Gospel: Text and Subtext*. Society for New Testament Studies, Monograph Series 72. Cambridge: Cambridge University Press, 1992.

Carroll, John T., and Joel B. Green. *The Death of Jesus in Early Christianity*. Peabody, MA: Hendrickson, 1995.

Carson, D. A., Douglas J. Moo, and Leon Morris. *An Introduction to the New Testament*. Leicester: Apollos, 1992.

Carson, Herbert M. *The Faith of the Vatican*. Durham: Evangelical Press, 1996.

Casurella, A. "Gospel." In *Dictionary of the Later New Testament and its Developments: A Compendium of Contemporary Biblical Scholarship*, edited by Ralph P. Martin and Peter H. Davids, 431–433. Downers Grove, IL: InterVarsity Press, 1997.

Chilton, Bruce. *Beginning New Testament Study*. London: SPCK, 1986.

Chisholm, Robert B. *From Exegesis to Exposition: A Practical Guide to Using Biblical Hebrew*. Grand Rapids, MI: Baker Books, 1998.

Clarke, Adam. *Clarke's Commentary*, volume 4, *Isaiah–Malachi*. Nashville, TN: Abingdon, 1970.

Cole, R. Alan. *Mark*. Tyndale New Testament Commentaries. Edited by Leon Morris. Downers Grove, IL: InterVarsity Press, 1989.

———. "Mark." In *New Bible Commentary*. 4th ed. Edited by D. A. Carson, R. T. France, J. A. Mortyer, and G. J. Wenham. Leicester: Inter-Varsity Press, 1994.

Conzelmann, Hans. *The Theology of Luke*. Translated by Geoffrey Buswell. London: SCM Press, 1982.

Cook, John G. *The Structure and Persuasive Power of Mark: A Linguistic Approach*. Atlanta, GA: Scholars Press, 1995.

Cornelius, E. M. "The Rhetorical Function(s) of Old Testament References in Mark 10:1–12." *Acta Patristica et Byzantina* 14, no. 1 (2003): 58–77.

Cotterell, Peter, and Max Turner. *Linguistics and Biblical Interpretation*. Downers Grove, IL: InterVarsity Press, 1989.

Croy, N. Clayton. *The Mutilation of Mark's Gospel*. Nashville, TN: Abingdon, 2003.

Dewey, Joanna. *Markan Public Debate: Literary Technique, Concentric Structure, and Theology in Mark 2:1–3:6*. Chico, CA: Scholars Press, 1980.

———. "Mark as Aural Narrative: Structures as Clues to Understanding." In *Sewanee Theological Review* 36 (1992): 45–56.

Dibelius, Martin. *From Tradition to Gospel*. Translated by Bertram Lee Woolfe. New York; Charles Scribner's Sons, 1934.

Dobson, John H. *Learn New Testament Greek*. 3rd ed. Carlisle, UK: Piquant, 2005.

Dockey, David S. *Holman Bible Handbook*. Nashville, TN: Holman Bible Publishers, 1992.

Donahue, John R. *The Gospel in Parable*. Philadelphia: Fortress, 1988.

Donahue, John R., and Daniel J. Harrington. *The Gospel of Mark*. Sacra Pagina Series, Volume 2. Collegeville, MN: Liturgical Press, 2002.

Doriani, Daniel M. *Getting the Message: A Plan for Interpreting and Applying the Bible*. Phillipsburg, NJ: P&R, 1996.

Duff, Jeremy. *The Elements of New Testament Greek*. Cambridge: Cambridge University Press, 2005.

Dunn, James D. G. *A New Perspective on Jesus: What the Quest for the Historical Jesus Missed*. Grand Rapids, MI: Baker Academic, 2006.

Duvall, J. Scott, and J. Daniel Hays. *Grasping God's Word: A Hands-On Approach to Reading, Interpreting, and Applying the Bible*. 2nd ed. Grand Rapids, MI: Zondervan, 2005.

Earle, Ralph. "Gospel of Mark." In *The New International Dictionary of the Bible*, edited by J. D. Douglas and Merrill C. Tenney, 622–623. Grand Rapids, MI: Zondervan, 1987.

Edwards, James R. *The Gospel According to Mark*. Pillar New Testament Commentary, edited by D. A. Carson. Grand Rapids, MI: Eerdmans, 2002.

Eliade, Mircea. *Myth and Reality*. New York: Harper & Row, 1963.

English, Donald. *The Message of Mark*. Leicester: InterVarsity Press, 1992.

Evans, C. F. "The New Testament in the Making." In *The Cambridge History of the Bible*, edited by P. R. Ackroyd and C. F. Evans, 232–284. London: Cambridge University Press, 1970.

Evans, Craig A. "How Mark Writes." In *The Written Gospel*, edited by Markus Bockmuehl and Donald A. Hagner, 135–148. Cambridge: Cambridge University Press, 2005.

Fee, Gordon D. *The First Epistle to the Corinthians*. Grand Rapid, MI: Eerdmans, 1987.

———. *New Testament Exegesis: A Handbook for Students and Pastors*. Philadelphia: Westminster, 1983.

Fee, Gordon D., and Douglas Stuart. *How to Read the Bible for All its Worth*. 3rd ed. Grand Rapids, MI: Zondervan, 2003.

Ferguson, D. S. *Biblical Hermeneutics: An Introduction*. Atlanta, GA: John Knox, 1986.

Ferguson, Everett. "Factors Leading to the Selection and Closure of the New Testament Canon: A Survey of Some Recent Studies." In *The Canon Debate*, edited by Lee Martin McDonald and James A. Sanders, 295–320. Peabody, MA: Hendrickson, 2002.

Fiore, Benjamin. "NT Rhetoric and Rhetorical Criticism." In *Anchor Bible Dictionary*, vol. 5, edited by David Noel Freedman, 715–719. New York: Doubleday, 1992.

Fiorenza, Elisabeth Schussler. "Rhetorical Situation and Historical Reconstruction in 1 Corinthians." *New Testament Studies* 33, no. 3 (1987): 386–403.

Fowl, Stephen E. "The Gospels and 'the Historical Jesus." In *The Cambridge Companion to the Gospels*, edited by Stephen C. Barton, 76–96. Cambridge: Cambridge University Press, 2006.

Fowler, Robert M. *Let the Reader Understand: Reader-Response Criticism and the Gospel of Mark*. Harrisburg, PA: Trinity Press International, 1996.

France, R. T. *The Gospel According to Mathew*. Tyndale New Testament Commentaries. Leicester: Inter-Varsity Press, 1985.

———. *The Gospel of Mark*. New International Greek Testament Commentary. Grand Rapids, MI: Eerdmans, 2002.

Funk, Robert W. *The Poetics of Biblical Narrative*. Sonoma, CA: Polebridge Press, 1988.

Gadamer, Hans-Georg. "Religious and Poetical Speaking." In *Myth, Symbol, and Reality*, edited by Alan M. Olson, 86–98. Notre Dame: University of Notre Dame Press, 1980.

Gamble, Harry Y. "The New Testament Canon: Recent Research and Status Quaestionis." In *The Canon Debate*, edited by Lee Martin McDonald and James A. Sanders, 267–294. Peabody, MA: Hendrickson, 2002.

Garland, David E. *Mark: From Biblical Text . . . to Contemporary Life.* NIV Application Commentary. Grand Rapids, MI: Zondervan, 1996.

Gerhardsson, Birger. *The Reliability of the Gospel Tradition.* Peabody, MA: Hendrickson, 2001.

Goldingay, John. *Isaiah.* New International Biblical Commentary 13, edited by Robert L. Hubbard and Robert K. Johnston. Peabody, MA: Hendrickson, 2001.

Gorman, Michael J. *Elements of Biblical Exegesis: A Basic Guide for Students and Ministers.* Revised edition. Peabody, MA: Hendrickson, 2009.

Gove, Philip Babcock, ed. *Webster's Third New International Dictionary of English Language: Unabridged.* Springfield, MA: Merriam Webster, 1961.

Gow, M. D. "Fall." In *Dictionary of the Old Testament: Pentateuch*, edited by T. Desmond Alexander and David W. Baker, 285–291. Downers Grove, IL: InterVarsity Press, 2003.

Gowler, David B. *What Are They Saying About the Parables?* Mahwah, NJ: Paulist Press, 2000.

Grant, R. M. "The New Testament Canon." In *The Cambridge History of the Bible*, edited by P. R. Ackroyd and C. F. Evans, 284–308. London: Cambridge University Press, 1970.

Green, Joel B. *The Death of Jesus, Tradition and Interpretation in the Passion Narrative.* Tubingen: Mohr Siebeck, 1988.

———. "Discourse Analysis and New Testament Interpretation." In *Hearing the New Testament: Strategies for Interpretation*, 2nd ed., edited by Joel B. Green, 218–239. Grand Rapids, MI: Eerdmans, 1995.

———. *How to Read the Gospels and Acts.* Downers Grove, IL: InterVarsity Press, 1987.

———. "Passion." In *Dictionary of Jesus and the Gospels: A Compendium of Contemporary Public Scholarship*, edited by Joel B. Green, Scot McKnight, and I. Howard Marshall, 601–604. Downers Grove, IL: InterVarsity Press, 1992.

Greenlee, J. Harold. *Introduction to New Testament Textual Criticism.* Revised ed. Peabody, MA: Hendrickson, 1995.

Gregory, Andrew. "Looking for Luke in the Second Century." In *Reading Luke: Interpretation, Reflection, Formation*, edited by Craig G. Bartholomew, Joel B. Green, and Anthony C. Thiselton, 401–415. Grand Rapids, MI: Zondervan, 2005.

Gregory, Andrew F., and Christopher M. Tuckett. "Reflections on Method: What Constitutes the Use of the Writings that Later Formed the New Testament in the Apostolic Fathers?" In *The Reception of the New Testament in the Apostolic Fathers*, edited by Andrew F. Gregory and Christopher M. Tuckett, 61–82. New York: Oxford University Press, 2005.

Guelich, R. A. "Gospel of Mark." In *Dictionary of Jesus and the Gospels: A Compendium of Contemporary Biblical Scholarship*, edited by Joel B. Green, Scot McKnight, I. Howard Marshall, 512–525. Downers Grove, IL: InterVarsity Press, 1992.

———. "Mark, Gospel of." In *The IVP Dictionary of the New Testament: A One Volume Compendium of Contemporary Biblical Scholarship*, edited by Daniel G. Reid, 770–784. Downers Grove, IL: InterVarsity Press, 2004.

Gundry, Robert H. *Mark: A Commentary on His Apology for the Cross*. Grand Rapids, MI: Eerdmans, 1993.

———. *A Survey of the New Testament*. 4th ed. Grand Rapids, MI: Zondervan, 2003.

Guralnik, David B., ed. *Webster's New World Dictionary of the American Language*. New York: Simon & Schuster, 1970.

Guthrie, Donald. *New Testament Introduction*. 4th ed. Downers Grove, IL: InterVarsity Press, 1990.

Hanson, James S. *The Endangered Promises: Conflict in Mark*. Atlanta, GA: Society of Biblical Literature, 1997.

Harrison, R. K. *Introduction to the Old Testament*. Grand Rapids, MI: Eerdmans, 1969.

Hatina, Thomas R. *In Search of a Context: The Function of Scripture in Mark's Narrative*. New York: Sheffield Academic, 2002.

Hays, Richard B. "The Canonical Matrix of the Gospels." In *The Cambridge Companion to the Gospels*, edited by Stephen C. Barton, 53–75. Cambridge: Cambridge University Press, 2006.

Herron, Robert W. *Mark's Account of Peter's Denial of Jesus: A History of Its Interpretation*. Lanham, MD: University Press of America, 1991.

Heston, Holly E. "The Implications of Orality for Studies of the Biblical Text." In *Performing the Gospel: Orality, Memory, and Mark*, edited by Richard A. Horsley, Jonathan A. Draper, and John Miles Foley, 3–20. Minneapolis: Augsburg Fortress, 2006.

Heath, Malcolm. "Invention." In *Handbook of Classical Rhetoric in the Hellenistic Period 330 B.C.–A.D. 400*, edited by Stanley E. Porter, 89–119. Leiden: Brill, 1997.

Hengel, Martin. "Eye-Witness Memory and the Writing of the Gospels: Form Criticism, Community Tradition, and the Authority of the Authors." In *The Written Gospel*, edited by Markus Bockmuehl and Donald A. Hagner, 70–96. New York: Cambridge University Press, 2006.

———. "The Four Gospels and the One Gospel of Jesus Christ." In *The Earliest Gospels: The Origins and Transmission of the Earliest Christian Gospels-The Contribution of the Chester Beatty Gospel Codex P45*, edited by Charles Horton, 13–26. London: T&T Clark, 2004.

———. *Studies in the Gospel of Mark*. Translated from German by John Bowden. Philadelphia: Fortress, 1985.

Hester, James D. "The Wuellnerian Sublime: Rhetorics, Power and Ethics of Commun(icat)ion." In *Rhetorics and Hermeneutics*, edited by James D. Hester and J. David Hester, 3–22. New York: T&T Clark, 2004.

Hooker, Morna D. "Mark." In *It Is Written: Scripture Citing Scripture: Essays in Honour of Barnabas Lindars*, edited by D. A. Carson and H. G. M. Williamson, 220–230. Cambridge: Cambridge University Press, 1998.

———. "Mark's Parables of the Kingdom (Mark 4:1–34)." In *The Challenge of Jesus' Parables*, edited by Richard N. Longenecker, 79–101. Grand Rapids, MI: Eerdmans, 2000.

Horbury, William. "'Gospel' in Herodian Judaea." In *The Written Gospel*, edited by Markus Bockmuehl and Donald A. Hagner, 7–30. Cambridge: Cambridge University Press, 2005.

Horsley, Richard A., Jonathan A. Draper, and John Miles Foley, eds. *Performing the Gospel: Orality, Memory, and Mark*. Minneapolis: Augsburg Fortress, 2006.

Huizenga, Leroy A. *The New Isaac: Tradition and Intertextuality in the Gospel of Matthew*. Leiden: Brill, 2009.

Hutardo, L. W. "Gospel (Genre)." In *Dictionary of Jesus and the Gospels*, edited by Joel B. Green, Scot McKnight, and I. Howard Marshall, 276–282. Downers Grove, IL: InterVarsity Press, 1992.

Jackson, Jared J., and Martin Kessler. *Rhetorical Criticism: Essays in Honor of James Muilenburg*. Eugene, OR: Pickwick, 1974.

Jaeger, W. "Early Christianity and the Greek Paideia: 1 Clement." In *Encounters with Hellenism: Studies on the First Letter of Clement*, edited by Cilliers Breytenbach and Laurence L. Welborn, 104–114. Leiden: Brill, 2004.

Jeffers, James S. *The Greco-Roman World of the New Testament Era: Exploring the Background of Early Christianity*. Downers Grove, IL: InterVarsity Press, 1999.

John, Bright. *A History of Israel*. 3rd ed. London: SCM Press, 1980.

Kahl, Werner. *New Testament Miracle Stories in Their Religious-Historical Setting*. Gottingen: Vandenhoeck und Ruprecht, 1994.

Kahler, Martin. *The So-Called Historical Jesus and the Historic, Biblical Christ*. Translated from the German by Cael E. Braaten. Philadelphia: Fortress, 1964.

Kealy, Sean P. *Mark's Gospel: A History of Its Interpretation from the Beginning until 1979*. New York: Paulist Press, 1982.

Keener, Craig S. *The IVP Bible Background Commentary: New Testament*. Downers Grove, IL: InterVarsity Press, 1993.

———. *Matthew*. IVP New Testament Commentary Series. Downers Grove, IL: IVP Academic, 1997.

———. *Miracles: The Credibility of the New Testament Accounts*. Vols. 1 and 2. Grand Rapids, MI: Baker Academic, 2011.

Kelber, Werner H. *The Oral and the Written Gospel: Hermeneutics of Speaking and Writing in the Synoptic Tradition, Mark, Paul, and Q.* Philadelphia: Fortress, 1983.

———. Review of *The Oral Ethos of the Early Church: Speaking, Writing, and the Gospel of Mark*, by Joanna Dewey. Review of Biblical Literature, 2016.

Kennedy, George A. *New Testament Interpretation Through Rhetorical Criticism.* Chapel Hill, NC: University of North Carolina Press, 1984.

Kilpatrick, George Dunbar. *The Principles and Practice of New Testament Textual Criticism.* Edited by James K. Elliott. Leuven-Louvain, Belgium: Leuven University Press, 1990.

King, Philip J., and Lawrence E. Stager. *Life in Biblical Israel.* Louisville, KY: Westminster John Knox, 2001.

Kingsbury, Jack Dean. *Conflict in Mark: Jesus, Authorities, Disciples.* Minneapolis: Augsburg Fortress, 1989.

Klein, William W., Craig L. Blomberg, and Robert L. Hubbard. *Introduction to Biblical Interpretation.* Nashville, TN: Thomas Nelson, 1993.

Koester, Helmut. *Ancient Christian Gospels: Their History and Development.* London: SCM, 1990.

———. "From the Kerygma-Gospel to Written Gospels." *New Testament Studies* 35, no. 3 (July 1989): 361–381.

Koptak, Paul E. "Intertextuality." In *Dictionary for Theological Interpretation of the Bible*, edited by Kevin J. Vanhoozer. Grand Rapids, MI: Baker Academic, 2005.

Kubo, Sakae. *A Reader's Greek-English Lexicon of The New Testament and a Beginner's Guide for the Translation of New Testament Greek.* Grand Rapids, MI: Zondervan, 1975.

Kurian, George Thomas, ed. *Nelson's New Christian Dictionary.* Nashville, TN: Thomas Nelson, 2001.

Landes, George M. *Building Your Biblical Hebrew Vocabulary: Learning Words by Frequency and Cognate.* Atlanta: Society of Biblical Literature, 2001.

Lane, William L. *The Gospel According to Mark.* New International Commentary on the New Testament. Grand Rapids, MI: Eerdmans, 1974.

Lategan, Bernard. "Textual Space as Rhetorical Device." In *Rhetoric and the New Testament: Essays from the 1992 Heidelberg Conference*, edited by Stanley E. Porter and T. H. Olbricht, 397–408. Sheffield: Sheffield Academic Press, 2001.

Levine, Donald N. *The Flight from Ambiguity: Essays in Social and Cultural Theory.* Chicago, IL: University of Chicago Press, 1985.

Lillegard, Norman. "(Revelation, Interpretation) Authority: Kierkegaard's Book on Adler Norman Lillegard." In *Hermeneutics at the Crossroads*, edited by Kevin J. Vanhoozer, James K. A. Smith, and Bruce Ellis Benson, 225–239. Indianapolis: Indiana University Press, 2006.

Lindemann, A. "Paul in the Writings of the Apostolic Fathers." In *Paul and the Legacies of Paul*, edited by W. S. Babcock, 24–45. Dallas, TX: Southern Methodist University Press, 1990.

Loos, H. Van Der. *The Miracles of Jesus*. Leiden: Brill, 1965.

Loveday, Alexander. "What is a Gospel?" In *The Cambridge Companion to the Gospels*, edited by Stephen C. Barton. Cambridge: Cambridge University Press, 2006.

Lund, N. *Chiasmus in the New Testament: A Study in Formgeschichte*. Chapel Hill, NC: University of North Carolina Press, 1942.

Lundin, Roger. "Interpreting Orphans: Hermeneutics in the Cartesian Tradition." In *The Promise of Hermeneutics*, edited by Roger Lundin, Clarence Walhout, and Anthony C. Thiselton, 1–64. Grand Rapids, MI: Eerdmans, 1999.

Luter, A. B. "Gospel." In *Dictionary of Paul and His Letters: A Compendium of Contemporary Biblical Scholarship*, edited by Gerald F. Hawthorne, Ralph P. Martin, and Daniel G. Reid, 369–372. Downers Grove, IL: InterVarsity Press, 1993.

Marshall, Christopher D. *Faith as a Theme in Mark's Narrative*. Society for New Testament Studies Monograph Series, 64. Cambridge: Cambridge University Press, 1989.

Marshall, I. Howard. *Luke: Historian and Theologian*. 3rd ed. Downers Grove, IL: IVP Academic, 1988.

Martin-Asensio, Gustavo. "Hallidayan Functional Grammar as Heir to New Testament Rhetorical Criticism." In *The Rhetorical Interpretation of Scripture: Essays From the 1996 Malibu Conference*, edited by Stanley E. Porter and Dennis L. Stamps, 84–107. Sheffield: Sheffield Academic Press, 1999.

Marxsen, Willi. *Mark the Evangelist: Studies on the Redaction History of the Gospel*. Translated by James Boyce, Donald Juel, William Poehlmann, and Roy A. Harrisville. Nashville, TN: Abingdon Press, 1969.

Matera, Frank J. *Passion Narratives and Gospel Theologies: Interpreting the Synoptics Through Their Passion Stories*. Mahwah, NJ: Paulist Press, 1986.

Mauser, U. *Christ in the Wilderness: The Wilderness Theme in the Second Gospel and Its Basis in the Biblical Traditions*. London: SCM, 1963.

McDonald, Lee Martin. "The Gospels in Early Christianity: Their Origin, Use, and Authority." In *Reading the Gospels Today*, edited by Stanley E. Porter, 150–178. Grand Rapids, MI: Eerdmans, 2004.

Mclay, R. Timothy. *The Use of the Septuagint in New Testament Research*. Grand Rapids, MI: Eerdmans, 2003.

Metzger, Bruce M. *A Textual Commentary on the Greek New Testament*. London: United Bible Societies, 1971.

Moeser, Marion C. *The Anecdote in Mark, the Classical World and the Rabbis*. Journal for the Study of the New Testament Supplement Series 227. London: Sheffield Academic Press, 2002.

Moo, Douglas J. *The Old Testament in the Gospel Passion Narratives*. Sheffield: Almond Press, 1983.

Moreschini, Claudio, and Enrico Norelli. *Early Christian Greek and Latin Literature: A Literary History from Paul to the Age of Constantine*. Peabody, MA: Hendrickson, 2005.

Moritz, Thorsten. "Book of Mark." In *Dictionary for Theological Interpretation of the Bible*, edited by, Kevin J. Vanhoozer, 480–485. Grand Rapids, MI: Baker Academic, 2005.

Motyer, J. Alec. *The Prophecy of Isaiah: An Introduction and Commentary*. Downers Grove, IL: InterVarsity Press, 1993.

Muilenburg, James. "Form Criticism and Beyond." *Journal of Biblical Literature* 88, no. 1 (1969): 1–18.

Needham, N. R. *2000 Years of Christ's Power: Part One: The Age of the Early Church Fathers*. Revised ed. London: Grace Publications, 2002.

Norris, Richard A. "The Apostolic and Sub-Apostolic Writings: The New Testament and the Apostolic Fathers." In *The Cambridge History of Early Christian Literature*, edited by Francis Young, Lewis Ayres, and Andrew Louth, 11–19. Cambridge: Cambridge University Press, 2004.

Nyende, Peter. "Hebrew Exegesis – Literary readings of Hebrews." PhD Seminar, NEGST, AIU, March 2015. Author's notes.

Osborne, Grant R. *The Hermeneutical Spiral: A Comprehensive Introduction to Biblical Interpretation*. 2nd edition. Downers Grove, IL: IVP Academic, 2006.

Packer, J. I., and M. C. Tenney, eds. *Illustrated Manners and Customs of the Bible*. Nashville, TN: Thomas Nelson, 1980.

Padgett, A. G. "Marcion." In *Dictionary of the Later New Testament and Its Developments: A Compendium of Contemporary Biblical Scholarship*, edited by Ralph P. Martin and Peter H. Davids, 705–708. Downers Grove, IL: InterVarsity Press, 1997.

Patrick, Dale, and Allen Scult. "Rhetoric and Ideology: A Debate Within Biblical Scholarship Over the Import of Persuasion." In *The Rhetorical Interpretation of Scripture: Essays from the 1996 Malibu Conference*, edited by Stanley E. Porter and Dennis L. Stamps, 63–83. Sheffield: Sheffield Academic Press, 1999.

Paul, Ian. "Metaphor." *Dictionary for Theological Interpretation of the Bible*, edited by Kevin J. Vanhoozer, 507–510. Grand Rapids, MI: Baker Academic, 2005.

Perelman, Chaim. *The Realm of Rhetoric*. Translated by William Kluback. Notre Dame, IN: University of Notre Dame Press, 1982.

Perelman, Chaim, and L. Olbrechts-Tyteca. *The New Rhetoric: A Treatise on Argumentation*. Translated by John Wilkinson and Purcell Weaver. Notre Dame, IN: University of Notre Dame Press, 1969.

Phillips, Peter M. "Rhetoric." In *Words and The Word: Explorations in Biblical Interpretation and Literary Theory*, edited by David G. Firth and Jamie A. Grant, 226–265. Downers Grove, IL: InterVarsity Press, 2008.

Pietersma, Albert, and Benjamin G. Wright, eds. *A New English Translation of the Septuagint*. New York: Oxford University Press, 2007.

Piper, O. A. "Gospel." In *The Interpreter's Dictionary of the Bible*, edited by George Arthur Buttrick, 442–448. Nashville, TN: Abingdon, 1962.

Porter, Stanley E., and Dennis L. Stamps. "Introduction: The Malibu Conference and the Ongoing Debate." In *The Rhetorical Interpretation of Scripture: Essays from the 1996 Malibu Conference*, edited by Stanley E. Porter and Dennis L. Stamps, 17–20. Sheffield: Sheffield Academic Press, 1999.

Rahlfs, Alfred. *Septuaginta: Id est Vetus Testamentum Graece iuxta LXX interpretes edidit Alfred Rahlfs*. Two volumes in one. Stuttgart: Deutsche Bibelgesellschaft, 1979.

Ramm, Bernard. *Protestant Biblical Interpretation*. Grand Rapids, MI: Baker Books, 1970.

Reed, Jeffrey T. "Discourse Analysis." In *Handbook to Exegesis of the New Testament*, edited by Stanley E. Porter, 189–217. Boston: Brill Academic, 2002.

Rees, Thomas. "Barabbas." In *International Standard Bible Encyclopaedia*, vol. 1, edited by Geoffrey M. Bromiley, 171–172. Grand Rapids, MI: Eerdmans, 1979.

Rhoads, David. *Reading Mark Engaging the Gospel*. Minneapolis: Augsburg Fortress, 2004.

Rhoads, David, Joanna Dewey, and Donald Michie. *Mark as Story: An Introduction to the Narrative of a Gospel*. 2nd ed. Minneapolis: Augsburg Fortress, 1999.

Richardson, Alan. *The Miracle Stories of the Gospels*. London: SCM Press, 1941.

———. "Miracle, Wonder, Sign, Powers." In *A Theological Word Book of the Bible*, edited by Alan Richardson, 152–155. New York: Macmillan, 1950.

Riches, John. "Editor's Foreword." In *The Miracle Stories of the Early Christian Tradition*, by Gerd Theissen, viii. Philadelphia: Fortress Press, 1974.

Ricoeur, Paul. "The Function of Fiction in Shaping Reality." *Man and World* 12, no. 2 (1979): 123–141.

———. *Hermeneutics and the Human Sciences*. Edited by John B. Thompson. Cambridge: Cambridge University Press, 1981.

Robbins, Vernon K. *Exploring the Texture of Texts: A Guide to Socio-Rhetorical Interpretation*. Valley Forge, PA: Trinity Press, 1996.

———. *Jesus the Teacher: A Socio-Rhetorical Interpretation of Mark*. Philadelphia: Fortress Press, 1984.

———. *The Tapestry of Early Christian Discourse: Rhetoric, Society and Ideology.* London: Routledge, 1996.

Robinson, James M. *The Gospel of Jesus: In Search of the Original Good News.* New York: HarperCollins, 2005.

Roskam, H. N. *The Purpose of the Gospel of Mark and its Historical and Social Context.* Leiden: Brill, 2004.

Runge, Steven E. *Discourse Grammar of the Greek New Testament: A Practical Introduction for Teaching and Exegesis.* Peabody, MA: Hendrickson, 2010.

Ryken, Leland. *How to Read the Bible as Literature . . . and Get More Out of It.* Grand Rapids, MI: Zondervan, 1984.

———. *Words of Delight: A Literary Introduction to the Bible.* Grand Rapids, MI: Baker Academic, 1987.

Ryken, Leland, James C. Wilhoit, and Tremper Longman III. *Dictionary of Biblical Imagery: An Encyclopaedic Exploration of the Images, Symbols, Motifs, Metaphors, Figures of Speech and Literary Patterns of the Bible.* Downers Grove, IL: InterVarsity Press, 1998.

Sailhamer, John H. *The Pentateuch as Narrative: A Biblical-Theological Commentary.* Grand Rapids, MI: Zondervan, 1992.

Schmidt, K. L. "Die Stellung der Evangelien in der Allgemeinen Literaturgeschichte," In *Eucharisterion: Studien zur Religion und Literatur des Alten und Neuen Testaments. H Gunkel Festschrift*, 50–134. Gottingen: Vandenhoeck, 1923.

Schmidt, T. E. "Taxation, Jewish." In *Dictionary of New Testament Background*, edited by Craig A. Evans and Stanley E. Porter. Downers Grove, IL: InterVarsity Press, 2000.

Schneck, Richard. *Isaiah in the Gospel of Mark I–VIII.* Vallejo, CA: BIBAL Press, 1994.

Schreiner, Thomas R. *New Testament Theology: Magnifying God in Christ.* Grand Rapids, MI: Baker Academic, 2008.

Schweitzer, Albert. *The Kingdom of God and Primitive Christianity.* London: Black, 1968.

———. *The Quest of the Historical Jesus: A Critical Study of its Progress from Reimarus to Wrede.* Translated by W. Montgomery. London: Black, 1910.

Schweitzer, Eduard. *The Good News According to Mark.* Atlanta, GA: John Knox, 1970.

Searle, John R. "Introduction." In *The Philosophy of Language*, edited by John R. Searle, 1–12. London: Oxford University Press, 1971.

———. *Speech Acts: An Essay in the Philosophy of Language.* Cambridge: Cambridge University Press, 1969.

Seid, T. "Synkrisis in Hebrews 7: The Rhetorical Structure and Strategy." In *The Rhetorical Interpretation of Scripture: Essays from the 1996 Malibu Conference,* edited by Stanley E. Porter and Dennis L. Stamps, 322–347. Sheffield: Sheffield Academic, 1999.

Shiner, Whitney Taylor. "Applause and Applause Lines in the Gospel of Mark." In *Rhetorics and Hermeneutic*, edited by James D. Hester and J. David Hester, 129–144. New York: T&T Clark, 2004.

———. *Proclaiming the Gospel: First-Century Performance of Mark*. Harrisburg, PA: Trinity Press, 2003.

Shul, A. *Die Funktion der Alttestamentlichen Zitate und Anspielungen im Markusevangelium*. Gutersloh: Mohn, 1965.

Smith, James K. A. "Limited Inc/arnation: Revisiting the Searle/Derrida Debate in Christian Context." In *Hermeneutics at the Crossroad*, edited by Kevin Vanhoozer, James K. A. Smith, and Bruce Ellis Benson, 112–129. Bloomington, IN: Indiana University Press, 2006.

Snodgrass, Klyne R. "The Gospel of Jesus." In *The Written Gospel*, edited by Markus Bockmuehl and Donald A. Hagner, 31–44. New York: Cambridge University Press, 2005.

———. "Reading and Overreading the Parables in Jesus and the Victory of God." In *Jesus and the Restoration of Israel: A Critical Assessment of N. T. Wright's Jesus and the Victory of God*, edited by Carey C. Newman, 61–76. Downers Grove, IL: InterVarsity Press, 1999.

Spencer, F. Scott. "Preparing the Way of the Lord: Introducing and Interpreting Luke's Narrative: A Response to David Wenham." In *Reading Luke: Interpretation, Reflection, Formation*, edited by Craig G. Bartholomew, Joel B. Green, Anthony Thiselton, 104–105. Grand Rapids, MI: Zondervan; Milton Keynes: Paternoster, 2005.

Stamps, Dennis L. "Rethinking the Rhetorical Situation: The Entextualization of the Situation in New Testament Epistles." In *Rhetoric and the New Testament: Essays from the 1992 Heidelberg Conference*, edited by Stanley E. Porter and Thomas H. Olbricht, 193–210. Sheffield: Sheffield Academic Press, 2001.

———. "Rhetoric." In *Dictionary of New Testament Background: A Compendium of Contemporary Biblical Scholarship*, edited by Craig A. Evans and Stanley E. Porter, 953–959. Downers Grove, IL: Inter Varsity Press, 2000.

Stanton, Graham. N. *Jesus and Gospel*. Cambridge: Cambridge University Press, 2004.

Stein, Robert H. "The Genre of the Parables." In *The Challenge of Jesus' Parables*, edited by Richard N. Longenecker, 30–50. Grand Rapids, MI: Eerdmans, 2000.

———. *Mark*. Baker Exegetical Commentary on the New Testament, edited by Robert W. Yarbrough and Robert H. Stein. Grand Rapids, MI: Baker Academic, 2008.

Streeter, Burnett Hillman. *The Primitive Church*. New York: Macmillan, 1929.

Swartley, W. M. "Intertextuality in Early Christian Literature." In *Dictionary of the Later New Testament and Its Development*, edited by Ralph P. Merlin and Peter H. Davids, 536–542. Leicester: Inter-Varsity Press: 1997.

Tate, W. Randolph. *Biblical Interpretation: An Integrated Approach*. Grand Rapids: Baker Academic, 1991.

Taylor, Vincent. *The Formation of the Gospel Tradition*. New York: St. Martin's Press, 1960.

Thayer, Joseph H. *Thayer's Greek-English Lexicon of the New Testament: Coded to Strong's Numbering System*. 4th ed. Peabody, MA: Hendrickson, 2005.

Theissen, Gerd. *The Gospels in Context: Social and Political History in the Synoptic Tradition*. Translated by Linda M. Maloney. Edinburgh: T&T Clark, 1991.

———. *The Miracle Stories of the Early Christian Tradition*. Edited by John Riches. Philadelphia: Fortress, 1983.

Theron, Daniel J. *Evidence of Tradition*. Grand Rapids, MI: Baker Books, 1957.

Thiselton, Anthony C. "Communicative Action and Promise in Interdisciplinary, Biblical, and Theological Hermeneutics." In *The Promise of Hermeneutics*, edited by Roger Lundin, Clarence Walhout, and Anthony C. Thiselton, 133–253. Grand Rapids, MI: Eerdmans, 1999.

———. *First Epistle to the Corinthians*. New International Greek Testament Commentary. Grand Rapids, MI: Eerdmans, 2000.

———. *Interpreting God and the Postmodern Self: On Meaning, Manipulation and Promise*. Edinburgh: T&T Clark, 1995.

———. *New Horizons in Hermeneutics: The Theory and Practice of Transforming Bible Reading*. Grand Rapids, MI: Zondervan, 1992.

———. *The Two Horizons: New Testament Hermeneutics and Philosophical Description with Special Reference to Heidegger, Bultmann, Gadamer, and Wittgenstein*. Exeter: Paternoster, 1980.

Tolbert, Mary Ann. *Sowing the Gospel: Mark's World in Literary-Historical Perspective*. Minneapolis: Fortress, 1989.

Tomasino, Anthony J. *Judaism before Jesus: The Events and Ideas that Shaped the New Testament World*. Downers Grove, IL: InterVarsity Press, 2003.

Unnik, W. C. Van. "Studies on the So-Called First Epistle of Clement: The Literary Genre." In *Encounters with Hellenism: Studies on the First Letter of Clement*, edited by, Cilliers Breytenbach and Laurence L. Welborn, translated by L. L. Welborn, 115–181. Leiden: Brill, 2004.

Upton, Bridget Gilfillan. *Hearing Mark's Endings: Listening to Ancient Popular Texts through Speech Act Theory*. Leiden: Brill, 2006.

Vanhoozer, Kevin J. *First Theology: God, Scripture and Hermeneutics*. Downers Grove, IL: InterVarsity Press, 2002.

———. *Is There a Meaning in This Text?: The Bible, the Reader, and the Morality of Literary Knowledge*. Grand Rapids, MI: Zondervan, 1988.

———. "A Lamp in the Labyrinth: The Hermeneutics of 'Aesthetic' Theology." *Trinity Journal* 8, no. 1 (1987): 25–56.
Verbin, John S. Kloppenborg. *Excavating Q: The History and Setting of the Sayings Gospel*. Edinburgh: T& T Clark, 2000.
Verbrugge, Verlyn D., ed. *New International Dictionary of New Testament Theology*. Abridged ed. Grand Rapids, MI: Zondervan, 1996.
Vines, Michael E. *The Problem of Markan Genre: The Gospel of Mark and the Jewish Novel*. Atlanta, GA: Society of Biblical Literature, 2002.
Vorster, W. S. "The Production of the Gospel of Mark." *HTS Theological Studies* 49, no. 3 (1993): 385–396.
Waldron, Samuel E. *Baptist Confession of Faith: A Modern Exposition*. Darlington, England: Evangelical Press, 1989.
Walhout, Clarence. "Narrative Hermeneutics." In *The Promise of Hermeneutics*, edited by Roger Lundin, Anthony C. Thiselton, and Clarence Walhout, 65–132. Grand Rapids, MI: Eerdmans, 1999.
Wallace, Daniel B. *Greek Grammar beyond the Basics: An Exegetical Syntax of the New Testament*. Grand Rapids, MI: Zondervan, 1996.
Walton, J. H. "Flood." In *Dictionary of the Old Testament: Pentateuch*, edited by T. Desmond Alexander and David W. Baker, 315–326. Downers Grove, IL: InterVarsity Press, 2003.
Wardlaw, Terrance R. "Discourse Analysis." In *Words and the Word: Explorations in Biblical Interpretation and Literary Theory*, edited by David G. Firth and Jamie A. Grant, 266–317. Downers Grove, IL: IVP Academic, 2008.
Watson, D. F. "Rhetoric, Rhetorical Criticism." In *Dictionary of the Later New Testament and Its Development: A Compendium of Contemporary Biblical Scholarship*, edited by Ralph P. Martin and Peter H. Davids, 1041–1051. Downers Grove, IL: InterVarsity Press, 1997.
Watts, Rikk E. *Isaiah's New Exodus and Mark*. Tubingen: Mohr Siebeck, 1997.
———. "Mark." In *Commentary on New Testament Use of the Old Testament*, edited by G. K. Beale and D. A. Carson, 111–251. Grand Rapids, MI: Baker Academic, 2007.
Wegener, Mark I. *Cruciformed: The Literary Impact of Mark's Story of Jesus and His Disciples*. Lanham, MD: University Press of America, 1995.
Wellek, Rene, and Austin Warren. *Theory of Literature*. New York: Harcourt, Brace & World, 1956.
Westminster Assembly. *The Westminster Confession of Faith*. Glasgow: Free Presbyterian Publications, 1995.
Whitacre, Rodney A. *A Patristic Greek Reader*. Grand Rapids, MI: Baker Academic, 2007.
Wiesel, Elie. "Myth and History." In *Myth, Symbol, and Reality*, edited by Alan M. Olson, 20–30. Notre Dame, IN: University of Notre Dame Press, 1980.

Wilkins, M. J. "Teaching, Paraenesis." In *Dictionary of the Later New Testament and Its Development: A Compendium of Contemporary Biblical Scholarship*, edited by, Ralph P. Martin and Peter H. Davids, 1156–1159. Downers Grove, IL: InterVarsity Press, 1997.

Williams, James G. *Gospel Against Parables: Mark's Language of Mystery*. Sheffield, England: Almond, 1985.

Williamson, H. G. M. "Preaching from Isaiah." In *Reclaiming the Old Testament for Christian Preaching*, edited by Grenville J. R. Kent, Paul J. Kissling, and Laurence A. Turner, 141–156. Downers Grove, IL: IVP Academic, 2010.

Witherington, Ben. *The Gospel of Mark: A Social-Rhetorical Commentary*. Grand Rapids, MI: Zondervan, 2000.

Wittgenstein, Ludwing. *Philosophical Investigations*. Translated by G. E. M. Anscombe. Oxford: Blackwell, 1953.

Wolterstorff, Nicholas. *Divine Discourse: Philosophical Reflections on the Claim that God Speaks*. Cambridge: Cambridge University Press, 1995.

———. "Resuscitating the Author." In *Hermeneutics at the Crossroads*, edited by Kevin J. Vanhoozer, James K. A. Smith, and Bruce Ellis Benson, 35–50. Bloomington, IN: Indiana University Press, 2006.

Wrede, William. *The Messianic Secret*. Translated by J. C. G. Greig. Cambridge: James Clarke & Co., 1971.

Wright, D. F. "Creeds, Confessional Forms." In *Dictionary of the Later New Testament and Its Development: A Compendium of Contemporary Biblical Scholarship*, edited by Ralph P. Martin and Peter H. Davids, 255–260. Downers Grove, IL: InterVarsity Press, 1997.

Wright, N. T. *Jesus and the Victory of God*. London: SPCK, 1996.

———. *The New Testament and the People of God*. London: SPCK, 1992.

Wuellner, Wilhelm. "Arrangement." In *Handbook of Classical Rhetoric in the Hellenistic Period 330 B.C.-A.D. 400*, edited Stanley E. Porter, 51–87. Leiden: Brill, 2001.

———. "Reconceiving a Rhetoric of Religion: A Rhetoric of Power as the Power of the Sublime." In *Rhetorics and Hermeneutics,* edited by James D. Hester and J. David Hester, 23–77. New York: T&T Clark, 2004.

Yamada, Kota. "The Preface to the Lukan Writings and Rhetorical Historiography." In *The Rhetorical Interpretation of Scripture: Essays From the Malibu Conference*, edited by Stanley E. Porter and Dennis L. Stamps, 154–172. Sheffield: Sheffield Academic Press, 1999.

Young, Frances. "Christian Teaching." In *Early Christian Literature*, edited by Frances Young, Lewis Ayres, and Andrew Louth, 91–104. Cambridge: Cambridge University Press, 2004.

———. "Towards a Hermeneutic of Second Century." In *The Cambridge History of Early Christian Literature*, edited by Frances Young, Lewis Ayres, and Andrew Louth, 105–111. Cambridge: Cambridge University, 2004.

Langham Literature, with its publishing work, is a ministry of Langham Partnership.

Langham Partnership is a global fellowship working in pursuit of the vision God entrusted to its founder John Stott –

> *to facilitate the growth of the church in maturity and Christ-likeness through raising the standards of biblical preaching and teaching.*

Our vision is to see churches in the Majority World equipped for mission and growing to maturity in Christ through the ministry of pastors and leaders who believe, teach and live by the word of God.

Our mission is to strengthen the ministry of the word of God through:
- nurturing national movements for biblical preaching
- fostering the creation and distribution of evangelical literature
- enhancing evangelical theological education

especially in countries where churches are under-resourced.

Our ministry

Langham Preaching partners with national leaders to nurture indigenous biblical preaching movements for pastors and lay preachers all around the world. With the support of a team of trainers from many countries, a multi-level programme of seminars provides practical training, and is followed by a programme for training local facilitators. Local preachers' groups and national and regional networks ensure continuity and ongoing development, seeking to build vigorous movements committed to Bible exposition.

Langham Literature provides Majority World preachers, scholars and seminary libraries with evangelical books and electronic resources through publishing and distribution, grants and discounts. The programme also fosters the creation of indigenous evangelical books in many languages, through writer's grants, strengthening local evangelical publishing houses, and investment in major regional literature projects, such as one volume Bible commentaries like the *Africa Bible Commentary* and the *South Asia Bible Commentary*.

Langham Scholars provides financial support for evangelical doctoral students from the Majority World so that, when they return home, they may train pastors and other Christian leaders with sound, biblical and theological teaching. This programme equips those who equip others. Langham Scholars also works in partnership with Majority World seminaries in strengthening evangelical theological education. A growing number of Langham Scholars study in high quality doctoral programmes in the Majority World itself. As well as teaching the next generation of pastors, graduated Langham Scholars exercise significant influence through their writing and leadership.

To learn more about Langham Partnership and the work we do visit **langham.org**

www.ingramcontent.com/pod-product-compliance
Lightning Source LLC
Chambersburg PA
CBHW051537230426
43669CB00015B/2626

Africa has millions of consummate storytellers with an ingrained sensitivity to storytelling conventions. Dr. Karura is one of them, and it is stimulating to read him interpreting the rhetoric of Mark. He employs several hermeneutical approaches – rhetorical criticism, speech-act theory, discourse analysis – to examine how the Markan text aims at convincing, convicting, and transforming the readers. In short, he reads the book as a *paraenesis* "meant to catalyze reader-response to the oral gospel." Portions of the text receiving especially close attention are Old Testament citations (Mark 1:2–3; 4:12), miracle stories, the parable of the sower, and the passion narrative. I warmly welcome the publication of Karura's study.

John F. Evans, DTh
Former Head of Biblical Studies Department,
Africa International University, Nairobi, Kenya

This innovative and enduring book tackles an important topic which has been almost unnoticed in Markan scholarship. It is a contribution to research on Mark's gospel, especially its opening words, "the beginning of the gospel of Jesus Christ, the Son of God." The author has ably revealed that "the beginning of the gospel" does not refer to the written gospel but to the "good news" that was orated. Certainly, before the gospel was written down, it was preached orally. The author pointedly and convincingly underscores that Mark's text was written to urge its readers to believe in the oral gospel preached in its author's environs. Using rhetoric biblical interpretation, he creatively argues that the Old Testament quotations, miracle stories and the passion narrative were used specifically as rhetorical devices to catalyze audience response to the oral gospel. This book is highly recommended due to its scholarly insights and eloquence. It is one of the best books on the relationship between oral gospel and written gospel.

Rev. Kabiro wa Gatumu, PhD
Associate Professor and Senior Lecturer, Faculty of Theology,
St. Paul's University, Nairobi, Kenya

It is a good and joyful thing when a former student leaves the nest and joins the scholarly world as a colleague. It is also a good thing when Majority World scholars can bring their perspective on biblical studies to a discussion long dominated by Western voices. Particularly relevant to this work is the rich tradition of storytelling that flourishes in many Kenyan cultures, which Dr. Karura first encountered as a child hearing stories from his parents. This has enabled him to approach aspects of the Markan text which have been less apparent to scholars whose orientation toward the Scriptures is rooted in more text-centered, cultural traditions. I, though one of his teachers, am glad to learn from his strengths, for "as iron sharpens iron, so one man sharpens another."

Joshua Harper, PhD
Department of Applied Linguistics,
Dallas International University, Dallas, Texas, USA

In *Catalyzing Reader-Response to the Oral Gospel*, Mwaniki Karura has shown that presuppositions regarding the origins and goal of a text have a direct bearing on how it is understood and interpreted. He argues that the rhetorical situation of the Gospel of Mark, and therefore its content and structure, is different from the essential gospel as proclaimed by Jesus and the early preachers post-resurrection. The written "gospel" of Mark was meant to point its audience to the "oral gospel," the *kerygma*. He further argues that all the New Testament writings attained the role of Scripture and primary memory of the gospel in the later patristic milieu. This work assists in moving biblical studies from disembodied literary and historical-critical studies, to the realms of language, communication, participants and skopos, and then on to pragmatic intent.

I happily recommend this book to students of the history of Christianity, students of biblical studies, students and practitioners of missions, and all those who want to acquire solid grounding in their understanding of the Scriptures as repositories of Christian faith. There is much to ponder here for the casual inquirer in the transmission of the Bible, the student of the Bible and even the seasoned biblical scholar.

Misheck Nyirenda, PhD
Global Translation Advisor, United Bible Societies
Former Associate Professor,
Pan Africa Christian University, Nairobi, Kenya

dominated by Western voices. Particularly relevant to this work is the rich tradition of storytelling that flourishes in many Kenyan cultures, which Dr. Karura first encountered as a child hearing stories from his parents. This has enabled him to approach aspects of the Markan text which have been less apparent to scholars whose orientation toward the Scriptures is rooted in more text-centered, cultural traditions. I, though one of his teachers, am glad to learn from his strengths, for "as iron sharpens iron, so one man sharpens another."

Joshua Harper, PhD
Department of Applied Linguistics,
Dallas International University, Dallas, Texas, USA

In *Catalyzing Reader-Response to the Oral Gospel*, Mwaniki Karura has shown that presuppositions regarding the origins and goal of a text have a direct bearing on how it is understood and interpreted. He argues that the rhetorical situation of the Gospel of Mark, and therefore its content and structure, is different from the essential gospel as proclaimed by Jesus and the early preachers post-resurrection. The written "gospel" of Mark was meant to point its audience to the "oral gospel," the *kerygma*. He further argues that all the New Testament writings attained the role of Scripture and primary memory of the gospel in the later patristic milieu. This work assists in moving biblical studies from disembodied literary and historical-critical studies, to the realms of language, communication, participants and skopos, and then on to pragmatic intent.

I happily recommend this book to students of the history of Christianity, students of biblical studies, students and practitioners of missions, and all those who want to acquire solid grounding in their understanding of the Scriptures as repositories of Christian faith. There is much to ponder here for the casual inquirer in the transmission of the Bible, the student of the Bible and even the seasoned biblical scholar.

Misheck Nyirenda, PhD
Global Translation Advisor, United Bible Societies
Former Associate Professor,
Pan Africa Christian University, Nairobi, Kenya

Africa has millions of consummate storytellers with an ingrained sensitivity to storytelling conventions. Dr. Karura is one of them, and it is stimulating to read him interpreting the rhetoric of Mark. He employs several hermeneutical approaches – rhetorical criticism, speech-act theory, discourse analysis – to examine how the Markan text aims at convincing, convicting, and transforming the readers. In short, he reads the book as a *paraenesis* "meant to catalyze reader-response to the oral gospel." Portions of the text receiving especially close attention are Old Testament citations (Mark 1:2–3; 4:12), miracle stories, the parable of the sower, and the passion narrative. I warmly welcome the publication of Karura's study.

John F. Evans, DTh
Former Head of Biblical Studies Department,
Africa International University, Nairobi, Kenya

This innovative and enduring book tackles an important topic which has been almost unnoticed in Markan scholarship. It is a contribution to research on Mark's gospel, especially its opening words, "the beginning of the gospel of Jesus Christ, the Son of God." The author has ably revealed that "the beginning of the gospel" does not refer to the written gospel but to the "good news" that was orated. Certainly, before the gospel was written down, it was preached orally. The author pointedly and convincingly underscores that Mark's text was written to urge its readers to believe in the oral gospel preached in its author's environs. Using rhetoric biblical interpretation, he creatively argues that the Old Testament quotations, miracle stories and the passion narrative were used specifically as rhetorical devices to catalyze audience response to the oral gospel. This book is highly recommended due to its scholarly insights and eloquence. It is one of the best books on the relationship between oral gospel and written gospel.

Rev. Kabiro wa Gatumu, PhD
Associate Professor and Senior Lecturer, Faculty of Theology,
St. Paul's University, Nairobi, Kenya

It is a good and joyful thing when a former student leaves the nest and joins the scholarly world as a colleague. It is also a good thing when Majority World scholars can bring their perspective on biblical studies to a discussion long